Ships, Ports, and Pilots

Ships, Ports, and Pilots

A History of the Piloting Profession

ROGER CLANCY

McFarland & Company, Inc., Publishers
Jefferson, North Carolina, and London

To my oceanographer son Mike,
in whom I have always been well pleased

The present work is a reprint of the library bound edition of Ships, Ports and Pilots: A History of the Piloting Profession, *first published in 1984 by McFarland.*

LIBRARY OF CONGRESS CATALOGUING-IN-PUBLICATION DATA

Clancy, Roger, 1903–
Ships, ports, and pilots : a history of the piloting profession / Roger Clancy.
p. cm.
Includes index.

ISBN 978-0-7864-7380-9
softcover : acid free paper ∞

1. Pilots and pilotage—History. I. Title.
VK1515.C58 2012
387.1'66 84-42600

BRITISH LIBRARY CATALOGUING DATA ARE AVAILABLE

On the cover: Pilot exists cargo ship to pilot ship (Stephen Schauer/Lifesize/Thinnkstock)

Manufactured in the United States of America

McFarland & Company, Inc., Publishers
Box 611, Jefferson, North Carolina 28640
www.mcfarlandpub.com

Table of Contents

Foreword

This is the complete story and annotated history of the profession of piloting—guiding—big ships in and out of seaports, avoiding all of the hidden dangers abounding there, close to land, in the seaward approaches to the ports. Sandbars, sunken wrecks, underwater rocks, coral reefs, ridges—one or more or all of them are sure to be there, somewhere, out of sight. Only the certified local port pilot knows where they are and where they *ain't*.

This is one of the oldest and most respected professions in the world today. It was needed and in existence far back in ancient times, long before the beginning of the Christian era. The book goes back and takes it from there, tracing its history down through the centuries, noting the ramifications and gradual changes, and supplying various ancient sets of maritime laws, relevant in one respect or another, that were encountered along the way. The book should be of great use in any legal reference collection. Among the general public, however, piloting is one of the lesser known professions. Hence this book.

In the preparation of it, I received a great deal of help, and I wish to express my appreciation, especially to the following: Captain Ernest A. Clothier, president of the American Pilots' Association, for his encouragement and for his gift of a copy of that organization's publication, *State Pilotage in America*; the Second Bank-State Street Trust Company of Boston for their illustrated booklet *Pilots and Pilot Boats of Boston Harbor*; the Sandy Hook Pilots' Association for their brochure *What Is a Sandy Hook Pilot?*; the Tampa Bay Pilots' Association for their brochure, *The Florida Pilots*, and various pilots who have chatted with me through the years, too numerous to acknowledge.

I grew up on the south shore of Long Island close to the Atlantic Ocean and its estuaries, tributaries and inlets. Boats, especially sailboats, were a big part of my life during that time, in inside waters and outside waters as well. At the beginning of World War II, I enlisted in the U.S. Coast Guard at Bayshore, near Fire Island Inlet, and went to sea the day after I enlisted on antisubmarine patrol off Long Island on a converted yacht. Later I was transferred to a newly-built 83-foot patrol boat and went to Cuba and the Caribbean on her as boatswain's mate first class and third in command. Later I went to the Hawaiian Islands on an LST landing ship and operated a fire-fighting boat at a port there. I was at Nawiliwili on Kauai when the war ended. After the war, I settled on the east coast of Florida, on the oceanfront, with a view of the ocean from every room in the house that I built there, and stayed 20 years. I have been a federally licensed captain of deep-sea sport fishing boats, a commercial fisherman, a shrimper, a yachtsman, a writer of salt-water magazine articles and stories. I have salt water in my blood.

R.C.

One

The Needs and the Origins

Mother Nature, in forming our continents and coasts thousands of years ago, paid no attention to uniformity or consistency of design. As a consequence, no two seaports anywhere in the world are exactly alike, neither in their shoreline configurations nor their underwater topographies, or the depths, widths, and meanderings of their navigable channels; and the hidden dangers of any given port's approaches will always be distinctly peculiar to it.

Thus the near approaches to the entrances of most major seaports and their sheltered harbors, especially those ports and harbors at the mouths of great rivers, are booby-trapped with a wide variety of unseen hazards such as shoals and sandbars, reefs and ridges, rip currents and eddies, narrow channels with sharp turns, and submerged wrecks and sunken rocks—not to mention the frequent hazard of unforeseen traffic jams. It therefore would be foolhardy and extremely dangerous for the captains and crews of big ships from overseas to attempt to bring them in or take them out at will without the help of resident local pilots who are well-acquainted with the waters and the safe though hidden and devious channels.

It is for this reason that port authorities the world over have seen to it that dependable safe guidance by experienced and expert pilots is readily available to arriving and departing ships at all times; *and this inshore ship handling is the most exacting part of marine navigation*! A small error in mid-ocean generally matters very little because there is sufficient time and space and deep water to permit of its correction before any harm is done; but a small error in the near approaches to a bay, river mouth, or harbor entrance could be disastrous—not only for the ship and its lading, but also in many cases for the port of call and its commerce. At many ports, the grounding or sinking of one large vessel anywhere along their main entrance channels could stagnate shipping in and out of them for weeks and even months. The traversing of those last few miles (the *first* few miles of an outward-bound passage) nearly always is a difficult and demanding operation.

The taking of bearings and the setting of courses must be done with precision, and the pilot must be unremittingly aware of the drift and set caused by currents, tides, and winds. Landmark objects on shore and artificial aids to navigation such as buoys, beacons, lighthouses, light-ships, and range markers must be positively identified as they are made use of—at night as well as in the daytime—and the ship's speed through the water must be computed accurately as it is timed from one fix to another. There can be topographical features or sets of circumstances that make it mandatory for ships to run on a certain course from a certain point at a certain speed for a certain number of minutes—no more and no less!—and then make a sharp turn "right on the dot," the only possible way to get through safely without delay. Each ship's draft or depth in the water and the varying depths of the bay or other estuary must be known and borne in mind, and since each piloted vessel may be approached by various other vessels coming from all directions, important decisions regarding speed and course changes must be made instantaneously. In poor visibility weather, all of the radar pips must be identified *immediately*.

Only a local expert can cope with these local problems successfully, and the certified licensed port pilot is such an expert. He has devoted a good part of his life to the preparation and training necessary to qualifying for a place in this important profession, and what he knows of the port's approaches and their dangers is comparable to the doctor's knowledge of the human body and the diseases and trauma that affect it injuriously. Just like the medical profession, too, the pilotage profession has been growing and forming and acquiring its core of substantive skill and knowledge and ethical tenets *for thousands of years*.

The dangers—the rocks and the shoals and the wrecked ships and the meandering channels, all hidden from view, usually—were there outside safe harbors everywhere in the world far back in antiquity, just as they are there now. The same navigational needs that we have now, fundamentally, also were there then, and it is well known from ancient writings and records that professional pilots were there too, to guide ships and their precious cargoes of property and people around the rocks and shoals and wrecks and along the hidden winding channels. The need for such specialists undoubtedly was recognized back then along with the need to guarantee, in part at least, the safe passages of those ships and their precious cargoes. And so there has come to us from the cradle of civilization, in relatively unchanged form, a profession that is as essential today as it was then before the dawn of history.

The real beginnings of transportation by waterborne vessels are so far back in the early stages of civilization as to be lost in antiquity—

so that it would be next to impossible for anyone to state with accuracy what was the certain time in ancient history when the first vessels were first put to use as transports carrying human beings or other cargo across a body of water. Likewise, it would be almost impossible for anyone to say with certainty when or at what point in the long and motley history of ancient ships and shipping the first pilot appeared on the scene. We do know for certain that it was thousands of years ago.

The Bible speaks of pilots in several places, and we find the concept of pilotage in ancient classical writings, those of Homer and Virgil presenting specific accounts of the workings of the profession. Almost without exception, all of these references to pilots by the ancients were deferential, commendatory, and admiring—unlike some defamatory references in certain legal documents of some thousand years later. In Virgil's great classic, *The Aeneid*, Plainurus, the pilot who guided Aeneas's fleet of ships, is eulogized again and again by the author. In Homer's *Iliad*, written many hundreds of years earlier, Thestor, "the pilot who guided the ships of the Achaeans to Ilium" is called "the best of augurs, a man who knows the past, the present, and the future." For us, this would translate into: "a good man at predicting the weather and plotting courses that keep ships from going aground or foundering on submerged rocks or wrecks."

The following paragraph is an excerpt from an antiquated maritime book, *Ocean, River, and Shore Navigation*, by the brothers A. Willcock and J.W. Willcock, published in London in the year 1863:

> The Egyptians of Memphis, 3500 years before the Christian era, and centuries before that period, the Egyptians of Thebes navigated the bounteous Nile. Their river was then a great highway, and during no inconsiderable portion of the year, its northern regions were a wide expanse of water dotted with towns and villages extending to the sea.... During one short period, the Pharaohs held dominion over the eastern part of the Mediterranean Sea ... a ship was the religious emblem of Egypt ... but their ships probably were manned by Phoenician mariners, those from the coasts of Asia Minor, Arabia, and the Isles of Cyprus and Crete....

It is certain that guides or pilots for ships were on the scene, perhaps in great numbers, long before the beginnings of the Christian era; and if we are to believe the historical records that tell us of the splendiferous oar-and-sail ships of the ancient Phoenicians and Egyptians, it seems very likely that professional pilots were guiding ships through areas of navigational dangers within sight of land 3000 years and more before the coming of Christ.

Two

Rhodes

The island of Rhodes, located off the southwestern corner of Asian Turkey, in the confluence of the Mediterranean and Aegean Seas, has a long and glorious maritime history, along with the two Mediterranean islands of Cyprus and Crete, not quite close enough to be called neighboring or sister islands, but close enough to have had a great influence on the commerce and culture of the city-state of Rhodes.

In that previously mentioned historical work by the brothers Wellcock, we find this:

> From about B.C. 2000 to B.C. 1550 ... the rule of the Phoenicians or peoples of a kindred race extended almost along the whole northern coast of Egypt, the whole coast of Syria, and the coast of Asia Minor perhaps as far as Rhodes; and that island, with Crete and Cyprus, was under the influence of Phoenician habits and sentiments, the love of commerce by land and sea....

The home territory of the Phoenician civilization was the eastern Mediterranean coastal area that now is Lebanon—just around the corner, one might say, from the mouth of the Nile and Egyptian shipping and commerce; and most historians are in general agreement on the once-upon-a-time cordial relationships existing between those ancient Phoenicians and the Egyptians. It becomes quite evident that the Phoenicians gained seafaring and trading knowledge from the Egyptians, used it well, and passed it on to the inhabitants of Cyprus, Crete, and Rhodes.

The encyclopedia tells us that the Phoenicians were an *inland* Middle East people who had migrated westward to the seacoast, that by the year 1250 B.C. they were well established as navigators and traders, and that they sailed and traded all over the Mediterranean and even into the Atlantic.

> From Cyprus, the tide of commerce flowed on to Rhodes fertilizing the seacoasts as it flowed. It wafted into this celebrated colony the institutions which took root and flourished there. This little island gave few colonies to commerce, but it preserved and concentrated its laws, and performed a part more important than any other Phoenician or Grecian state.

Again this is an excerpt from the Wellcock history, and the "part more important" to which it refers is this little Mediterranean island's establishment and promulgation of the oldest formal set of maritime laws on record, The Naval Laws and Statutes of the Rhodians. Ancient historians have agreed on the year 408 B.C. as the date of the founding of the city-state of Rhodes. It reached its maritime greatness in the third and second centuries B.C. It is apparent that the stream of nautical knowledge and experience flowed from Egypt to Phoenicia to Cyprus to Rhodes and other Mediterranean ports of call over a period of some 3000 years.

This set of laws, promulgated long before the beginning of the Christian era, was adopted by the conquering Romans and was highly respected by them. Noteworthy for us is Article II of the first segment, fragmented and recovered only in part, which reads: "The Wages of the Pilot shall be a Portion and a half."

In the Wellcock history, we find this:

> The commercial ordinances of Rhodes, derived perhaps from her Phoenician progenitors, established themselves among the codes of imperial Rome and laid the foundations of the medieval and still accepted rules of the sea. This little state still reigns as the only recognized ruler of oceans which she never knew; to the Atlantic and the Pacific, she has given the law. Of the laws, one portion is distinctly adopted in the fourteenth book of the digest which contains the Roman institutions as to the conduct and contracts of the mariners and the owners of ships.

In a learned jurisprudence treatise, *Dominion of the Sea*, written by one Justice Alexander over 250 years ago, there are these commetaries concerning the Roman adoption of the Naval Laws and Statutes of the Rhodians:

> ...even the Victorious Romans themselves ... paid so great a Deference and Respect that, to the immortal glory of their Authors, they (the laws) were honored with the singular Approbation of the Roman Emperors as well as their Senate.
>
> The Laws of the Rhodians were so much esteemed among the

> Ancient Romans that they were unanimously received as the Rule of all Maritime Affairs, except in cases where they were directly opposite to the Native Laws of their (conquered) Country. And as the Fraud and Dishonesty of Men had found means to elude the true Design and Intent of the first Rhodian Legislators, the Romans took care to reform such Abuses by some explanatory Additions to the aforesaid Laws which, as long as that Monarchy lasted, they always held in great Veneration.

Thus these Naval Laws and Statutes of the Rhodians became the maritime laws and statutes of the great Roman Empire, with only minor changes and additions, and with certain adaptations to avoid conflict with the working laws of the conquered nations over which it held dominion. They undoubtedly were put in force throughout the broad expanse of the empire and became an integral part of the commerce and culture of the Roman era.

We, today, seafarers or landlubbers, realizing it or not, are under the influence of that ancient set of maritime laws established on the island of Rhodes, and many persons might be disposed to say that this was a more important accomplishment than the construction and erection of the famed and fabled Colossus of Rhodes. This was a gigantic bronze statue of Helios, the sun god, in the harbor of the city of Rhodes, now the capital of that proud and illustrious little island colony. Certainly that giant statue at the harbor entrance was a welcome guide for mariners, though not the sort for mariners with which we will be concerned throughout these pages.

It is unfortunate that the record of those ancient Rhodian laws was not found in its complete form but only in two fragmentary segments, with portions of both segments missing and lost to history and mankind—though not altogether irretrievably, as we shall see. One segment, referred to as "Section I" by the archaeologists, contains 21 articles of the maritime law, while the other segment, called "Section II," contains 51 articles, distinct and legible.

Those 21 articles of Section I deal with such things as: wages of crewmen and officers, passengers and their treatment, monies aboard ship, oaths of service, loans and interest, relationships between crewmen, officers, and merchants, space aboard ship, and other related matters.

The articles of Section II are concerned with the areas of theft, quarreling, fighting, corporal punishment, lightening of ships in storms, shipwreck, negligence, damages, charter parties, stowage, consignments, demurrage, laying to anchor or mooring, collisions, spoilage of cargo, death at sea, and a long list of other maritime matters.

Since we find only one meager reference to pilotage and pilots in these Naval Laws and Statutes of the Rhodians—that very succinct Article II that deals with the wages of pilots—it seems to be quite probable that some of those portions that were lost may have been concerned directly or indirectly with those seagoing guides, though that may never be confirmed with absolute certainty based on documentary evidence.

However, the fact that later maritime laws based on the Rhodian concept, those of the Romans and the northern Europeans in particular, covered piloting and the conduct of pilots in great detail gives us ample reason to believe that some of those lost portions of this important set of laws were "not altogether irretrievably" lost to us.

It is not only the later laws of the Romans and the northern Europeans, but also the writings of historians, that tell us about the existence of piloting and its being held in high esteem at the time of the establishment of the Rhodian laws. For example, Justice Alexander, writing about that period, those laws, and that profession of piloting in his book, *Dominion of the Sea*, has this to say:

> ...it was usual for the Pilots not only to direct the Ship's course but to steer her too themselves, as indeed they are still obliged to do among us, when the Ship has any dangerous Place to pass through, or is so near to any Shoar, that a more than ordinary Skill is requisite to bring her off safe.

This would indicate that the term "pilot," or its equivalent in whatever language, as used in that period, referred to a professional seaman who was qualified to do much more than merely steer a straight compass course on the open sea, a not too difficult assignment ordinarily. It seems to have been acknowledged even then and earlier in history that a member of a ship's complement designated as pilot and charged with the responsibility of guiding her through areas of nautical dangers close to land needed a knowledge and skill above and beyond that normally required for the handling of a ship out on the open sea and that, when one so skilled was not available from the regular crew of a vessel, a local pilot would be brought out from shore to do the job.

However, for many hundreds of years, there was scarcely any distinction between pilots with special skills and accurate knowledge of local port conditions and those pilots (so-called) who stayed with ships as crew members throughout long voyages. That distinction, of necessity, had to come about eventually, and it did come about long after the hey-day of Rhodes. The distinction was clear-cut and lasting. Bar, bay, harbor, and river pilots became a type of mariner distinctly set aside from all others, and they merited special consideration in the regulatory laws of maritime nations.

Nevertheless, the superior skill and knowledge of those pilots attached to ships as regular crew members in those ancient times were highly respected, and that solitary brief reference to pilots in the original Rhodes laws attests to that: "The wages of the Pilot shall be a Portion and a half." This meant that the pilot received as his pay one-half more than the regular share of an ordinary seaman at the end of a voyage. This was fairly high pay, since the captain or master himself received only a double share—of course not counting all of the shares that went "to the ship," if he happened to be the owner as well.

Three

Oléron

Oléron is a small island in the Bay of Biscay just off the middle Atlantic coast of France. It is in the Department of Charente and near the mouth of the Charente River. Like Rhodes, it too is famous for the set of maritime laws promulgated from it, the Naval Laws of Oléron, though this landmark legislation was enacted some 1500 years after the Rhodian laws were first published. Unlike Rhodes, this island can boast that its set of laws, first called "The Roll of Oléron," has been preserved in its entirety and is the oldest complete and available body of maritime regulations in existence.

The religious Crusades to the Holy Land of that era were responsible for this turn of events and this distinction given to this little island, only 68 square miles in area. Many of the Crusaders, especially those high in the royal houses and governments of their countries, were very much impressed by the maritime customs and regulations of the Near East countries. They saw a need for the overhaul and revision of the laws of the sea in their own and other northern European countries, in order to incorporate some of the more desirable features of the system existent in the eastern Mediterranean, where the laws of the Rhodians and the Romans were in use and working well.

Two of these observant crusaders were King Richard I of England, who had led the Third Crusade to the Holy Land with two other monarchs, and his mother, Queen Elinor, the Duchess of Guyenne. On his way home to England by ship, the king put in to Oléron with his retinue and his mother.

Guyenne was a province of southwest France under English rule at that time. Its area comprised territory that later was all of five different departments (political subdivisions similar to the states of the United States) in the region of Bordeau and that little island of Oléron. A random historical reference to Queen Elinor refers to Oléron as "her beloved isle."

While he was here, according to some historians, King Richard wrote those laws and regulations and had them published and established. They came to be known in England as: "An abstract of the Naval Laws of Oléron instituted by Richard I, King of England, in his return from the Holy Land in the End of the Eleventh Century for the better Regulation of Merchants, Owners, and Masters of Ships and Mariners; and all Sea-faring Persons in Maritime Affairs." The wording and the spelling are those of Justice Alexander in his juridical treatise, *Dominion of the Sea*.

While the English have attributed these laws to King Richard, French historians have attributed them to his mother. According to Justice Alexander:

> Queen Elinor ... returning from her voyage to the Holy Land at the same time that the Customs of the Sea in the East inserted in the Book of the Consulat were in Vogue and Credit all over the Levant, ordered the first Project of Judgements or Laws to be drawn up, which were called the *Roll of Oléron*, from the name of her beloved Isle, which was to be a Law in all the Southern Sea and to decide all Disputes relating to Navigation.

"Southern Sea" undoubtedly referred to that part of the Atlantic Ocean that was south of England and west of France, for their authenticated world was comparatively small in those days, and in line with its limited scope, the Irish Sea was called the "Western Sea" around that time.

However, the writings of other historians have made it appear doubtful that either the king or his mother had much to do with the actual formation of the Laws of Oléron, except for their having sojourned there and contributed pertinent information gained from their Crusade experiences.

According to the Wellcocks, as they write of Oléron:

> ...Its lawyers and merchants appear to have made this collection (about the year 1190) from their own observances and convictions, and the information as to Rhodian, Italian, and Saracenic institutions derivable from the Code and Collections of Amalfi and Barcelona. Common acceptance, not regal authority, has made it part of the European Law ... the Collection was progressive and not completed til about 1266.

The contradictions concerning the authorship of the set of laws called the *Roll of Oléron* was never resolved authoritatively. Eventually they came to be known as the "Naval Laws of Oléron," were adopted as such into England's "Black Book of the Admiralty," and are referred to as such in matters of jurisprudence dealing with maritime crimes and regulations.

These laws covered nearly every facet of maritime legality known to the Admiralty at that time, from shipwreck to misconduct of masters and crewmen. There were forty-seven articles in all, *and three of them dealt exclusively with pilotage.*

None of these three dealt with the wages or pay of pilots or with considerations, comforts, or conveniences to be accorded them. Instead, all three of them dealt with appropriate harsh punishments to be meted out to pilots when they failed to do their jobs or do their jobs well, either through ignorance, neglect, poor judgment, or malice aforethought.

The punishment described in these articles was rather severe. Article XXIII read:

> If a pilot undertake the Conduct of a Vessel, to bring her to Saint Malo or any other Port, and fail of his duty therein, so as the Vessel miscarry by reason of his ignorance in what he undertook, and the merchants sustain damage thereby, he shall be obligated to make full satisfaction for the same, if he has wherewithal, and if not, lose his head.

In other words, if he couldn't pay, he couldn't stay.

Article XXIV augmented the severity of that punishment by stating that it could be handed out by the captain or crew or merchant charterers without any legal trial or official process whatever:

> And if the Master or any one of his Mariners or any one of the Merchants cut off his head, they shall not be bound to answer for it: but before they do, they must be sure that he had not wherewith to make satisfaction.

Article XXV was not concerned with the *beheading* of pilots but only with the *hanging* of pilots — by the neck until they die — not from yardarms but from "high gibbets" erected on shore at or near the places where they had brought ships to ruin *on purpose*. This article was rather long-drawn-out in language and rather clumsily worded. It seems to have been a prodigious attempt to mandate against a certain underhanded practice in which several conspirators, one of whom would be a certified pilot, would arrange to wreck a ship, by accident supposedly, so that, under the unusual salvage customs of the time, it might be looted without interference or reprisal. This article is worth a complete reading, for its plaintive awkwardness, if for nothing else:

> If a Ship or other Vessel arriving at any place, and making in towards Port or Harbour, set out her Flag, or give any other Sign to have a Pilot come aboard, or a Boat to tow her into the Harbour, the Wind or Tide being contrary, and a Contract be made for piloting the said Vessel into the said Harbour accordingly; but by reason of an unreasonable and accursed Custom, in some Places, that the third or fourth Part of the Ships that are lost shall accrue to the Lord of the Place where such sad Casualties happen, as also the like Proportion to the Salvors, and only the Remainder to the Master, Merchant, and Mariners: The Persons contracting for the Pilotage of the said Vessel, to ingratiate themselves with their Lords, and to gain themselves a part of the Ship and Lading, do, like faithless and treacherous Villains, sometimes even willingly and out of Design to ruin Ship and Goods, guide and bring her upon the Rocks, and then feigning to aid, help and assist the now distressed Mariners, are the first in dismembering and pulling the Ship to Pieces, purloining and carrying away the Lading thereof, contrary to all Reason and good Conscience. And afterwards, that they be the more welcome to their Lord, do with all good Speed post to his House with the sad Narrative of this unhappy Disaster; whereupon the said Lord with his Retinue appears at the Place and takes his Share; the Salvors take theirs; and what remains the Merchants and Mariners may have. But seeing that this is contrary to the Law of God, our Edict and Determination is that, notwithstanding any Law or Custom to the Contrary, it is said and ordained, the said Lord of that Place, the Salvors, and all others that take away any of the said Goods, shall be Accursed and Excommunicated and punished as Robbers and Thieves as formerly hath been declared. But all false and treacherous Pilots shall be condemned to suffer a most rigorous and unmerciful Death; and high Gibbets shall be erected for them in the same Place or as nigh as conveniently may be, where they so guided or brought any Ship or Vessel to Ruin, as aforesaid; and thereon these accursed Pilots are with Ignominy and much Shame to end their Days; which said Gibbets are to abide and remain to succeeding Ages at that Place, as a Visible Caution to other Ships that shall afterwards sail thereby.

The severity of those punishments dealt out to erring pilots, as compared to that meted out to other malefactors within the seafaring fraternity, would seem to belie the assertion made herein elsewhere to the effect that pilots of those times were held in very high esteem. On the contrary, this would seem to be indicative of the great value placed upon the skill and know-how of the people in the piloting profession and upon the strict code of ethics to which all of them, ordinarily, scribed. It was like saying that pilots were trusted so much and so reverently that it would be an unpardonable offense if any were to betray that trust through default in any form.

There is cause to wonder and marvel at the fortitude of those brave souls who dared to offer their services as pilots in those times in the face of those punishments prescribed *just for them*.

Four

The High and Mighty Pilots

During the first centuries of the Christian era, long before the Roll of Oléron had come into being of course, Arab mariners were extensively engaged in professional ship guiding services in the Middle East and the Indian Ocean. Hundreds of years later, when Marco Polo made his historic first voyage to the Orient in the year 1271, Arab pilots were still around. They evidently had some somewhat superior knowledge in maritime affairs, and their Arab confreres were among the first to use the ship-born magnetic compass intelligently. The Polos—father, son, and uncle—employed Arab pilots to guide them in the Indian Ocean, and it is recorded that, on the way home from Peiping to Venice many years later, Marco Polo made exceptionally good and fortuitous use of charts prepared by those Arab sailormen.

Some 200 years still later, Arab pilots were still around and some were used by Vasco da Gama, the famous Portuguese mariner on that historic first voyage around the Cape of Good Hope and the African continent to India and the Far East.

Throughout most of the Middle Ages, the term *pilot*—which is to say, the equivalent designation in the various languages and dialects—was in use mainly to refer to the steersman of a vessel, the man at the tiller or helm (the ship's wheel would not come into existence until many years later). He was a specialist of no great importance afloat or ashore. In the later years of that period, however, when the navigational responsibilities had increased immeasurably and were discharged in admirable fashion by a long line of capable pilots, the label designated the sailing master or chief navigator of a vessel or fleet of vessels.

Christopher Columbus and Ferdinand Magellan both were called "Pilot" with great respect and admiration, though it is well known that both made use of subordinate navigators to guide their expeditions in the New World. Columbus's chief pilot on his first two westward voyages was Juan de la Cosa, a Spaniard, who also was the owner of the flagship *Santa Maria*, on board which he had a berth and a sort of command post. Magellan's chief pilot, assigned to the flagship *Trinidada* as "King's Pilot," was Esteban Gomez, a fellow Portuguese. Apparently the skills and the navigational abilities of all pilots then were so highly regarded that it was considered very complimentary to call the expedition commanders "Pilot" too.

By the time of Magellan and Drake, the piloting profession was well established, though the pilots of those days had a somewhat different status than the pilots of modern and very ancient times. In those times, the label was applied to a sailorman who was a highly-regarded, permanent member of a ship's complement or crew and was responsible for determing the ship's courses throughout an entire voyage, both on the open sea and in the close confines of the approaches to a new and unfamiliar port of call. Also, he was expected to participate in general overall charting operations and the compiling of New World navigation data for the king or queen of the country being represented in the expedition. In appreciation of his skill and accomplishments, he might be given a high and prestigious post in the government of that country.

It was the custom then for a royal house to appoint a Chief Pilot, King's Pilot, *Pilote Major*, or "Grand Pilot of the Realm," making him an overlord of all maritime expeditions and explorations to whom all fleet captains and pilots must report. For example, Amerigo Vespucci, the Italian explorer and navigator after whom America was named, was appointed *Chief Pilot of Spain* in 1508 and made responsible for the preparation of nautical charts to be used by all of Spain's ship masters. Orders were given to all of those sailing to new and unfamiliar regions of the New World and India to report all discoveries of islands, bays, rivers, harbors, straits, currents, shallows, deeps, natural landmarks, etc., to the Chief Pilot so that pertinent charts could be prepared and kept up-to-date.

Explorer Sebastian Cabot became *Grand Pilot of England* by appointment of King Edward VI in 1549. He was one of those who had made official reports to Vespucci, most of them undoubtedly covering the coast of North America, which he had explored so thoroughly for Spain. He also worked for the Portuguese at one time. He was commissioned by Don Emanuel, King of Portugal, to discover the reported new route to the Moluccas, the "Spice Islands" of the Pacific, by way of the Straits of Magellan, but he failed to do this. Vespucci also was given the same assignment by the same Portuguese king, and he too failed. Those and other, similar failures, by Italians, Portuguese, Spaniards, all served to enhance the reputation of Ferdinand Magellan.

Englishman Richard Hakluyt, famous medieval historian who devoted his life to the collection and preservation of documents containing firsthand information on important voyages of discovery and exploration, tells of this royal appointment in these words:

> King Edward the Sixth, that prince of peerless hope, with the advice of his sage and prudent counsaille, before he entered into the Northeasterne discovery, advanced the worthy and excellent Sebastion Cabot to be Grand Pilot of England, allowing him a most bountiful pension (of 166 pounds) by the year during his life.

Esteban Gomez, on the flagship of Magellan's fleet, had been named "King's Pilot," which title gave him prestige and made him one of the top men in the expedition but not *the* top man. In South America, after a mutiny had been put down, he was transferred to the *San Antonio*, the heaviest ship of the fleet.

Later, when all five ships of the fleet, one of them wrecked, were already in the Straits of Magellan on their perilous journey through to the Pacific Ocean, Gomez, worried about a shortage of provisions and the possibility of starvation, and feeling that the expedition's mission had been accomplished by their discovery of the Straits, persuaded the commander of the *San Antonio* to desert. They sailed back to Spain with most of the provisions and elaborate tales of Magellan's tyrannical abuses and his executions of members of the expedition without good and sufficient reason allegedly.

Sir Francis Drake, on his greatest voyage, had a top-notch pilot, Nuna da Silva, a Portuguese, to whom the whole world is indebted, not only for his navigational accomplishments but also for his accurate and excellent log and records keeping. Historians have been deeply grateful and appreciative of the neat logs and colorful writings he left behind. Originals, in his own handwriting, may be found in the *Archivo General de Indias* at Seville, Spain, a vast depository of documents concerning the Spanish and Portuguese voyages and conquests that began with the opening of the Far East, the discovery of America, and the partitioning of the earth's areas.

Before teaming up with Drake, Nuna da Silva had been master and pilot of the Portuguese ship *Maria*, very probably an armed merchantman like so many other ships of the times. He met up with Drake in the vicinity of the Cape Verde Islands off Africa at the beginning of Drake's epic voyage around the world. Drake attacked the *Maria*, defeated her, and took her as a prize, along with her cargo and her master, da Silva. Both the ship and her master became accepted members of the English expedition, the *Maria*'s cargo and her ship's stores became a welcome assist, and da Silva became a loyal friend of Drake as they sailed across the South Atlantic to South America and through the Straits of Magellan into the broad Pacific.

Arriving there, the fleet, now only three ships instead of six, was beset by terrible troubles in the form of adverse winds and currents and prolonged, generally dirty weather. Attempting to sail westward, they were driven far to the south and east, to an area much further south than Cape Horn, and were blown almost back into the Atlantic. For two whole months, they fought their way back, as if they were ships of a later era beating their way "around the Horn." Two more ships were lost in the struggle and only the flagship, the *Pelican*, was left. Nuna da Silva's log told the whole story with remarkable accuracy, as was proved over and over again in later years.

Eventually winning the battle, Drake and da Silva found a safe anchorage and fair winds at a small island a little way north of the Pacific mouth of the Straits and about 15 miles off the mainland. Here Drake changed the name of his ship to *Golden Hind*, after the heraldic device of his patron, Sir Christopher Hatton, then Vice Chamberlain to the Queen and later Chancellor of England. After some rest and recuperation for all hands, Drake proceeded to sail northward up the entire west coast of South America, making captures on the way, to Mexico and California, and thence across the Pacific and around the world to England and knighthood.

Da Silva was set free and put ashore in Mexico, where the poor fellow met a sad fate that included imprisonment and the torture of the inquisition, for the Spaniards had heard about him, much to their bitter annoyance, and those Spaniards of "New Spain," which included nearly all of South and Central America and Mexico, counted it a stroke of good fortune when he was delivered right into their hands. They believed even then that Drake was still leading a sizable armada along the Pacific coast to prey on their ships and cities. Just prior to da Silva's capture at Guatulco, Mexico, Gaspar de Vargas, the Chief Alcalde (combination mayor-judge) had reported to the Viceroy of New Spain as follows:

> Drake carries with him a Portuguese pilot who is very skillful. It seems that it is he who governs and directs this armada. This Portuguese speaks the English language as though it were his own, and he is the General's all in all.

(In those times, the flag officer of a fleet usually was given the title of *Captain-General*.)

When the Spaniards got all the information they could out of Nuna da Silva regarding the activities and future plans of Francis Drake, he was released and sent to Spain. It is recorded that he later went to England to live, under an assumed name, that he was paid in full for the property taken from him by Drake, and that the correctness of his written record of the famous voyage was vouched for by Drake and members of the crew of the *Golden Hind*.

This record was the basis for various books and narratives concerning the expedition. Especially noteworthy were those published by Richard Hakluyt, who usually managed to get his stories of great voyages into print while many of the principals were still alive and available for interviewing at first hand. Because of da Silva's astuteness in keeping a log, Hakluyt was able to publish an account of the voyage that gave actual courses, positional fixes, chronologies, landfalls, anchorages, and arrivals and departures of Drake's *Pelican/Golden Hind*, leading the expedition, all cross-checked and corroborated.

Those high and mighty pilots of those adventurous and perilous times are far removed from the category of port pilots with which we are concerned, and actually they are an entirely different breed, a vanished or extinct breed in truth. For that reason therefore, it seems best that we have done with them — but not before the telling of this one last little anecdote:

In 1683, a respectable, knowledgeable English navigator and pilot by the name of Cowley joined an expedition under John Cooke and William Dampier, celebrated adventurer, on a ship named *Revenge*. It was a smallish bark with a crew of 52 and an armament of 8 cannon, and Cowley supposed it to be just another armed trader or merchantman. Once at sea, however, he was informed that the object of the enterprise was straight-out piracy and nothing else, and he was forced to become an accessory to captures, blood baths, looting, and plain and fancy buccaneering. From pilot to pirate!

Five

Transition

For centuries, as has been noted heretofore, the pilot who directed a ship's courses across a far-flung ocean also brought her into each port of call, except when his unfamiliarity with the near approaches to any port made that a dangerous thing to do—dangerous for the ship and its cargo, that is. This was true in so many cases that there grew up a practice of taking along an extra pilot who was especially skilled in ship handling within the confines of bays and estuaries containing hidden dangers in the form of sunken wrecks, shallows, sandbars, and other underwater obstructions, along with generally scanty maneuvering room.

Eventually, it came to be realized and acknowledged that safe and efficient pilotage in such cases required the local knowledge of resident local pilots rather than the techniques of traveling pilots no matter how skillful they might be. Ultimately, the term *pilot* began to be applied only to those local ship guides who permanently engaged in the occupation of conducting ships safely over bars and shoals and around submerged rocks and wrecks and other hazards into secure anchorages in sheltered harbors. Thus they were set apart from those others who had been called "pilot"—in whatever language—down through the centuries.

The transition was a long time in the making—hundreds of years in fact. Although the ancient Naval Laws and Statutes of the Rhodians made no clear distinction between pilots with special knowledge and skills pertaining to local, individual seaports and those expert ship handlers who stayed with ships throughout long voyages, The Naval Laws of Oléron (about A.D. 1200) saw to it that the function of piloting by the typical bay or bar pilot was set apart definitely from all other forms of maritime activity.

Here is a commentary from Justice Alexander's book, *Dominion of the Sea*, on this differentiation back in medieval times:

> The Original calls these Pilots *Locmen*; for when those Laws were written, there were Officers aboard all Ships called *Pilots* who went the whole Voyage, whereas the Locmen were like our Pilots, Mariners hired at every River to guide the Ships; for dwelling at the Place, the Locmen was supposed to know the Shoar better than the Ship's Pilot, who perhaps was never there before: for which reason, he commonly required the Master to have a Locman, to avoid Rocks, Shelves, Shoals, and Sands which he must be well-acquainted with by long using the River. That of Roan is very dangerous on this account, and there are sworn Pilots every two Leagues to guide Ships up the Seine. They are very necessary all over Brittany.

These locmen or bar pilots, often called lodesmen as well, were once quite numerous on the coast of France and could indeed be found every two leagues (every six nautical miles). "Sworn pilots," in this commentary, undoubtedly meant just that—that they had sworn an oath affirming that they knew the waters well and knew their business, for which they had been given official certification. They were numerous also, at about the same time, in the British Isles and the Baltic countries and in Holland, the little country with the big maritime heritage.

The Dutch were not only one of the very first peoples to pioneer in the concept of an organized, regulated, professional ship guidance system for the seaports of their country, but they also were responsible for the word *pilot* coming into our English language, just as they were responsible for the origination of *yacht* and *sloop* and other nautical words of ours.

It has been established authoritatively that *pilot* derives from the Old-Dutch *piloot*, which derives from two Dutch words *pijl* and *lood*, meaning "pole" and "lead," the mineral substance. With the Dutch people, however, *pijl* also is the designation for anything vertically straight, straight-up-and-down, perpendicular, plumb. That is how they got *piloot*. A man who measured the various depths of a port's approaches by means of a light line fastened to a lead weight periodically sunk to the bottom from the deck of a vessel underway was a *pijl-lood* man, because he got his measurements when the line was taut and straight-up-and-down between the bottom and the surface. To better appreciate the probable facility with which the two words married and became one, one should keep in mind the fact that the Dutch letter *J* is pronounced like the English letter *Y*. We got *yacht* from the Dutch word *jagt*, meaning "chase" or "hunt" and pronounced "yacht." The English people adopted *piloot* and revised it into *pilot* as a matter of course, Anglicizing it, so to speak, as they did with so many other foreign words. Dutch pilots often are called "loods" familiarly, in the same way that a carpenter's mate in the U.S. Navy is called "chips."

The Dutchmen's pioneering into the concept of an organized pilotage system introduced a new element into the evolution of the art and science of guiding ships through dangerous areas close to land. It implied a distinction between the random use of part-time pilots, qualified or not, and the regular use of an organized system of pilotage by a group of certified, well-qualified pilots offering their services on a permanent, continuing basis. This innovation evidently was the forerunner of professional pilotage as we know it today.

Another maritime first for this little country of Holland was the very earliest record of a professional pilot, one who publicly announced that he was a professional and an expert and ready, willing, and able to guide sailing ships in and out of the seaports of Holland for pay. This was a man named Franz Naereabout, who must have realized that the slow and tedious process of creeping into a port using the lead line over and over again could be supplanted by a swift, sure, safe passage guided by experienced, expert pilots who were in constant possession of a complete store of up-to-date knowledge regarding all characteristics and peculiarities of the approaches to the various ports.

By making use of marker buoys, beacons, range lights, stakes, signs, natural landmarks on shore, gossip clearing houses, and even, as some have alleged, a kind of sixth sense compounded from borrowings from each of the original five, they could stick to pre-determined, well-traveled, and well-tried paths and conduct ships safely in and out of harbors, easily avoiding each and every danger spot, as if they were using the electronic sounding devices later to be invented. This is the essence of modern piloting, except that most ships of today *do* have electronic depth-measuring devices on board and in operation most of the time that they are underway in unfamiliar waters close to land. That alleged sixth sense often has been referred to by the use of the phrase "He smells his way in."

In the book *Pilot Lore from Sail to Steam*, there are these paragraphs about this first professional pilot and this transitional period, in which was created the prototype organization for the modern, organized, world professional pilotage systems now in existence:

> For ages the navigators of the Old World had been familiar with the plumb and sounding line—even though we cannot state, even approximately, the date when the plumb and sounding line's efficacy was first discovered by a navigator—but it was not until Franz Naerebout, born in Gees, Province of Zeeland in 1749, announced himself as being a professional *pijl lood*, ready to take the sailing ships of his day in and out of the seaports of Holland, the approaches to which he had studied until he knew the location of every danger spot, that pilotage, as such, became a science and an art.

> The Dutch Society for the promotion of the General Welfare has reared an appreciative memorial over the grave of Franz Naerebout, the original professional pilot, who had been offered a huge salary by the British government to serve under the British flag but who refused the tempting bait and remained loyal to his own beloved tricolor until his peaceful end in 1818.

The Dutch people paid this homage to his life and work because they realized that his achievements were of great importance to Holland and the entire world, for, considering the great span of all the centuries during which piloting in random, haphazard forms had existed, this creation of the first organized and regulated pilotage system was long overdue. Truly it may be said of Franz Naerebout that he was the father of professional organized pilotage systems as they exist today. There is a monument to his memory in Bellamy Park, Vlissingen (Flushing), Holland, on which an inscription in Dutch reads as follows:

> FRANZ NAEREBOUT, 1749–1818
> Heroic Saver of Shipwrecked
> Skillful Seaman, Undaunted Pilot

In addition, there is a special charity fund in his name for the support of relatives of certain pilotage staff members who died in World War I and for certain living members who have become ill and incapacitated.

Six

Britannia

The need to have some system of pilotage established and in good working order at the principal ports of England, Ireland, and Scotland was recognized in very early times, even before the time of Franz Naerebout of Holland. Government and the entire mariner fraternity were in full realization of the fact that, without the help of a local pilot to guide the steersman, a ship laden with a precious cargo such as spices from the Indies, lemons from Italy, figs from Greece, oranges from Spain, or very important persons from anywhere in the world could founder or get aground at the entrance to a seaport because of such things as a sudden squall or shift in the wind direction or a bit of careless steering while in the vicinity of a hidden reef, sunken wreck, or adamantine rock formation. They realized that the economic and political well-being of the empire depended on the safe passage of such ships in and out of these ports.

They realized also that there could be no substitute for an intimate, personal knowledge of a port's hidden dangers, the reefs, shoals, rocks, wrecks, and meandering channel paths that lie about its entrance. They therefore encouraged not only the formation of associations of local pilots at the various ports but also the instituting of the concept of "compulsory pilotage," whereby ship masters are compelled by law to use the services of local pilots at certain ports. Various forms of this compulsory pilotage idea are now in effect at various ports all over the world.

The development of pilotage systems and organizations in the British Isles was not as rapid or profound as that which took place in Holland, and professional British pilot organizations were slow in coming. When they did come, they followed the guild ideology in general in their operation. The very nature of the occupation and its local sore need for fraternity, mutual cooperation, and solidarity of purpose and outlook fostered this adoption of the guild pattern, since it seemed best fitted for the type of organization required for the services to be rendered.

The fraternity and mutual cooperation of the traditional merchant and craft guilds of medieval England were copied in the forming of the novel pilot associations, and all of this has remained with them down through the years. Pilots' associations of today still retain the basic features of the guild system, even though many outside observers prefer to regard them merely as tight, ultra-exclusive trade unions; but vestiges of the traditional, fraternal, social, and benevolent features of the medieval guild societies are clearly in evidence in them.

The following is part of a treatise by Grosvenor M. Jones, writing in the U.S. Government publication, *Pilotage in the United States*, put out by the Department of Commerce:

> The earliest form (of pilotage in England) consisted, in all probability, of certain guilds or associations of pilots established at important maritime centers, such as the ports of the English Channel, the Thames, and at Kingston-upon Hull, Newcastle-on-Tyne, and Leith. The primary object of these guilds was the organization of mariners engaged in the trade of the port for their mutual protection and advantage. Later, at each of the districts and places above named, a corporation was established by royal charter, the principal objects of which were, so far as regards pilotage: to provide for the piloting of vessels in and out of the ports under the jurisdiction of the corporation by a body of duly licensed pilots; to prevent unqualified persons from undertaking to pilot vessels at all; and, lastly, to provide for the regulation of the bodies of licensed pilots. These corporations most frequently took the name of the Trinity House of the port or district under their jurisdiction. Thus the Trinity House of Hull is believed to have been established in 1369 and was incorporated in the reign of Henry VIII (1549).

The original Trinity House was a fraternity of seamen connected from early times with the River Thames. They were described in the charter of incorporation granted in the name of the Holy Trinity by King Henry VII on May 20, 1514 as "The Shipmen of Mariners of England."

Its present charter, granted by King James I in 1685, refers to it as: "The Guild, Fraternity, or Brotherhood of the Most Glorious and Undivided Trinity and of Saint Clement in the Parish of Deptford Stronde in the County of Kent." The first appointed master was the founder of the corporation, Sir Thomas Spert, Controller of the Navy.

The corporation is now the general lighthouse authority for England and Wales, the Channel Islands, and Gibraltar; it also is the principal pilotage authority for England and Wales, and its functions in both these respects are controlled by statute. Other Trinity Houses were established under those ancient charters at Hull, Newcastle, and Leith.

Thus the Trinity Houses of England, forerunners of that great maritime nation's pilotage system.

Once established, the pilot guilds of England outlived all economic, social, and political upheavals, including the upsets of the great industrial revolution of the years 1760 to 1800. The industrial revolution in England, with its massive social and economic changes, had almost no effect on the occupation of guiding ships in and out of seaports. That was because the pilot guilds were service guilds rather than craft guilds, all of which suffered mightily and eventually disappeared because of the machinations of the mass-production moguls of industry.

Artisans and skilled craftsmen were replaced by hordes of mere workmen, each of whom would then perform, ordinarily, only one single small part of the work that went into the making of such things as wagons, barrels, shoes. For example, one man would do no job other than drive nails into the heels of shoes all year long and never make a complete pair of shoes that year or ever in his life. Another would put hoops on barrels all day, every day, day after day, and never produce or learn how to produce a complete barrel. True craftsmanship went into a decline and eventually down the drain in deference to the tidal-wave demand for mass production.

In the piloting business, however, there could be neither mass production, with an ever-increasing apportionment of tasks and duties, nor any elite group of merchants or manufacturers or money moguls to control the dispensing of its services. The job of each pilot would continue to be the whole job of bringing the whole ship all of the way in, rather than bringing part of the ship part of the way in. There could be no machines coming into the picture to replace manual labor, for machines could neither board a ship and talk to the master, mate, or quartermaster nor suddenly know that it was necessary to tell one of them: "A little more to leeward" or "Now you must steer directly toward that tallest tower of that green-and-yellow castle yonder."

No inventive genius could design any mechanical devices that would take the place of the pilot's knowledge of the coastal waters near the entrance to a port, the dangers lying submerged there, and the maneuvers to be used in circumventing those dangers. His stock in trade was his training, experience, knowledge, and skill—all acquired through long years of tussling with the sometimes unamiable elements and the cantankerousness of ships and men and the sea. His was a profession apart from the common cacophony of commerce ashore, and although pilots of those days may have looked askance, anxiously and fearfully, at the continuing economic upheavals brought about by the industrial revolution, there was no need to worry, for the upheavals halted at the edge of the sea, as the economic invasion turned aside there. It was as if the watery territory beyond was deemed scarcely worthwhile or vulnerable enough to warrant an assault upon it.

Industry and society made no noticeable effort to change the pattern of activity of the pilot groups, undoubtedly because it was evident that their activities were too highly individualized. Thus the guild pattern prevailed in the profession—down to the present day in fact, and it seems to be as practical now as then.

Some of its advantages are: the voluntary basis of associating, the fraternalism in membership, the highly-developed interdependence of members, the dedication to democracy, the mutual determination of working condition and remuneration, the common treasuries for the common good, the acceptance of regulation by a sovereign body, the common ownership of assets, and joint efforts for the common welfare and protection.

Those Trinity House and corporation pilot groups, strictly regulated by the British government, existed at only a few of the British Isles ports, the larger and more important ones. Elsewhere pilots, competent or not, pursued their profession as individuals or in small unorganized groups. All of them nonetheless came in for government regulation eventually, because of the influence of the Naval Laws of Oléron undoubtedly.

The Naval Laws of Oléron, to which reference is often made in English jurisprudence, had a forceful impact on English maritime legislation, probably because it had been a beloved English king, Richard I, and his mother who supposedly had drafted them originally. They were incorporated into the "Black Book of the Admiralty," that massive compendium of maritime customs and regulations, almost in their entirety, though not quite in their original forms.

The articles that dealt with pilotage and prescribed fitting punishments to be meted out to recalcitrant pilots for malfeasance or misfeasance were altered and amended somewhat to make some of these punishments a little less severe than those in the originals—*but only a little* less severe, as the following amended article, quoted verbatim, will show:

> A managing owner of a ship or vessel who shall let or shall have let it for freight to go any places, in which neither himself nor anyone on board the ship can certify that he knows the navigation will have to hire a pilot who knows the navigation, and that pilot shall affirm and say to the managing owner of the ship that he knows and is certain of his knowledge of those localities in which the managing

owner shall wish to go. And if that pilot shall say that there is no place amongst those parts, where the managing owner wishes to go or shall have let his ship go for freight, which he does not know thoroughly, and that pilot shall perform for the managing owner of the ship all that he has promised well and diligently, the managing owner of the ship or vessel is bound to pay all the wages which shall have been agreed upon between them without any dispute; further, he is bound to give more than he has promised, according to the good qualities and values that shall be in that pilot, because that pilot has performed for that managing owner of the ship all that he has promised. Nevertheless, all the covenants which have been made between the managing owner of the ship and that pilot ought to be all formally entered in the register book of the ship or vessel, because there ought not to be any dispute between the managing owner of a ship or vessel and the person who shall be taken as pilot does not know those parts in which he has said and promised and agreed to pilot the ship or vessel, he who has been taken as pilot, and has promised this to the managing owner of the ship or vessel, and cannot fulfill any things of what he has promised, in such case ought to lose immediately his head, without any remission and without any mercy: and the managing owner of the ship may cause his head to be cut off, and is not obliged to complain to the authorities of the place unless he chooses, because the pilot has deceived him and has placed in peril of destruction the managing owner of the ship and those who depend on him, and in addition the ship and all the goods on board. Nevertheless, it shall not rest solely on the judgement of the managing owner of the ship or vessel that he who shall have been taken as pilot ought to lose head or ought not; on the contrary, it ought to rest on the judgement of the mate and the merchants and all the ship's company. And if all the above mentioned or the greater part see fit and adjudge that he lose his head, he ought to lose it, and if it does not seem fit to them that he ought to lose it, he ought not to lose it; but it shall be done precisely as they adjudge, whether it ought to be done so or not: because if by chance at times a man went as pilot at the discretion of many managing owners of ships, they might well wish that some against whom they had a spite should lose their heads, and in order that the wages which they had promised to pay and ought to pay should remain in their hands, for there are managing owners of ships who are destitute of sense as well as other persons and still more, there are many managing owners of ships who do not know when they should go forward and when backward, nor what the sea is and what it is not. And, therefore, it would be an evil that a man should be put to death at the caprice or the judgement only of the managing owner of the ship or vessel. Wherefore, every man

> who holds himself forth as a pilot ought to beware before he does so that he can and knows how to perform all that he shall promise, in order that the punishment above stated shall not devolve upon him, nor any other loss.

The wording and specifications of that British maritime law, in reality only a slightly watered-down version of one of the harshest of the Naval Laws of Oléron, was some concession to the profession, but altogether they scarcely would lead anyone to believe that the British Admiralty was going soft on pilots at that time.

No such mellowing is going to be encountered, in any investigation into the art and science of pilotage, until one has left the British Isles and the isles of Oléron and Rhodes and has gone to still another isle, the island of Gotland in the Baltic Sea, where still another set of maritime laws once was promulgated.

Seven

Wisby and the Laws

The island of Gotland is off the lower east coast of Sweden, right smack in the middle of the Baltic Sea, about mid-way between Sweden and Latvia in Russia. It was conquered and acquired by Sweden in 1280, when the Viking Age was just about coming to an end. Gotland is important to this investigation into the occupation of piloting only because of the one-time magnificence and fame of its principal city and capital, the port city of Visby, generally known as Wisby to non-Swedes, and the set of maritime laws that was promulgated there.

Wisby, later famous for having given to the world this new, complete body of maritime laws, the celebrated Laws of Wisby, all of which were enlightened, progressive, and comprehensive, then was famous as a free port and city of astoundingly great commerce and trade, with very noticeable international aspects. For many years, it was the hub and focal point of northern hemisphere trading and the most renowned market-place in all of Europe.

Many factors helped to make this so. It had a fine, roomy harbor, a temperate, pleasant climate, a centralized, isolated location, and an almost complete independence of any continental control or influence. It was a free port in the fullest meaning of the term and a sanctuary for traders of all kinds—ship masters, merchants, importers, artisans, slave traders, pirates, thieves, and scalawags. It was inevitable that all of them and this city should prosper enormously. Wisby was indeed a true city-state and became at one time a veritable dynasty and capital city of the sea.

The Wellcocks, in their historical work, *The Ocean, the River, and the Shore*, long ago explained a good portion of the phenomena of Wisby thusly:

> The island of Gothland in the Baltic, situated midway between Sweden and Courland (Latvia), with a commodious Harbor on its

> western side, and a climate more genial than the neighboring Lands, independent or almost independent of any continental power, offered an asylum for industry and commerce ... the arts and merchandise not only of Sweden, Russia, Denmark, Prussia, Finland, Vandalia, and Saxony, which touched the surrounding seas, but also of Scotland, England, Flanders, France, and Spain, enriched the sumptuous merchants of Wisby and adorned their marble Halls. For about a century and a half, in the alliance of the Hanse, she remained Mistress of the Baltic and prescribed the Laws which Commerce still reveres.

Over 150 years before the publishing of that Wellcock book, Justice Alexander, writing in his book, *Dominion of the Sea*, also explains some of the phenomena of Wisby very well — as follows:

> They flourished more and more and grew great by their Trade and Navigation, to which they gave themselves up in entirety; insomuch that this Town was a long while the Axis and the most celebrated Market of Europe; there being no city so full of Merchants and so famous for its commerce. Hither came Swedes, Russians, Danes, Prussians, Livonians, Germans, Finlanders, Vandals, Flemings, Saxons, English, Scots, and French to trade. Each nation had their own Quarter, and particular Streets for their Shops and Warehouses. All strangers were safe and welcome there, and enjoy'd the same Privileges as the Townsmen themselves ... the Ruins of it are now to be seen, and under them are often found Tables of Marble, Porphyry, and Jaspar; witness of the ancient Splendor and Magnificence of the Citizens. The houses were covered with Copper; the Windows gilt with Gold, and all that is said or that is discover'd of it, shows the inestimable Riches of the Inhabitants in Times past ... 'twas in this City of Wisby that the Sea Laws and Ordinances, which the Swedes brought with Credit, were compos'd. They were received as righteous and just, and were kept in the Teutonic language until now. Germans, Swedes, Danes, Flemings, and all the People of the North observe them. But none have been so curious as to preserve the Date and the Remembrance of the Time when they were compos'd and publish'd.

Some 50 pages back in that same book, Alexander had written:

> The Citizens of the Magnificent City of Wisbuy in the Isle of Gothland, in the Baltick Sea, upon the Foundation of the Laws of Oléron, built the Ordinances and Regulations which take their Name from Wisbuy.

For several hundred years prior to the founding of the free port of Wisby around the year 1288, throughout most of the Viking Age, that is, the entire Baltic Sea was like a private lake for the Swedes, another factor in the phenomenal growth and preeminence of that market city. For mariners on Sweden's coast, which is nearly all on the landlocked Baltic and its tributary Gulf of Bothnia between Sweden and Finland, the North Sea and the open Atlantic was a long haul away and in part a winding, twisting, troublesome, dangerous one at that. Included in the troubles were tolls and tariffs exacted by the Danes for the use of certain straits and passages as shortcuts to and from the open sea. Swedish sea rovers therefore did most of their roving—and plundering—by voyaging eastward across the Baltic and up the rivers of eastern Europe, mostly in what is now Russia.

According to the renowned Swedish historian and archaeologist, Eric Oxenstierna, author of many books dealing with the early history of northern Europe and Scandinavia, and author of *The Norsemen*, a book so widely acclaimed that it has been published in German, English, French, Spanish, Japanese, and Swedish, those *Svea*, or Swedish Vikings:

> ...advanced in their light ships across eastern Europe as if its meadows and forests were the open sea. Sailing up the Duna and Memel rivers, they beached their shallow-draft vessels and carried them overland to launch them again in rivers flowing south—the Dneiper and the Volga....

The Danes, on their peninsula, faced both the North Sea and the Baltic Sea, but they seldom went into the Baltic because of the conveniently accessible rich prizes that awaited them as they island-hopped and raided throughout the British Isles and in France and Germany. As for the Norwegians, all of their seaports were right on the North Sea or the Atlantic Ocean, so that it was merely a hop-skip-and-a-jump to the Shetland and Orkney Islands, to Scotland and its numerous islands, and to the Irish Sea with its rich prizes along its western and eastern shores.

It is little wonder then that the Danish and Norwegian vikings seldom came into the Baltic, and they came only on those rare occasions when they were bent on trading instead of plundering. When they did come to trade, they certainly must have found the Baltic, with its safe harbors and Norse-speaking custodians, the Swedes, a nice place to do business. Ultimately, when that very commonplace occupation of plundering, accompanied by bloodshed, killing, maiming, raping, burning, and kidnapping was universally denounced and declared to be an illegitimate one that had to go and did go, Danish and Norwegian vikings, abjuring this amphibious form of piracy, turned procedurally to the Baltic Sea and inevitably to Gotland and Wisby, as traders of one sort or another.

Wisby flourished for about 150 years, a member of the Hanseatic League during most of that time, and very probably its most illustrious member. It was only natural that a set of maritime laws should be developed there, in view of its preeminence as a seaport, and it was only natural that they should be patterned after the Naval Laws of Oléron, which had come into being only a short time before the founding and rapid ascendancy of Wisby.

However, there were modifications and sharp changes from the pattern, some of which eliminated many of the harsh restrictions and punishments allocated to pilots. The new set of laws thus raised the status of pilots a little in the social scale and made piloting an occupation of less personal risk than in prior times.

The Laws of Wisby comprised 70 articles covering every conceivable maritime need of the times. Four of the articles dealt specifically with pilotage, that is to say, with the new kind of local or bar, bay, harbor, and river pilot. These four articles are given here:

> ARTICLE XLIV: If it is thought convenient in any River, or off any dangerous Coast, to take aboard a Pilot of the Country, and the Merchant opposes it, yet if the Master, the Ship's Pilot, and the Major Part of the Seamen are of another Opinion, he may be hir'd, and the Pilot shall be paid by the Ship and Cargo, as Averidges are calculated for Goods thrown overboard.
>
> ARTICLE LXIII: If a Pilot or Mariner buys a Ship or is made Master of one, he shall be discharged from his own Master, paying him back what he received from him; and it shall be the same if he marries.
>
> ARTICLE LIX: When a Ship is at Anchor before an Harbour with which her Pilot is not well acquainted, the Master ought to hire one at the Place to carry his Ship into it, who shall be paid by the Ship and the Cargo.
>
> ARTICLE LX: When a Ship is in an Harbour or River, and the Master does not know the Coast nor the River, he ought to take a Pilot of that Country to carry her up the River or Harbour, which Pilot shall be maintained by the Master, and paid by the Merchant.

It becomes thus quite apparent that the laws of Wisby embodied within them a progressiveness and enlightenment, especially in the area of piloting procedures, that was far beyond any concernment embodied in earlier maritime laws. Not only did they improve the public image and societal standing of pilots and the profession of pilotage, but they also promulgated the concept of compulsory pilotage. It is said that they had a compelling influence on the latter development of this essential element of the art and science of ship handling.

Two of these Wisby articles, the 44th and the 59th are looked upon as having been the forerunners of the custom of compulsory pilotage, now almost universal, and existent at a majority of the world's seaports. The practice devolves from the long-accepted premise that sovereign bodies of maritime nations have the right and indeed the obligation to operate at all times under the assumption that all ship masters and their crews have an inadequate knowledge of underwater conditions at each and every nation's various seaports and that the exigencies of maritime commerce make such an assumption essential.

Article 44 decrees that the master of a ship, his pilot, and the majority of the crew can overrule the merchant charterers and hire a local pilot against their wishes and at their expense. In a way, this was compulsory, since the charterers were being compelled by the ship's complement or crew, backed up by the law, to hire local pilots at various ports of call. However, this was not entirely equivalent to the compulsory pilotage of modern times, since the owners or charterers were not being compelled *by the government* to hire a local pilot.

Article 59 decrees that the master "ought" to hire a pilot where his knowledge of local conditions is inadequate. Many persons have asserted that *ought* here, considering those times and those customs, was equivalent to *must* and that the content of the article implied an obligation bordering on compulsion.

Compulsory pilotage, in early times, had its widest acceptance and most substantial growth in the British Isles. As early as 1687, when the charter of the Newcastle Trinity House corporation was granted, compulsory pilotage already was a general practice in Great Britain—for ships of foreign nationalities, that is. British maritime legislation then was highly protective and discriminatory—*and retaliative*—in line with the general state of the world's commerce of course.

One part of the Newcastle Trinity House charter decreed compulsory pilotage for foreign vessels in no uncertain terms:

> ...forasmuch as in ports beyond the seas all manner of merchants, strangers resorting to thither, are compelled to take pilots belonging to the same respective ports or otherwise to pay the duty of pilotage there usually due and accustomed, it is also decreed and stipulated that foreign ships refusing or neglecting to take on board a licensed pilot should be liable to pay pilotage dues as if they had taken on such pilots.

Eight

The Hanseatic League and More Ship Laws

In the twelfth and thirteenth centuries, following the break-up of the old feudal system in most of Europe, a new mercantile and trading era flourished. With a sprightly new money economy taking the place of the old serfdom system, merchants became in effect more powerful and influential than the old feudal lords. Since much of the commerce was maritime in nature and was expanding at a rapid rate, there had to be more and more centers to accommodate it physically and financially. These centers had to be seaports of necessity, and they prospered and grew big all over Europe and in the Mediterranean and Near East countries.

Many of the favorably situated and lavishly endowed centers formed themselves into leagues and confederations that promoted and regulated commerce among them for their mutual benefit and aggrandizement, and this in turn led to the formulation of various codes of conduct for those engaged in maritime commerce. There were the *Statutes of Trani*, the *Statutes of Marseilles*, the *Usages of Tortosa*, the *Sea Laws of Barcelona*, and others, but none of these were of a stature great enough to merit further consideration here.

However, the contemporary *Laws of the Hanse Towns*, which applied to that famous federation of northern European cities, in all of which the paramount language was Germanic rather than Latin or Nordic, do merit some consideration here. The federation was known as the Hanseatic League and it comprised some 70 cities, one of which, Lubeck in north Germany, was predominant. In fact, Lubeck was made the chief of the Hanse Towns by official royal decree, that of Emperor Frederick I, in 1161 when it was given a "free city" charter. It was at Lubeck that the *Sea Laws of the Hanse Towns* were promulgated, in the German language, in 1597.

The Hanseatic League got its name from the *Middle High German* word *hanse*, meaning a guild or alliance of merchants similar to a present-day chamber of commerce. It was in fact, at first, a league of various merchant groups of free Germanic cities whose business dealings were overseas for the most part. It later became a league of the cities themselves contrived to protect their commerce in general. Some of the more important member-cities were Danzig, Brunswick, Hamburg, and Lubeck.

The member-cities all had special commercial privileges in trading with one another, and through agreements and rules, they acted in concert to advance trade, not only in their own countries but also with nations abroad. They greatly increased their trade with the Near East and Mediterranean countries, as well as with nearby nations such as England and France. It was only natural that they would someday promulgate their own magisterial set of maritime laws.

There are 60 articles in the Laws of the Hanse Towns, as handed down to us by historians. Many of them appear to have been patterned after the Laws of Wisby, but some of them seem to revert back to earlier laws such as the Naval Laws and Statutes of the Rhodians for their content and slant. This is quite noticeable in the articles pertaining exclusively to pilotage, of which there are only three, articles 16, 27 and 55, in the entire body of 60.

These articles made no distinction between pilots who are part of a ship's company and those local bay and harbor pilots at the various ports of call, who often were called "locmen" or "lodesmen" in those days. In fact, local pilots as such are not mentioned specifically anywhere in these laws. Also, they make no reference to any obligation on the part of shipmasters to hire local pilots or to assume any responsibility for not hiring them, an obligation inherent in the concept of compulsory pilotage, already in vogue at the time.

It is known definitely, however, that the use of bay and harbor pilots was a traditional practice in the shipping circles of the Hanse Towns, and it is safe to assume that in at least a few of these port cities, there was an obligation, bordering on compulsion, to make use of the services of a qualified local pilot when entering or leaving them. Nevertheless, it is strange but true that these local pilots are not mentioned in the laws as a separate and distinct class, and no clauses anywhere in the articles say that shipmasters "ought" or "should" or "must" hire a local pilot.

The three articles pertaining to pilotage are as follows:

> ARTICLE XVI: Before the master hires any mariner or pilot, he ought to acquaint the owners with what wages he is to give them and have their allowance of it, under penalty of 25 crowns.

> ARTICLE XXVII: He who shall be found incapable of discharging his duty as a pilot or mariner, for which he has received wages, shall forfeit all that was promised to him and be besides punished according to his demerit.
>
> ARTICLE LV: The master or the pilot may each load 12 barrels (of salt) on their particular account; the officers six each, and the seamen four each, and the boys two each.

The first two definitely put pilots and mariners (seamen) in the same category, and all three articles contain the implication that the pilots being referred to were regular members of the ship's company or crew.

Nine

The French and Their Pilots

Throughout the long history of ships and shipping, it has always been the custom — and hard and fast rule, even in very ancient times — for someone aboard every ship, no matter how small, to keep an accurate, chronological, running account — a log, in other words — of each and every sea voyage, long or short, and these accounts are the stuff of history.

However, there always have been sea voyages that were just too, too short to merit any such careful log or record keeping. Mostly, these were the short trips of pilot boats taking pilots out of harbors or into them and the short trips of pilots aboard ships that they were conducting into harbors or out of them. The pilots left no running accounts or stuff of history — they generally had too little time and perhaps too little temperament for such a chore — and so there are consequent great gaps of time and place and circumstance, especially during the medieval and Renaissance eras, in the story of piloting.

It is for this reason principally that this narrative has been concerned (unduly so, it might seem) with one-after-another set of maritime laws compounded along the way down through the ages. The continuity is served by them. They fill in some of the gaps. They are pegs on which to hang the skein of the story.

In this regard, and at this point, there is yet another set of maritime laws to be considered. They are the Sea Laws of France, considerably more advanced and enlightened than any of those previously dealt with, and the evident forerunners of much of modern maritime jurisprudence. They were promulgated at Fontainebleau in August of 1681 by King Louis XIV of France.

> To settle the Laws of Maritime Contracts, which have hitherto been uncertain, to regulate the Jurisdiction of the Officers of the Admiralty and the principal Duties of Seafaring People, and to es-

> tablish a good Polity in the Ports, Coasts, and Roads that are within the extent of our Dominions.

Such was the preamble.

The Sea Laws of France are a large body of laws and very comprehensive, covering a great variety of maritime matters. They are comprised of 54 major sections, and each section is made up of a number of articles. One section deals entirely with pilots and has 18 separate articles listing rules and regulations for them.

All of these 18 articles, as recorded in Alexander's *Dominion of the Sea*, published in 1709, are presented here, with explanatory comments following some of them:

> ARTICLE I: In places where it is found necessary to establish Pilots, Lodes-men to conduct Vessels into and out of the Entries of Ports and navigable Rivers, their Number shall be regulated by the Officers of the Admiralty, with the Advice of the Aldermen and the most eminent Merchants of the Place.

It should be obvious that the term, *the Place*, had a broad meaning and wide usage at the time and here refers to any important seaport and its environs and government. The "Aldermen" were the *elder* men, those elected to the City Commission or whatever was the legislative governing body of the seacoast municipality. "Lodesmen," derived from the Dutch word *lood*, meaning "lead," the mineral substance, was the regional name for local port pilots. It is evident that the regulating of the number of pilots operating out of individual seaports was of primary importance even then, as it has been all down through the years up to the present time—to prevent free-for-all scrambles and chases for business, unfair and cutthroat competition, and much exploitation and possible injuriousness to ship owners and masters.

> ARTICLE II: No person shall exert that Function till he's arrived to the age of five and twenty, and receiv'd before the Officers of the Admiralty, after having been examined in their Presence and in that of two Aldermen or eminent Merchants, and two antient Pilots, with the like Number of antient Masters of Ships.

Nowadays of course we would say: "No person shall *exercise* that function" rather than "No person shall exert that function," and nowadays we would write "*senior* pilots and *senior* masters of ships" rather than "*antient* (ancient) pilots and *antient* masters "of ships." Also we would say "accredited" before the officers of the Admiralty rather than "*receiv'd*" before the officers of the Admiralty.

However, nowadays also one may find that the make-up of our examining boards looking into the capabilities and competency of prospective pilots is strikingly similar to the make-up of those examining boards of that by-gone period first covered by those Sea Laws of France.

> ARTICLE III: The pilots, Lodes-men, shall be examined of the Knowledge and Experience they ought to have of the Fabrick and Working of Ships, and of the Courses of the Tide, of the Currents, Shelves, Rocks, and other Impediments that may render difficult the Entry of the Rivers, Ports, and Harbours in which they are established.

The "Fabrick and Working of Ships" most certainly was meant to infer the design, construction, and underway characteristics of ships, generally and variously, very important knowledge for pilots then as now. And of course then as now, prospective pilots were required to prove their knowledge of the waters of the ports "in which they are established." This would include their knowledge of all of the "Impediments," which we now generally call "obstructions" or "hazards."

> ARTICLE IV: They shall be olbiged to have their Shallops always provided with Anchors and Oars, and to be in a Condition to go and succour Ships upon the first Order or Signal, under Pain of 10 Livres, and greater Penalty, according to the Exigence of the Case.

A shallop was a small, light, fast sailing vessel, a kind of ship's boat or tender or messenger vessel. Although it was responsible for the word *sloop* coming into our language, it was not always "sloop-rigged," as we say today. The shallops or sloops of those times carried many different sailing rigs, and the name was indicative only of their hull design, their lightness, speed, and maneuverability, and the type of work that they did.

> ARTICLE V: We forbid, under Pain of Corporal Punishment, all Mariners, not being receiv'd Pilots, Lodes-men, to offer themselves to conduct Ships into or out of Ports or Rivers.

> ARTICLE VI: However, the Masters of Ships, for want of Pilots, may make use of Fishermen to conduct them.

> ARTICLE VII: If a Pilot comes aboard a Ship, where there is already a Fisherman, before she be past the dangerous Places, the Pilot shall be receiv'd, but the Fisherman's hire shall be deducted from his.

> ARTICLE VIII: A Pilot undertaking to conduct a vessel while he's drunk shall be fined in five Livres, and he shall not exert the Function of Pilot during one Month.

> ARTICLE IX: We enjoin the Pilots to conduct first the Ships that first require their Service, and we forbid them to prefer the most remote to the nearest, under pain of five and twenty Livres.

> ARTICLE X: We likewise forbid them to go farther than to the Roads to meet Vessels coming in to Ports and Harbours, to go aboard of Ships without the Master's consent, and to leave the Ships they bring in till they come to an Anchor and moor'd in the Port: and those they carry out, until they're in the High-Sea, under Pain of the loss of their Wages, and a Fine of thirty Livres.

> ARTICLE XI: The Master of the Ship shall be oblig'd, as soon as the Pilot gets aboard, to tell him how much his vessel draws, under Pain of five and twenty Livres Fine, to the Benefit of the Pilot, for every foot concealed.

Here definitely is landmark legislation. From that time on, down to the present day, the established basic measure of compensation for piloting services has been, almost universally, a given charge of so much a foot of draft of each individual vessel. This was and is only natural and fair, since the greater the tonnage and the heavier the cargo burden, both of which account for the deepness of the draft, the greater the demands on the men guiding the ship through the hazards of the port's approaches. Here was a handy yardstick for figuring costs.

This basic principle of compensation for services rendered has been modified only sparingly down through the centuries, and the modifications never have tended to eliminate these charges of so much for each foot of draft, but only added additional charges for extra services rendered. There have been, for example, added fees for such things as "swinging ship to calibrate compass or direction finder," "standing by with pilot boat," "being detained in quarantine," "being carried out to sea against one's wishes," and other operational activities considered to be over and above the normal routine actions related to the task of bringing a ship in or taking one out.

> ARTICLE XII: In every Port, there shall be made at the Suit of our Attorney, with the Advice of the Magistrates or two eminent Merchants, a Regulation for the Wages of Pilots; which shall be inserted in a publick Writing, and a Copy of which shall be in the Admiralty-Office and another affixed upon the Key.

Here is more landmark legislation, for the determining and fixing of pilotage fees by some governmental authority has been an imperishable fact of life for hundreds of years, throughout the world and in the coastal waters of the United States.

> ARTICLE XII: The Pilots and Mariners shall not exact greater sums than those specified by the Regulation, under Pain of Corporal Punishment, except it be in Time of Storm and imminent Danger; in which Case the Officers of the Admiralty, with the Advice of two Merchants, may tax their Wages higher, having Regard to the Work they have done, and the Danger they have run.
>
> ARTICLE XIV: We declare null, all Promises made to Pilots and Mariners while in Danger of Shipwreck.

(No fair gouging!)

> ARTICLE XV: We injoin the Pilots daily to view the Roads of the Places where they are established, to hoise the Anchors left there, and within four and twenty Hours afterwards, to make their Declaration to the Officers of the Admiralty.
>
> ARTICLE XVI: If they discover any Alterations in the Channels and ordinary Passage of Ships, or that the Buoys and Sea-Marks are not right placed, they shall be obliged, under Pain of ten Livres, to acquaint the Officers of the Admiralty and the Master of the Key therewith.

It was the same then as now. Present-day pilots are obliged to inspect buoys and other channel and range markers, checking on their stability and effectiveness and on the correctness of their location. Also, after checking, they are obliged to do something about any damages or misplacement found.

> ARTICLE XVII: It shall be free for the Masters and Captains of French or Foreign Ships, to take such Pilots as they please to conduct them into Ports and Harbors, without being oblig'd to make use of the same to conduct them out again.
>
> ARTICLE XVIII: A Pilot that ignorantly runs a Ship aground shall be whipped by the Hand of the Hangman and forever depriv'd of his Employment; and as for such as maliciously and designedly run a Ship upon a "Rock or Bank or Shore, he shall be punished with Death, and his Body hung upon a Mast that shall be planted near the Place of the Shipwreck.

Rather severe, that last one, as were some of the Naval Laws of Oléron. Nevertheless, it will be noted, these Sea Laws of France were quite comprehensive, considering the era in which they were promulgated, and considerably more advanced and less punitive than those of eariler periods.

Ten

Early American

In tracing the history of pilotage in America, we need to go far back, long before the establishment of the United States of America—*even further back than the year 1694*, in which, incredible as it may seem, the Sandy Hook Pilots Association of New York Harbor, still in existence at the present time, began its life!

Firstly, there were the pilots of Columbus and Ponce de Leon, even though they may not have been, strictly speaking, in the category of "port pilots" under consideration here. It is recorded that Alammis, a pilot on one of Columbus's ships, long after the fateful year of 1492, was one of the first mariners to encounter the forceful flow of the *North Atlantic Equatorial Counter Current*, otherwise known as the Gulf Stream. Somewhere at sea between Cuba and Florida, attempting to transit the Florida Straits on a southerly course with fair but light winds attending, his ship could make no headway against this current, and the frustrated pilot and crew assumed that it "rose" in the Gulf of Mexico at the other end of the straits "somewhere off Cuba." Other mariners, of those and later times, readily concurred in this assumption and the current was given the name *Gulf Stream* in consequence.

After Ponce de Leon discovered Florida in 1513, he went exploring on its Altantic and Gulf Coasts, putting in to various ports, it must be assumed. He therefore must have carried among his crewmen the first genuine pilot to gain first-hand experience with seaports of the American mainland, such as they were.

In the writings of a certain Franciscan missionary, Father Escobedo, and particularly in his epic poem *La Florida*, there are numerous references to pilots, most of whom were not identified by name. However, he does call one of them by name and refers to him as "the expert and famous pilot, Gines Pinzon, who enjoyed the full confidence of the king."

In Havana in 1587, this Gines Pinzon set a course for Saint

Augustine and brought a ship safely there. On the ship were twelve Franciscan friars, one of whom was Father Escobedo. In the following year, a ship commanded by Captain Vincente Gonzalez made a voyage *from* Saint Augustine to the coast of Virginia with this same Pinzon on board as pilot and navigator.

Certainly one ought to concede that this man Pinzon "knew" that port of Saint Augustine, qualified as an able pilot for it, and must be considered to be an ancestral progenitor, along with Ponce de Leon's unknown pilots, of the Florida State Pilotage System, with emphasis on that word *state*, a key word in any consideration of pilotage in America. The system consists of twelve individual pilots' associations, at twelve deep-water ports, banded together in a parent *Florida State Pilots Association*, and composed of well-qualified, professional, licensed pilots performing their services at fourteen seaports on the Atlantic and Gulf coasts of Florida. They will be dealt with in more depth later in this history.

During what may be called the "British Period" in North America, that era of settlement and colonization that existed before the American Revolution, pilotage had been instituted at the principal ports of the colonies, but written records of the activity or profession are so very scanty that much of its story is by way of conjecture and supposition. This is especially true of the Port of New York, and this circumstance seems rather strange, since the commodious harbor there was and is the greatest on the North American Continent.

Its history dates back to April of the year 1524, when it was discovered by an Italian, Giovanni da Verrazano, in the employ of the French, trying to find a new route and passage to India. In no part of that British period and, before that, for many years after the city's original founding by the Dutch, who named it "Nieuw Amsterdam," are there any significant records or narratives dealing with pilots at the Port of New York.

The history of piloting there, according to one information source, "...dates from the time of Hendrick Hudson, who undoubtedly used his '*pijl lood*' earnestly and repeatedly from the time he sighted the then virginal slopes of the Atlantic Highlands (of New Jersey) until he had passed through the Lower Bay, the Narrows, the Upper Bay, and finally cast his anchor somewhere in the Hudson River. There was no welcoming greeting from a pilot boat off Sandy Hook for Hendrick, and so the first investigative casting of the lead in the waters of what later became New York City was done by the intrepid Dutch shipmaster from a little lead-heaving platform off the rail (the starboard rail undoubtedly) of the famous little "*Halve Maan*" (*Half Moon*).

It is quite certain moreover that bay and harbor pilotage did continue to develop in the New York area from that time on, even though there is no continous running account or solid history. According to that same information source just previously quoted,

> There is no authentic record of any pilot keeping a lookout for ships off Sandy Hook in the early days of the Colonies, although it is believed that the British, quick to see the advantage of having an experienced pilot such as Franz Naerebout had proved to be, undoubtedly established a piloting system in the port of New York after they had changed its name from that of *Nieuw Amsterdam*, even though these pilots may not have been organized as a body of men under local or governmental control.

The reference to Franz Naerebout is inept or worded incorrectly, since the British gained control of *Nieuw Amsterdam* in 1664 and the famous Dutch pilot did not begin his piloting operations until a hundred years later — around 1770 if he began when he was 21 years old. Of course, even with this being so, the British still would have had a few years, prior to the American Revolution, in which to develop an efficient pilotage system modeled after that one pioneered by Naerebout in Holland. Perhaps the historian who originally authored that paragraph meant to say "...such as Franz Naerebout *would prove himself* to be" or perhaps he did say that and was misquoted by a later writer transcribing his statements.

Following the birth of the new nation, this efficient pilotage system or a similar replacement one did exist in the New York area and did continue to develop and grow. It was stimulated and paced by an ever-increasing convergence of ships of all nations upon that great seaport. The New York Harbor pilots, highly skilled and proud of it, were always available, not only for the conducting of ships in and out of the port, but also for participation in official state functions and ceremonies.

They were very much in evidence on the occasion of George Washington's arrival at New York for his second inauguration as President of the United States. The record states that our first president:

> ...ARRIVED AT Elizabethtown (Elizabeth, New Jersey), where he was met by the Congress deputation and other dignitaries upon the occasion of his second inauguration. These all, with General Washington, embarked in the barge, manned by thirteen pilots in white uniforms commanded by Commodore Nicholson and with John Randall as coxswain, and proceeded in stately fashion across the bay to the Battery, where the citizenry welcomed them with loud acclaim.

It must have been an impressive and glorious sight.

Other than these few early references to piloting in the New York area, there is scarcely any record or narrative of the activity prior to 1837. That was the first year in which a continuous running account of piloting operations began to be maintained. Before that, nearly all is blank, and New York is not the only port thus deprived. Much of the early story of piloting in many other American ports never was actually recorded in writing or print and much of what was recorded was lost or destroyed.

Eleven

After the *Mayflower*

Although the records of pilotage at Plymouth Colony and at Massachusetts Bay Colony in Boston Harbor are indeed very scanty, and for good and sufficient reasons, the history of piloting in Boston Harbor may be said to have begun in 1633, when Captain John Gallop, an early free-lance bar pilot, successfully conducted the good ship *Griffen* into the harbor with the Reverend John Cotton and Elder Thomas Leverett on board. Gallop's Island, near the outer limits of Boston Bay, is named after this John Gallop. He later was acclaimed for his valiant actions in the colonists' battle with the Narrangansett Indians near Block Island.

Strangely enough, however, it was an Indian, Tisquantum, better known as "Squanto," a member of the Pawtuxet tribe, who actually was one of the first—if not *the* first—pilots to do duty on the Massachusetts coast, and he did so long before the debut of John Gallop, though this Indian was not essentially a bar pilot conducting ships into the harbor from the open sea. Because of his knowledge of local shoreline conditions, he was used by Governor Bradford as a pilot on the ship *Swan* on a voyage to Monomoyick Bay. He also aided the colonists by being an interpreter and by helping them with their crop plantings and growings.

It would be unthinkable to discuss the early history of pilotage in Boston Harbor without including a comment on the famous old Boston Light on one of the Brewster Islands to eastward and westward of Gallop's Island in the confluence of Boston Bay and Massachusetts Bay. That is because the two were immeasurably associated with each other. It seems that, inevitably, pilots became lighthouse keepers and lighthouse keepers became pilots.

The lighthouse first was lit on September 14, 1716, and the first keeper was a pilot named George Worthylake, who was paid 50 pounds per year for his services as keeper. He earned additional money by acting as a regular, accredited pilot of Boston Harbor. Following Worthylake, a pilot named John Hayes became keeper in 1718. He was followed by pilots Robert Saunders and Robert Ball. Ball was appointed in 1733 and served for 40 years. Eventually that Brewster Island berthing the light became known as "Lighthouse Island" and still is known by that name.

Tending the light and the lighthouse was only a part-time job in actuality, and most keepers, being qualified bar pilots, spent a good deal of their time conducting ships in and out of the harbor. *Keeper of the Light* was nonetheless a favored position, much to be desired, and many sought it constantly. The pilot who was keeper of the light could spot incoming ships far offshore, could make ready his plans and his equipment to go out to meet them, and could then go aboard them and earn pilotage fees that supplemented and usually exceeded his lighthousekeeper's pay.

It is appropriate to mention here a history-making episode, small and insignificant though it may seem to be. It is recorded that Keeper Robert Ball, after having been entrenched in this half-unofficial, dual position for many years, and finding it very much to his liking, became very much annoyed at the small army of freelance pilots who were crowding in on his piloting business. They especially had the opportunity to do this during those times when he was busy tending the light, and some of them even went so far as to collect tolls from vessels just for passing the light without any pilot aboard.

In order to protect his profitable position from such villainous encroachments, Ball petitioned the colonial authorities to create the post of *established pilot* of Boston Harbor, which they did, appointing him as the first established pilot. It was then decreed that any would-be pilot caught muscling in on his territory would be required to pay half of his collected fee to Ball as penalty.

As a condition to his appointment, however, Ball was required at all times to keep two pilot boats on station in the outer harbor, both of which must be readily distinguishable and identifiable as such and must be seaworthy and able in all weathers. Although this could have been somewhat of an expense to him, it was offset by his getting a corner on the market, so to speak, by the very fact of his two boats being there with experienced pilots aboard—all by official edict—and all others could go hang or do their piloting somewhere else. This affair was the forerunner of one certain aspect of the piloting profession that became solidly entrenched and persisted down to the present day. It is the practice of pilots owning and maintaining pilot boats and keeping them on station on the open ocean at strategic positions outside seaports, with penalties for the ships disregarding their offer of pilotage services and of course penalties for the pilots failing to offer or give these services.

The pilotage monopoly of Robert Ball and his successors could not last forever however. As commerce in Boston Harbor and elsewhere in the state continued to grow prodigiously, it became necessary to appoint large numbers of qualified pilots for Boston and other ports. This was done by legislative action and the creation of a new law in 1783.

The new law covered such ports as Gloucester, Marblehead, Newburyport, Plymouth, Martha's Vineyard, and Nantucket Island, and it provided that appointments of new pilots were to be made by the governor with the advice of his council. This again was landmark legislation, paving the way for the growth and development of a comprehensive pilotage system in Massachusetts, by that time a member state of the United States of America.

Twelve

The Virginians

The earliest known pilot in the Virginia territory of the American colonies was one John Clark, a very unfortunate fellow. The following references to him and his misadventures were found in the *Maryland Historical Magazine* and in *State Pilotage in America*, a complete and comprehensive historical review published by the American Pilots' Asssociation under the able editorship of Captain W. Hilton Lowe, the association's president at one time, to all of whom the author of this book is indebted for much of the information contained in it:

> Although there probably was at least one man in the original group of Virginia colonists with a superior knowledge of the waters of the bay entrance and the James River by the time the second supply arrived, the first formal mention of a pilot, an unfortunate fellow named John Clark, is not found until four years later. In 1611 a Spanish vessel, dispatched to spy out the condition of the colony, arrived at Hampton Roads. Claiming that their vessel was 'lost,' three of the crew came ashore to request the aid of a pilot to get her back to sea; the Governor "knew well what the visitors were up to, and eager to rid himself of the very unwelcome guests, he sent Clark to con (conduct) them out of the Capes. The pilot was no sooner in the boat at the Capes, than they carried him off to Spain. There he languished in a dungeon for years, with the Inquisition ever in his eye, before the English government succeeded in having him released. This same John Clark was the mate of the *Mayflower* when in 1620 she wandered into Plymouth Bay instead of Chesapeake Bay, her intended destination. It is regrettable that the first known pilot in Virginia should have been dispatched on a mission so disastrous to him personally.

"The Capes" of course refers to Cape Charles and Cape Henry, at the mouth of Chesapeake Bay, its northern and southern "jaws."

Here in Virginia, as in Boston Harbor and most others of the coastal colonies, the genesis and development of the pilotage profession followed the same definite pattern almost identically. First there were the very early pilots, intrepid, independent loners, pioneering in this chancy occupation without any governmental recognition or support. Then there came an increase in maritime commercial activity with an accompanying increase of recognition of the status of pilots and a big demand for more of them. Then came the increase in the number of available pilots, who were recruited much too early and were, in many cases, inexperienced, untrained, and irresponsible.

Then came the rivalry among the pilots themselves and the competition, rough, tough, and cutthroat, accentuated by free-for-all ocean races, brawls, skullduggery, and damages to ships and shipping. Then there came cncerted calls for an end to the disorder and for the official appointment of an "established pilot" or Chief Pilot as an expedient in maintaining order, and this was done forthwith. Finally there came an action by the colonial governing bodies to set up some system for commissioning or warranting pilots and exercising some control over them.

In Virginia, this was done in 1669, by a law passed by the House of Burgesses. The *Maryland Historical Magazine* tells about it thusly:

> To prevent untrained and irresponsible persons from practicing as pilots, the House of Burgesses in 1669 passed an act which stipulated that no man could legally work (as a pilot) unless he be certified. The would-be pilot must present evidence of his good character and equally important prove his knowledge of the Bay's bottom by a certificate from five master mariners of 'experience, skill, and judgement.' By 1702, two pilots had been qualified for the James River, John Lowery and Israel Vaulx; one for the York River, William Seyers; two for the Rappahannock, Garet Minor and James Jones; but none had been commissioned for the Potomac or the eastern shore rivers.

Of course this piece of legislation was ancillary to another act, passed by the House of Burgesses in 1660, and the conditions and events leading up to the enactment of this prior legislative action are described in this excerpt from the pages of the *Maryland Historical Magazine*:

> With an increasing traffic entering the Capes, one would assume there was demand enough for pilots to be assured of an adequate small size and consequent easy draft of the vessels first used in the Virginia trade. As the vessels became larger and as the settlements spread along every waterway, the need for pilots became very evident. About 1600, complaints were made that there were no pilots working, and to make matters worse, there was a complete absence

> of 'beacons," as channel markers were then called, on the shoals and even in the most important stream, the James River. With attention called to these dangers to the all-important tobacco fleets, the House of Burgesses passed its first act to improve navigation in the Bay.
>
> This first act to improve navigation created a 'chief pilot' "For the James River who was to be paid 5 pounds for every vessel over 80 tons conned or, if his services were refused, 40 shillings. Evidently vessels under 80 tons were shoal enought to take care of themselves. The first man appointed to the office of chief pilot was Captain William Oewen. In addition to his duties as pilot, he also had to set out the maintain marker buoys along the channel from Willoughby Spit to Jamestown. These were financed by a charge of 30 shillings paid to the chief pilot by every vessel which anchored. His dual function gave him a full-time job, and Oewen soon was petitioning for permission to take on apprentices. Captain Oewen was succeeded by Captain Chichester, who was followed by his son William, thereby beginning a tradition of the profession, family dynasties of pilots.

Family dynasties of pilots truly is a tradition of the profession. For example, some of today's members of the Associated Branch Pilots' organization, the "bar" pilots of the Mississippi Delta, are great grandsons of pilots who were members of the same association 130 years ago; and pilot groups throughout our coastal states are full of members related to one another, distantly and otherwise.

By the Act of 1669, which barred unprofessional and incompetent individuals from engaging in the occupation, Virginia began moving toward a permanent, organized system that eliminated the irresponsible and unprofessional "would-be" pilots and made competency a watchword. This was good for morale and over-all efficiency. In this regard, the *Maryland Historical Magazine* has this to say:

> The commissioned pilots were extremely jealous of their rights and resented interlopers strongly.... To help prevent these imposters from passing themselves off as pilots, in 1721 the Virginia customs officials were required to post lists of the commissioned pilots in their offices.
>
> Over the years following the basic Act of 1660, commissioned pilots established themselves on practically every stream into which a sea-going vessel might enter. Of course increasing traffic density brought new problems, chiefly those concerning fees, and in 1775 pilotage as a whole was taken into consideration by the Virginia legislature, which enacted a bill regulating almost every phase.

Thus, even before the beginning of the Revolutionary War, Virginia's maritime interests had grown to a mature state with regard to pilotage regulation, and this must have stood this stalwart colony in good stead during that conflict.

Thirteen

More of Chesapeake Bay

The colonies of Maryland and Virginia, both bordering on Chesapeake Bay, could be said to have been close neighbors back in those early times, and one would suppose that the development of the pilotage profession in each was similar. That is true. It was similar but not coincidental. It is clear that the early history of the occupation in each territory was one of free-for-all competition and individual initiative by the pilots, with little or no attention being paid by the colonial governments, but Virginia was the first to give official recognition to the profession, and it did so over *a hundred years sooner* than did Maryland. In this connection, we have this, from the *Maryland Historical Magazine*:

> In the early years of both the Virginia and the Maryland colonies there was no difference in the conduct of the pilot's profession. The pilots of each as individuals acted on their own, getting jobs where and when they could and charging whatever the traffic would bear, with no regulation under law. Virginia began its official recognition of the profession in 1660; Maryland gave it no legal notice until after she became a state, well over "a century later." ...lack of attention does not mean that there were no Maryland pilots, and the very fact that they are seldom mentioned in the executive or judicial records is evidence that they must have been men of skill and respectability, and that they were on hand when needed. For example, when an expedition under Colonel William Burges set out, the leader was instructed to take a 'pilott' in order to reach the Indian town of Chicacone. A few years later Thomas Hebb of St. Mary's County—the birthplace of most of the early Maryland pilots—was held for trial in Virginia because he had piloted a vessel through Virginia waters without being the holder of a 'branch' (commission or license) from either colony.... Again the existence and importance of Maryland pilots was recognized by the Governor at the time of Queen Anne's

> War, when all Maryland pilots were ordered upon the first alarm of a hostile fleet in the bay to come to Annapolis *by land* to avoid the risk of capture by the enemy.

The statement "evidence that they must have been men of skill and respectability, and that they were on hand when needed" does not rule out the fact there were in those times, as previously noted, professed pilots who were not so skillful or respectable and those who were not always on hand when needed. Indeed, the first early pilot to be given an identity, some ten years after Lord Baltimore's settlers arrived, was one John Rablie, who demonstrated his lack of skill in a rather disastrous manner. The *Maryland Historical Magazine* tells about it thusly:

> Indeed some ten years must elapse after the landing at St. Mary's before the first Maryland pilot, John Rablie, appears in the record. Even he may well have been an amateur because, according to one vessel's owner, Rablie 'did not do the duty of pilot, but brought his ship aground & carried her beyond the port.' An understatement that, apparently, for when in 1644 Rablie sued for his fee ('15 lb. Sterl. in goods.... a new P. of shoes & new Saile for his sahllopp"), a witness stated, according to the official record: 'the shipp sailed by St. Michael's point (presently Point Lookout) on Saturday & the next morning she came aground about James Point on the eastern shore; & then returned back to St. Michael's point on Sonday night.' Certainly not a good testimonial to the skill or knowledge generally expected of a professional pilot.

There is definite evidence that there were pilots, skillful or not, actively engaged in the life of the colony ten years and more before the time of Rablie. Even then, the entire Chesapeake Bay area was becoming a main artery of traffic for ocean-going ships. However, the records of the period are so scanty that very few of these pilots have been given any identity or recognition. Even before Lord Baltimore's settlers arrived, there were pilots who were familiar with the waters of the Bay and the rivers tributary to it, and there is a recorded account of an individual's hiring a pilot and paying for his services a year before the arrival of the Baltimore expedition, but that pilot was not named or identified. Even the pilot who conducted the Baltimore ships up the Bay was never identified. The following excerpt from the *Maryland Historical Historical Magazine* may serve to point up this anonymity:

> The name of that very important fellow who piloted the *Ark* and the *Dove* up the Bay on March 1634 is yet to be learned. His

knowledge of the waters and shore may have had much to do with the choice of Maryland's first settlement. There were pilots even then who were familiar with the Bay and rivers because the year before Lord Baltimore's settlers arrived, William Claiborne had paid 10x. for the services of one. The pilot *de facto* for Baltimore's party may have been Henry Ffleet, who accompanied the expedition up from Jamestown, but if so, Ffleet after all was not a professional pilot but a trader who had had some experience in the Potomac River channels while on trading trips to the Indian towns.

Fourteen

After the Revolution

We have seen how some of the colonial governments regulated pilotage at their principal ports and did the job fairly well, eliminating irresponsibility, incompetence, and cutthroat competition from the pilot ranks in some measure. However, we have not been regardful of how it was in other than the principal ports, and we must assume that it was not quite as well regulated and was still subject to abusive exploitation by lone pilots and pilot groups of varying degrees of competency and responsibility.

After the Revolution, while the new nation was still in the travail of infanthood, this exploitation continued and increased as the rapid increase in maritime commerce brought about greater and greater demands for pilots to conduct ships in and out of ports that were new and unfamiliar to the captains and crews. The new nations growth pains tended to obscure this trend, and the invention of the steamboat heightened the demand all the more, so that many individuals of doubtful maritime background rushed in to fill the void, increasing the supply, though not necessarily the value of the pilots available for duty.

In the early 1800s, with the age of steam only a little way underway, much of the piloting profession in America was a free-for-all, hit-or miss affair and hundreds of pilots were independent free lances, each with his own sailing vessel for a pilot boat, or were members of free-lance groups owning pilot boats jointly. This set of conditions continued on up to the 1880s.

Pilots often engaged in the so-called "mad race to the sea," racing each other far offshore to incoming ships—with the grudgingly implied understanding that the first one to get to a ship and climb aboard was entitled to the job of guiding her in and earning a sizeable fee thereby. The nautical know-how or competence of the winners of these races was not always certifiable.

Competition was indeed very keen—and also cuttthroat and

rough-and-tough, with skulduggery and nasty brawls thrown in. Because of all this, very often, ships and their cargoes and passengers were placed in jeopardy. Groundings, delays, ship damage, cargo losses, law suits, criminal actions, and even bad collisions and loss of life were prevalent.

These conditions prevailed even at the Port of New York, where the stout and stable Sandy Hook Pilots' Association operated for the general welfare of the profession *in toto* but failed to alleviate these unhealthy conditions, mainly because of a lack of co-operation on the part of the small independent groups and individual loners forever competing with one another.

In this connection, commenting on some of the sets of laws enacted from 1853 to 1867 for the better regulation of pilotage at the Port of New York, *State Pilotage in America* has this to say:

> These acts were passed in the period of competitive pilotage and generally preceded pilots' associations as such. Thus is exemplified a system of control considerably advanced from the early colonial period, when mere licensing and qualifying of pilots was the function of state or local authority. Here we have controls not only as to licensing but extending to, among other things, the creation of boards of commissioners of pilotage, the regulation of pilot boats, and the regulation of fees and of certain rights or privileges of pilots. In no complete sense did this constitute a state pilotage system as we know it today.
>
> In this record of the New York situation, there is no mention of the elimination of competitive practices, the mad race to the sea, or any co-operative arrangements with any pilots' association, for New York had none at this stage. Only various small independent groups within the port appear to have been principally in evidence, and these operated for competitive purposes against other groups.

Also in this connection, there is this quotation from *A Report on Pilotage in the United States*, a monograph prepared by the Commandant of the United States Coast Guard in 1942:

> Up until about 1880, intense competition among the pilots prevailed at most ports, particularly those without a restriction on the number of pilots who might be licensed. Pilots cruised far out at sea in quest of business. Little effort was made to maintain pilot stations, and frequently pilots could not be had when wanted. In fact, the cutthroat competition among the pilots was unprofitable, wasteful, unsafe, and inefficient.

These general observations clearly indicate the looming approach and need of a turning point—a beginning of the end of the competitive struggles and the foul conditions at the ports. The turning point came in the early 1880s, and it came through the formation and development of pilot associations, regulated under law and working cooperatively with the law.

The ultimate step was taken when voluntary organizations, working together with the governing authorities, helped meld together a unified program of piloting activities under government regulation. This is the program that became the arrangement known as State Pilotage, undoubtedly because it had become woefully apparent that government regulation alone and by itself was not sufficient for providing a satisfactory service.

Fifteen

Pilot Licensing in America

In 1694, the Colonial Assembly of New York authorized the Governor of the colony to issue the first Sandy Hook Pilot license. The other colonies, at about the same time or even earlier, likewise enacted similar legislation empowering their local governments to provide for the licensing of pilots at their ports.

After the Revolution, when the colonies had become states, they continued in this practice, and the new Congress of the United Sates reaffirmed the legality and judiciousness of it on August 7, 1789 by an Act of Congress. This enactment provided that pilotage should continue to be regulated under the existing and future laws of the states "until further legislative provision shall be made by Congress.

This practice, well received and always working well, continued for some 60 years. Then, summarily, perhaps through misconception and a somewhat perverse ineptitude of the lawgivers, the "further "legislative provision" did come, scads and scads of it, and the final outcome was a permanent federal law providing for the universal licensing of all pilots by the federal government. This was contrary and counter to every facet of the state pilotage concept, which everlastingly called for the use of resident, local pilots with a complete, up-to-the-minute knowledge of local conditions surrounding the approaches to each particular port. There was no place in this concept for wandering, itinerant, peripatetic pilots empowered to guide ships in and out of ports that were totally unfamiliar to them.

In part, this rather adverse federal law came about because of the increase in the number of steam vessels engaged in ocean commerce and because of disputes between pilot groups of two states sharing the same common waterway boundary, for example Virginia and Maryland on Chesapeake Bay, Pennsylvania and Delaware on Delaware Bay, and New York and New Jersey on New York Harbor. Here it was a matter of which Sandy Hook pilots, the New Yorkers or the New Jerseyites, had the right to pilot which ships into the harbor.

That law still stands today—it is a federal *statute*—and all professional pilots must have a license from the federal government, since they are working in federally controlled waters, even though some might be river pilots exclusively, never operating on the open ocean. There is, for example, a group of them who work on the Mississippi River only, guiding ocean-going vessels back and forth between New Orleans and Baton Rouge. They are the "New Orleans-Baton Rouge Steamship Pilots' Association."

In addition to meeting the federal license requirement, all professional pilots with any job-status or seniority at important seaports are required to work under the regulations of state charters granted to their assoications, with the authorization of a commission or warrant, and this is tantamount to holding two licenses to perform the self-same service. Of course it is true that the state regulations are the governing regulations almost entirely. State laws regarding pilotage are operative as long as they are not in conflict with federal laws, but the power of the federal government in pilotage matters is exclusive only when it is exercised—which is seldom. That federal license is always required, however, no matter what.

In the United States, as in Great Britain, the federal government has established pilotage districts and authorities. Through them, the state governments control and regulate pilotage within their territorial limits, and this is a rather tight control and a strict, comprehensive regulation. The states actually control the licensing of pilots and many states make pilotage compulsory in certain cases and upon certain types of vessels. In the great majority of the coastal states, compulsory pilotage is decreed for all vessels, of foreign and domestic registry, engaged in foreign trade. It does not apply to those vessels engaged in the coasting (coast-wise) trade.

This tight control and comprehensive regulation by state officials was not always a fact of life however. It was practically absent during a long span of about 50 years, beginning with that first adverse legislation in 1837, designed merely to settle disputes between pilot groups of two or more states sharing a common, navigable, waterway boundary. This act of 1837 was the first pilotage law enacted by the federal government since the original decision of the first Congress to leave pilotage regulation to the individual states until it saw fit to determine otherwise. Although it was innocuous to some extent, this law was an opening wedge or foot-in-the-door for a certain element of the maritime community hostile to the established order of things. More and more adverse federal legislation followed until state control, or the system that we now know as *State Pilotage*, was practically nullified.

Many deplorable situations arose from this negation of that tried-and-true system. Some of these situations resulted from the machinations of over-eager, "would-be" pilots seeking only to get their hands on that federal license, by hook or crook, and then to make indiscriminate use of it in obtaining piloting jobs anywhere in the nation, regardless of their lack of knowledge of local port conditions.

Most of these individuals called themselves "federal pilots" with some pomposity. Most of them were called 'federal pilots" with scorn and derision by established, knowledgeable, "state" pilots still adhering to the tradition that the job of guiding big ships through dangerous waters close to land was a job for a local man with a complete, up-to-date knowledge of local conditions. It is reasonable to suppose that any charts that were available in those times would have been inadequate for making up for this deficiency on the part of those so-called federal pilots.

Many of these federal pilots belonged in a category eventually denominated as "political pilots" for good reason. They were incompetent political job seekers who demanded and received the federal pilot license from certain elected officials in return for political favors and support resulting in votes galore. These officials found it expedient to use their positions in this manner for the sake of more and better political gain and votes. Because of all this, many wholly incompetent pilots were able to join the ranks of the profession, with definite impairment of the service and its public image. These political pilots abounded and were most numerous at the Port of New York. According to Captain W. Hilton Lowe, former president of the American Pilots' Association, writing in *State Pilotage in America*:

> The regular pilots of those days were not held responsible for those conditions, as corrupt politics had entered into the field of pilotage. Men solely interested in financial gain were being granted licenses without any thought as to their qualifications for a hazardous profession which required experience and skill.
>
> There followed an interlude of shameful pilot performance at Sandy Hook. Instead of applying themselves to the task of maintaining an efficient pilot service devoted to the preservation of the lives and property of those who sailed to and from the Port of New York, these self-styled pilots spent their days cruising a few miles off the harbor entrance when the weather was fair, and playing cribbage in waterfront tap rooms when the weather was foul. Frequently, ships stood off the harbor entrance battling gale-swept seas and frantically signalling for a pilot, only to be left to stand off dangerous icy shores until the weather abated. Then, and not until then, these politico-pilots put to sea to earn the fees the law required the waiting ships to pay.
>
> It was inevitable that such an irresponsible pilot service could not

> long endure. The nature of a pilot's duties and the indispensability of his services to the safe movement of ships make his office wholly unadaptable to any system of political patronage. Consequently, it is not surprising that, during this era, many a fine ship piled up upon the beach with tragic loss of human lives."

The loss of many fine ships, including the packet ship *Mexico* and the barque *Bristol*, was directly attributable to the work of these unqualified politico-pilots, and one may well wonder how such deplorable conditions could obtain and persist. *State Pilotage in America* has the answer, as follows:

> "The answer lies in the fact that governmental regulation was not sufficient in itself to provide a satisfactory service. It required an organized effort on the part of the professional pilots themselves, working in co-operation with the governmental authorities, to accomplish the desired results. The growth and development of the port pilot groups was therefore inevitable. The tasks of creating more unity and co-ordination, eliminating wasteful competition, struggling against political interference, promoting higher professional standards, and increasing the general over-all efficiency—all were essential in achieving a better service.
>
> "It was soon found that port groups could not function alone in direct competitive practices, any more than the individual pilots themselves could. Other groups within the individual states had similar problems, and the sharing of experience and operating methods was a necessary element in promoting the efficiency of the whole service. Concerted effort within a particular state came to be recognized as essential. By such effort, not only would the best interests of the pilots be served but the advancement of commercial progress as well. This eventually gave birth to the state pilot organizations composed of the various port groups working together for the common good.
>
> The results achieved by the state pilot organizations speak for themselves, and the history of the development of commerce in the respective states would be incomplete indeed without their contributions and achievements. In this every pilot can take pride. Many of the state historical records show an appreciation of this, not only on behalf of government but from the business community as well. The weakness of un-coordinated effort within the states was thus surmounted by concerted action giving added strength of purpose to the entire program.

The main accomplishments of this "entire program," carried out by the port pilot associations and their parent organization, the American Pilots' Association, enlightened legislators, and business and commerical interests was the bringing of pilotage regulation and pilot commissioning back into the hands of the states and the establishing of the compulsory pilotage principle at most of our ports.

Sixteen

Trends in Compulsory Pilotage

We have seen how the concept of compulsory pilotage long ago, as early as 1687 in fact, began to be implemented in Europe, notably in England, Holland, and the countries bound by the Laws of Wisby, named for that great free port market city on the populous island in the Baltic Sea. We have seen also how this concept met with complete indifference and even opposition in other places, especially in the 70-odd cities of the Hanseatic League. Of the entire 60 articles in the *Sea Laws of the Hanse Towns*, only three dealt with pilotage, and none of these three made any reference to the compulsory pilotage principle, which obligates shipmasters to use the services of resident local pilots at ports of call or to assume complete responsibility in the event of not having done so.

The broadest acceptance and most substantial adoption of the compulsory pilotage principle seems to have been in England. This is substantiated in a published commentary, *Report on Pilotage in the United States*, issued by the U.S. Department of Commerce in 1917. It reads in part, pertinently, as follows:

> Pilotage was made compulsory in England almost from the beginning and was probably first imposed on foreign vessels. The fact that pilotage was made compulsory for ships of foreign nationality may be explained by the conditions of the times, when maritime legislation was highly protective and discriminatory. The British report on pilotage above referred-to calls attentions to the fact that the charter of the Newcastle Trinity House, which was granted in 1687, provided that *'forasmuch as in ports beyond the seas all manner of merchants, strangers resorting thither, are compelled to take pilots belonging to the same respective ports or otherwise to pay the duty of pilotage there usually due and accustomed,'* all foreign ships coming into British ports would have to do likewise,

> and it stipulated that foreign ships refusing or neglecting to take on board a licensed pilot should be liable to pay pilotage dues '*as if they had taken in such pilots.*'

Here is good evidence that the concept of compulsory pilotage had gained wide acceptance in Europe even at that early date, and there is further evidence that, shortly after the *Sea Laws of France* were adopted, France herself began to exercise more control of shipping at her seaports by adopting this compulsory pilotage idea. Certainly this early acceptance of the principle and the establishment of its legitimacy by those European countries had a direct and compelling influence on the early American colonies and states, as far as regards their acceptance of it.

The American colonies did accept the principal, and it was in vogue and wide usage long before, up to, and immediately after the American Revolution. After the war and the founding of the new nation, the practice was retained by the several states, and the new Congress of the new nation eventually approved of this and other pilotage regulation by the new states.

However, following the Act of 1837, the first pilotage law enacted by the Congress since its original decision to leave the regulation of pilotage to the states until it 'saw fit to determine otherwise,' there followed a period of about 50 years that was full of growing opposition to the whole compulsory pilotage program and fraught with many proposals for its modification or elimination.

The reasons for this opposition were various though never very clearcut. Most of it emanated from tugboat interests in the New England states seeking an arrangement whereby licensed, so-called federal pilots might be permanently employed on their tugboats and the tugboat skippers would do the jobs of towing and piloting all in one. Also, some opposition was simply a matter of avoiding pilotage fees.

Strangely and almost unbelievably, the most contentious and persistent opposition came from the State of Maine, with its stern and rockbound coast, a formidable, jagged long line of rocks, reefs, shoals, and tricky channels unmatched anywhere on the North American continent. It would seem that no other state could have felt the need of competent pilots and a compulsory pilotage system more than Maine. Yet, for almost 50 years congressmen from Maine, one after another, fought for the elimination of compulsory pilotage through national legislation.

Strangely too, much of the agitation against compulsory pilotage centered in large part around its elimination for sailing vessels. Here was a perversity that would seem to border on lunacy, since it must have been obvious and well known that sailing vessels did not have the maneuverability and power of steam vessels, and of course they never could go astern, that is to say, back up. Beset by sudden unexpected storms and adverse winds and currents, they could be pushed unawares onto ruinous rocks or shoals unless they were in the hands of competent pilots who knew the waters totally. Nevertheless, to quote *State Pilotage in America*,

> ...an acceptance of this fact, with adequate efforts to provide the necessary elements for the safety of life and property, seemed peculiarly absent in the early history of Maine.

In spite of the prestigious positions held by the Maine Congressmen, their forceful leadership, and their powerful influence, all their efforts failed, since the federal government, through the Congress, held that state laws then in effect with regard to pilotage were valid and just ones. Congress already had overturned some of its adverse legislation enacted during the period 1837–1884.

Regardless of all this, Maine, as a sovereign state, abolished compulsory pilotage entirely within her territorial limits. New Hampshire followed her in this, and other New England states modified their pilotage statutes to exempt certain classes and, in some cases, to make their systems almost entirely voluntary ones. Also, the state of Maryland, in some respects and by some definition a southern state, abolished compulsory pilotage for coast-wise vessels in 1852. This meant that Maryland was joining the North Atlantic states that had abolished compulsory pilotage for coastwise vessels.

The Potomac River at one time was considered to be the demarcation point between the Northern and the Southern states. All of the states south of the Potomac and on the Gulf of Mexico had compulsory pilotage laws and systems in effect. They believed that this was a necessity because of their generally shallow waterways and the shipping hazard created by shifting sands and straying channels. They resisted the efforts to have the systems eliminated by federal law, even though the Congress already had enacted legislation exempting *coastwise steam vessels* from the compulsory pilotage statutes of the states. *Coastwise sailing vessels* (in the South) remained under the state pilotage systems.

There is cause to wonder why the shipping interests of New England, of Maine in particular, fought so vigorously to have coastwise vessels freed of the obligation to hire port pilots, when it was common knowledge that sailing ships, of whatever rig, were extremely lacking in maneuverability, as compared with propeller-driven craft, could not back away from rocks or shoals when the wind was setting them on, and when beset by storms or adverse winds, could not maintain a set course to avoid obstructions.

The answer to that one is this: for financial and economic reasons. The New England states, with Maine as a focal point, were the axis of a very prosperous sailing ship trade, principally with the Southern states, during the last quarter of the 19th century and well on into the 20th century. Lumber, cotton, turpentine, phosphate were some of the things carried north in innumerable shiploads—and carried very economically. Manufactured products, furniture, fabrics, clothing, and machinery were some of the things carried south—very economically, using wind power only. Sailing vessels, principally schooners, did most of the carrying, even though the age of the steamship had been well underway for some time. The cost to the owners would be reduced further if there were no pilotage fees to pay.

As late as 1906, observers saw this trade thriving mightily and wrote about it in a booklet, *The Coastwise Trade*, prepared by the Gilbert Transportation Company. The following excerpt was quoted by Senator Sparkman of Florida, speaking before the House of Representatives on June 28th of that year:

> The coastwise trade is today making fortunes as it did of yore. It was at one time thought that the sailing vessel would be entirely superseded by the steamship; but the course of events had demonstrated that this was a mistaken surmise. Great as has been the development of the steamboat traffic, it has not by any means displaced the sailing vessel. This is especially true in regard to the coastwise trade. Experience has shown that there is a class of traffic which can be and always will be more profitably carried on by sailing vessels than by steamships. To handle this class of transportation, the demand for the sailing vessel is rapidly increasing.

It was this coastwise trade between the Northern and Southern states that gave rise to the conflicts over compulsory pilotage and led to the introduction of most of the controversial anti-pilotage legislation on the national level. It should be clear, therefore, that the purpose of the anti-pilotage bills sponsored by the New England states was to force the elimination of compulsory pilotage and pilotage fees in the Southern states, whose ports and products were so important to New England commerce, rather than to bring about any important changes in conditions at the North Atlantic ports.

Seventeen

Tugboats and a Tug-of-War

It might be a matter of some astonishment if one could know exactly how many normal, ordinary persons actually believe that port pilots and tugboat captains are one-and-the-same functionary. There are sundry indications that many persons do have that mistaken belief, and these people need to be informed that these are two separate hirelings performing two dissimilar functions, the one taking up where the other leaves off.

For a clearer understanding of this difference, there is this explanation in a brochure put out by the Sandy Hook Pilots' Association:

> The Sandy Hook pilot goes aboard ocean-going vessels—passenger liners, freighters, and tankers—either at the pier or on the open sea off the entrance to the harbor. Often at the risk of his life, he clambers up the side of a vessel on a rope ladder and makes his way to the bridge. He then assumes the conn to ensure the safety of the vessel with her precious cargo of human lives and goods. This is where his job really begins. He guides the vessel through traffic, rocks, reefs, shoals, and narrow channels to her destination. She is directed either to a safe anchorage or to a point directly off the end of a pier, at which time the tugboats take over and assist the ship into her berth.

All of this notwithstanding, however, there was a time in the history of pilotage in America when many persons sought to obtain the enactment of federal laws that would make that mistaken idea—of the dual identity of port pilots—an actual true fact. One of the earliest anti-pilotage bills introduced in Congress was the Dingley Bill, presented in 1883, 1884, and 1886. The chief provision of this bill, the one that caused the greatest concern among the organized state pilotage groups, would have given shipmasters the right to reject the services of pilots when they accept the services of tugboats. Congressman Nelson Dingley, Jr. of Maine, the sponsor of this bill, previously had introduced anti-pilotage legislation as early as 1874.

The Dingley Bill never became law, principally because the congressmen were made to realize that tugboat captains, whose primary function was the employment of their engine-powered vessels in the movement of ships by towing them astern or alongside and by pushing them ahead or around and about, principally in safe, deep-water harbors, and into and out of their dockside berths, could never be substitutes for experienced pilots and their expert guidance.

Although this bill never became law, by its continued, repetitive presentation, it gave impetus to other legislative proposals, all somewhat similar and all aiming to abolish or modify the existing compulsory pilotage system. One of these proposed the exemption of ships from compulsory pilotage requirements when they were towed into or out of harbors by tugs on board which there were crew members who were licensed as pilots by the federal government, the previously mentioned "federal" pilots, much maligned by the traditional or "state" pilots. Another bill proposed that all examining and licensing of pilots be done by the federal *Inspectors of Hulls and Boilers*.

The latter bill read, in part, as follows:

> Whenever the master or mate of a sailing vessel of the United States, claiming to be a skillful pilot, offers himself for a license, the inspectors (of Hulls and Boilers) shall make diligent inquiry as to his character and merits, and if satisfied from personal examination of the applicant, with the proof that he offers, that he possesses the requisite knowledge and skill, and is trustworthy and faithful, they shall grant him a license for the term of five years to pilot any vessel within the limits prescribed in the license.
>
> No state or municipal government shall impose upon any such pilot any obligation to procure a state or other license in addition to that so issued by the inspectors, or any other regulation which shall impede such pilot in the performance of his duties; and no pilotage charges by any state or municipal government shall be levied on any vessel so engaged in the coastwise trade, being towed into or out of any port in the United States by a vessel under command of a pilot licensed as provided for in this bill.

It should be apparent that the provisions of this bill could not guarantee the competence of those prospective pilots being examined and given those federal licenses, simply because the competence and knowledge of those doing the examining could not be guaranteed. There was cause to wonder about how much the Inspectors of Hulls and

Boilers knew about ship handling, tides and winds and currents, general all-round seamanship, and the specific workings of the ship guiding profession. If this bill had become law, it would have been tailored to the avid and unreasonable demands of the New England tugboat and cargo sailing ship interests, expecially those trading with the Southern states. This law would have dealt a telling and perhaps mortal blow to the cause of state pilotage, the proven, traditional, satisfactory system.

Needless to say, state and city pilot groups rose up to fight against these and other adverse legislative proposals and to exert a still more vigorous tug in the tug-of-war that had been going on between them and the anti-pilotage forces. They sought to do so on the national level, at Washington, at the seat of government, where the impact of public opinion was so forcefully felt. It was there of course that the federal pilotage law overriding all others had originated and there that it would be rendered ineffective and powerless.

As they set about doing this, they noticed that a vital something was missing in their ranks. That something was a unifying, guiding leadship supplied by a national association, a parent organization, headquartered in the nation's capital city, tying all the port groups and state groups together as one big family. The recognition of this deficiency led to the founding of just such a parent organization, the American Pilots' Association on September 30, 1884.

Eighteen

The American Pilots' Association

As of this writing, the American Pilots' Association has 52 member organizations, which are the various port groups on the Atlantic, Pacific, and Gulf coasts, and two associate member organizations, which are a Great Lakes group and a St. Lawrence Seaway group. The combined membership of all these groups is 935 pilots.

The association's headquarters is in the nation's capital, at 2000 K Street, NW, Washington, D.C. 20006. Its president is Captain Ernest Clothier, who succeeded Captain W. Hilton Lowe upon his retirement in 1964. In all, there have been eight presidents, six before these two, beginning with Captain Henry Harbinson of New York, one of the founders, who took office in 1884 and served for 13 years.

Captain Harbinson helped to nurture and guide the new organization during its troubled infancy and later helped in its development to a mature status throughout those early trying times when opposition to the now traditional "state pilotage" system was strong and was trying to modify and even abolish that system, to the detriment of the pilotage profession, American maritime commerce, and the general public welfare.

Captain Harbinson was followed in the presidency by Captains J. Edward O'Brien of Florida (1897–1911), Edward Turnure of New York (1911–1913), Benjamin Mitchell of Louisiana (1913–1933), and John S. Delano of Maryland (1933–1956).

Presidents Harbinson and O'Brien especially were impelled to fight long and hard and diligently to repel the attacks, by various vested interests, against the state pilotage system and its supplemental concept of compulsory pilotage *which*, as Captain O'Brien once explained, was "nothing more than pilotage under local laws designed to prevent recklessness in navigation."

A sound argument in favor of that compulsory pilotage concept and its aim "to prevent recklessness in navigation" is contained in this excerpt from a communication to the South Carolina legislature requesting its support in a concerted effort to defeat the Dingley Bill and other anti-pilotage legislation then before the national Congress. It was sent on behalf of the pilots of Charleston. It reads as follows:

> Gentlemen: To abolish compulsory pilotage on coastwise vessels will disorganize and destroy our usefulness in the ports of South Carolina. It will become a matter of bargain for the service of a pilot. Advantage will be taken by the master in good weather and by the pilot in bad weather (if there is any advantage to be had), and it will demoralize and destroy that high sense of honor of a pilot who believes that he has a lifetime right to pilot, if he does not do anything to forfeit his license. Our best material will seek other employment, leaving the commerce of our ports subject to the schemes of unprincipled men, thereby increasing the risk of insurance, and depriving us of large ships to carry our products to foreign ports, thereby making us a feeder for the larger deep-water ports of the northern states.
>
> The tides that wash our shores twice in every twenty-four hours are constantly shifting the sands, filling up channels and cutting out new channels, requiring pilots to be local men who are required by law to sound the bars at least once in two weeks and report in writing to the Harbor Master the depth of water found, the changes, etc. A pilot must be familiar with the courses of currents, the changes, the set of the tides, the rise and fall of tides, the winds, the effects of winds on tides, the effects of seas on ships of different size, shape, and build, which have to cross our shoal, sandy bar; which knowledge can only be obtained by long and constant practice.
>
> To pilot a ship of heavy draft over our bar requires a local state pilot aboard the ship.... We have to float ships across our bar with not more than one inch of water in excess of the ship's draft.... Compulsory pilotage means law, order, safety. The abolition of it means disorder, distress, and danger. I earnestly hope that you will use your best energies to defeat the Dingley Bill and other bills and allow the matter to be settled by the states, where it rightly belongs.

In 1886, just two years after its founding, the American Pilots' Association composed and presented to the Congress a lengthy and discursive statement, *Statement in Behalf of the American Pilots' Association Against the Abolition of Compulsory Pilotage*. In it, various allegations and legislative proposals by the opposition, represented in large part by the *Shipmasters and Shipowners Association*, were refuted with verve and telling effect. This latter organization might be said to have been the opposite number of the American Pilots' Association.

One adverse legislative proposal, that one which proposed substituting tugboats for pilots, was controverted in these words:

> One of the main arguments of the advocates of these bills is that steam tugs, under the command of United States licensed pilots, would be of more practical utility than the present system of pilot boats. To the ordinary observer, whose knowledge of tug service is confined to his observation of canal boats towed swiftly along the placid bosom of the canal ditch, or even vessels towed up or down a quiet river on a summer day, this argument seems forceful; but when it is remembered that the great need of pilotage is not on placid canals, or on summer days, but on dangerous coasts, of dark nights, when the winds blow and the waves rise and the tempest is at hand, then a different view is presented. And we contend that when the emergency is greatest, the tug will be wanting, while the pilot boat will be on hand. The ordinary tug is not capable of going to sea. They are built with low hulls, and houses on deck, one above the other, the top of the upper house being some 12 feet above the deck. The moment a big sea strikes them, over they go. They know this and therefore they never venture out to sea in bad weather and always come inside at night. That is the very time when the mariner needs a pilot.
>
> But suppose a tug, more venturesome than most of them, should fall in with a vessel in a heavy sea and undertake to tow her in. She could make no headway—ten chances to one the hawser would break, and if it did not, the weight of the tow and the drift of the current would exceed the power of the tug.... Of course powerful tugs can be and have been built that could tow vessels in heavy weather at sea, but their cost is so great as to render them unprofitable in any but large cities with heavy commerce.
>
> Another consideration and a most important one is: In the case of the pilot boat, the pilot is put on board the vessel itself. Whatever happens, he is there at the helm. If the vessel goes into port, he goes with her. If she goes to the bottom, he is with her. But with the pilot of the tug, he drops his hawser and takes care of himself, and the captain is left with his vessel, perhaps in a most critical position, to do the same.

All of this seemed to be saying that the tugs in most cases had as much need of local pilots as the vessels they towed.

The statement also belittled and controverted the proposal which would create great numbers of new "federal" pilots, some of whom were to operate tugs in replacing "state" pilots, by giving to boards made up of Inspectors of Hulls and Boilers the power to examine and license as "United States Pilots" any persons whom they might deem fit. These "boards" consisted of only two men, neither of whom was required to be a practicing or retired pilot, shipmaster, mate, quartermaster, any other functionary concerned with ship handling. The statement made capital of the obvious preponderance of this deficiency and emphasized other defects in the proposed system, the adoption of which would set the government on a course of unrestricted licensing of masters and mates of coastwise vessels, as well as tugboat operators, to be official, accredited port pilots. This part of the statement reads as follows:

> The adversaries of compulsory pilotage propose to substitute for the state pilots United States pilots, who are to be examined and licensed by the boards of local inspectors provided for in Section 4442 of the Revised Statutes. These boards were created for the purpose of inspecting steam vessels, and the law provides that they shall consist of two persons, one of whom shall possess the qualifications necessary for an inspector of boilers. But there is nothing in the Revised Statutes that requires or contemplates that either of them should have any knowledge of pilotage or of the marine topography of their respective districts.
>
> By what rule of fitness have these men been selected by the framers of these laws to examine and license pilots, to select the men who shall be entrusted with the lives and property that venture upon the waters of this country? The states require, first, an apprenticeship of years; second, a rigid examination, conducted by the oldest and most skillful pilots; but this bill proposes to entrust the pilotage of any and all vessels to any man who can produce a license signed by an inspector of hulls and an inspector of boilers. What can the examining board possible know about the subject upon which they are to examine the applicant?
>
> You might as well subject naval officers to an examination by a ship carpenter and fireman; army officers by a board of gunsmiths; or physicians by manufacturers of surgical instruments. But this is the serious proposition of these bills: men thus examined and thus certified are to take charge of the pilotage of this country, driving out those who have spent their lives in careful and laborious observation of the waters on which they live.
>
> But aside from any question of examination, can it be possible that these masters or mates of vessels, plying in all parts of the district covered by their licenses, can have the same accurate and current knowledge of all these ports as each home pilot now has of his own? Can they be cognizant of all the changes that wind and tides and storms can work on shifting sands, on buoys and lights, in their

> absence? To hold that they can is to aver that these extraordinary diplomas endow their recipients with either omniscience or omnipresence or both.

The presentation of this statement to Congress was not the first belligerent action of the American Pilots' Association — nor the last. At the organizational conference of pilot delegations at the Metropolitan Hotel in New York City on September 30, 1884, the following resolution, which actually signalized the founding of the association, was adopted:

> Whereas the coast approaches and ports of the United States of American are now, at the end of the 19th century, not less beset with dangers, storms, fogs, and shoals than of old times, and
>
> Whereas, never since the United States became a nation, has there been any abatement of the necessity for the pilot's calling or of the sincere respect for his services as a seaman expert, always on the alert to safeguard human life, whether at sea or by preventing the introduction of infectious diseases from fever-stricken passengers, and
>
> Whereas the wealth, safety, and strength of the United States is best preserved by a well-regulated mercantile marine once more carrying the stars-and-stripes into every part of the globe as in time past, and
>
> Whereas the abolition of compulsory pilotage would multiply the dangers and risks inevitable on the American coastline, and
>
> Whereas the past services of the pilots to their country deserve grateful recognition and at least just and proper compensation to be paid if legislators succeed in destroying compulsory pilotage, in other words, the pilotage system itself, and
>
> Whereas any effort to resuscitate and consolidate the American mercantile marine must be futile if the mainstay of that marine, the pilotage service, is abolished, now therefore be it
>
> RESOLVED that a committee of five, with power to add to their number, and with a president and secretary, be and is hereby formed for the purpose of frustrating any overt acts against the employment and livelihood of the pilots of the United States.

Membership in this national pilots association is restricted to "organized groups of bar, river, and harbor pilots holding licenses under the authority of the law of any state." The state groups are autonomous in their respective localities and in their dealings with the various state governments, local authorities, and industry groups; and the scope of the authority of the national association is confined to the responsibility given to it by these member groups.

Some of these responsibilities have been and are: the carrying on of active progress in the field of public relations, not only with the legislative and executive departments of the government, but also in the shipping industry, in labor and management circles, and in the broad area of public relations with the general public: the carrying on of a continuous research program into legislative, administrative, business, professional, and scientific activities, as these tend to affect the best interests of the pilotage profession: assisting in the solution of knotty or stubborn local problems, some of which could have a bearing on local matters throughout the entire nation, at times when this assistance may be requested by state or local groups.

One responsibility that it does *not* have is that of recommending or proposing rates to be charged the owners of vessels for their use of a pilot's services. Pilotage charges are determined locally by the local pilot groups, after consultations involving the various parties that are to be affected, adversely and beneficially.

Of course the universal, fundamental measure of compensation is that old-reliable one based on that old-reliable yardstick, a vessel's draft or depth in the water—a fixed amount of money for each foot of that draft. Other additional charges are made for the performance of other services such as docking and undocking, moving ships in port from one berth to another, and adjusting and calibrating compasses in "swing ship" exercises. There is no plan to achieve uniformity, neither on a nation-wide scale nor on an entire coast, since each local area has its own set of conditions, problems, and methods of operating.

The cordial working relationships between the association and the various state and port groups have been maintained down through the years under the "Articles of Association," which have provided the operational set-up for the groups in the alliance. The entire organizational structure has worked well over the years in solving the problems and achieving the goals of these groups.

The aims and objectives of the American Pilots' Association, as stated in Article II of its by-laws, are as follows:

> To promote the welfare and common business interests of licensed State pilots and pilot associations.
>
> To assist State pilots in their efforts to maintain the traditionally high standards of the State Pilotage system.
>
> To promote public safety and protect life and property on the inland and coastal waters of the United States.
>
> To co-operate with Federal and State authorities in the national interest in matters relating to pilotage.
>
> To gather and disseminate information pertaining and of interest to State pilots and State pilot organizations.

To co-operate with shipping and transportation industries and organizations in matters relating to pilotage and to promote common business interests.

To encourage and aid in the development of closer relationships between the general public and licensed pilots.

Nineteen

The War Goes On

In the prolonged struggle between the pilots dedicated to the preservation of the state pilotage system and those who would destroy it (ship owners and shipmasters, middle men, traders and brokers, the Maine bureaucracy, and certain foreign corporations), the pilots acquired many allies and champions for their cause. Among these sympathizers were the insurance and business interests, who decried the extra, unnecessary risks incurred when captains of heavily-laden ships refused the services of qualified port pilots and brought their ships into port under no guidance than their own or that of certain crew members.

At one time, for coastwise vessels, this was permissible and common practice at the ports of all the north Atlantic states and—for a very short time only—in the state of Maryland. There is of course a distinction to be made between those states that had a strict compulsory system, those that had a voluntary or choice system, and those that absolutely forbade compulsory pilotage. Of these last, there were only two, Maine and New Hampshire.

The Port of New York had a non-compulsory or voluntary system at one time, and herewith is one consequence, as reported in that previously mentioned Statement in Behalf of the *American Pilots' Association Against the Abolishment of Compulsory Pilotage*:

> In 1854 the captain of the *New Era*, a sailing vessel with about 400 souls aboard, bound to New York, refused to take a pilot under the non-compulsory system existing there at the time. He piloted his own ship, and sank her off the New Jersey shore, and 400 human beings were drowned near where Asbury Park now is. The result was the passage of the compulsory pilotage laws for the State of New York.

This statement was presented and read to Congress in 1886, the year in which nearly all the legislators from Maine, and especially

Congressman Dingley, were bent on pushing through legislation to abolish compulsory pilotage nationally. It was on this account, undoubtedly, that the following two reports of marine disasters, both of which took place on the coast of Maine, were included in the statement:

> The advocates of these bills point to the State of Maine, with her voluntary law, as an example for Congress to follow. In 1865, the Allan steamship *Bohemian* came on the Maine coast off Portland harbor in the afternoon. There was no pilot to be had, and the steamship laid off the port that night. The next day, the captain attempted to do his own pilotage. He struck a rock off the harbor and sank immediately, and 60 people were drowned in the rigging of that vessel, in sight of the inhabitants on shore. Since that time, the steamship lines of that port have appointed two pilots to look after their vessels at all times.
>
> Again, a stevedore was employed there by the owners of certain ships for pilot duty, because they thought the charges of the professional port pilot exorbitant. They paid the stevedore $1800 per year. In leaving Portland with one of these ships, he struck her on a reef, and the resulting damage was three or four hundred thousand dollars to ship and cargo. That would have paid for compulsory pilotage in Maine for all Eternity.

Many other marine disasters definitely resulting from deliberate negligence in making use of the services of a professional port pilot brought many more champions and allies to the side of the state pilots. These included local seaport city officials and high federal authorities, various labor unions, U.S. Coast Guard and U.S. Navy officialdom, and almost the entire business community, especially marine insurance companies and prominent shipping interests. Individuals and small groups in the rank and file of the general public also added their say-so and support.

Some of the ablest support came from a small group of congressmen on a certain congressional committee, the *Select Committee on Ship-building and Ship-owing Interests*. This was in 1886, in the first session of the 49th Congress, during which more anti-pilotage bills were being sponsored by Congressman Dingley of Maine. This small group—minority—of that committee showed its distaste for the proposed legislation in its Report of the Minority of the *Select Committee on Ship-building and Ship-owning Interests*. This report minced no words. Pertinent parts of it are given here:

> We, the undersigned, dissent from the report of the *Select Committee on American Ship-building and Ship-owning Interests*

recommending passage of the bill (H.R. 6390) to abolish compulsory pilotage for American sailing vessels for the following reasons:

1) Under said bill one may procure a license as a pilot without having navigated the waters on which he will pursue his calling and without showing any acquaintance with the channels of the ports on those waters.
2) The board which grants such licenses is composed of two men, one the inspector of boilers and the other the inspector of steamboat hulls. Neither of them is required to be expert in pilotage, nor do their duties as inspectors qualify them to make determinations as to the fitness of persons to discharge the responsible duties of pilots.
3) From the nature of things, a pilot perfectly acquainted with the entrance into one port may be a very dangerous reliance in another. Some ports are approached by stable and well-defined channels. The entrance to others often is intricate and tortuous, over bars constantly shifting and to be known only by frequent soundings and constant vigilance. The entrance by the steamboats, once learned, may be repeated at any reasonable interval in safety. On the other hand, the action of winds and waves upon the shifting bottom in a single storm may cause death and destruction to a vessel and crew not protected by the knowledge acquired and *only acquirable* by the local pilots.
6) A pilot on a steam tug towing a vessel cannot in all respects supply the need of a pilot on that vessel. In stormy weather, the hawser may part. Sometimes, to avoid pulling the vessel onto an obstruction, the hawser must be thrown off or instantly cut. When so detached, the sailing vessel is without a pilot and may encounter danger from her *inertia* or winds and waves. The hawser is at least 50 fathoms (300 feet) long. If the channel be winding, the tug may be on one side of a shoal trying to pull around it, the sailing vessel on the other side. Then the tendency is to pull the vessel upon the shoal, and a pilot is needful on her to prevent such a disaster...
7) As a rule, the inspectors are not familiar with each and every port in their districts and yet, under this bill, they could license pilots for every port in their districts. Of course they cannot know the men's fitness for the work...
8) Many maritime insurors object to the passage of this bill. The abolition of compulsory pilotage would increase the hazards of marine insurance and the dangers to life...property and passengers might be sacrificed through the parsimony of ship owners or the mistakes or rashness of ship masters.
9) Passage of this bill will destroy efficiency of pilots. Under the state regulations, one must serve in the lower branches and prove himself capable and trustworthy before he can be a "full branch" pilot.

> A full-branch pilot's badge justly has been designated "the blue ribbon of the ocean." But if the training and experience of years and the study of the dangers and difficulties peculiar to a port must pass for naught, and licenses be granted as this bill proposes, the title of pilot will be degraded and the service will deteriorate...
>
> 12) The people of the several states are anxious for commerce at their several ports, and they may well be trusted to deal with the matter in the future, as they were so trusted in the past. They will not allow unjust fees to be collected. Without these local pilots, there will be great difficulty in preventing selfish strangers from dumping debris or ballast along our ocean paths. Without them, selfish strangers, to avoid quarantine may conceal and carry into our cities diseases breeding wide-spread death. These pilots, though local, serve the country at large, especially as they police the water-gates to the country. All these duties they must perform by law. We had best let well enough alone.

This Report of the Minority was so logical and forceful that it was well received by the legislature, and both houses of that body rejected this bill and several almost-identical bills introduced later on. The proponents, principally New England shipping interests, fought hard to get the bills passed, and the burden of their song, as always, was that owners and masters of American coastwise vessels were being compelled to pay fees to pilots whose services were not needed, that this practice was going on only in the Southern states and not in the North, and that this was a discriminatory practice since there rightfully should have been reciprocity between the two coastal areas.

In their report to Congress, the majority—the anti-pilotage faction—of that same Select Committee, had this to say:

> Ten states only, to wit, Maryland, Virginia, North Carolina, South Carolina, Georgia, Florida, Alabama, Mississippi, Louisiana, and Texas, altogether...still insist on compelling American coasters to pay fees to pilots whose services are not needed.
>
> A Maryland, Virginia, or Georgia coasting vessel, for example, may enter and leave the ports of Maine, New Hampshire, and even New York without being compelled to pay a State pilot whose services are declined; but a Maine, New Hampshire, or Massachusetts coaster, in entering the ports of Maryland, Virginia, or Georgia, must pay compulsory fees to a State pilot who is not used when the vessel is piloted by its own master or is towed in by a steamer under the charge of a United States pilot.

It was that "United States pilot" entity and all the intimations associated with it that was the bone of contention among the disputants.

Twenty

Accidents and Eloquence

When a United States Government vessel accidentally gets hard aground at a seaport entrance, especially if it is a big and important ship of the Navy, it becomes a matter of great distress and embarrassment, not only for the officers and crew of the ship, but also in the chain of command on up to the top admirals and the office of the Secretary of the Navy. This has happened over and over again down through the years, and in consequence the Navy has modified its appertaining regulations from time to time. It eventually became permissible and even advisable that Navy ship commanders hire civilian pilots to guide their men-of-war into harbors and out of them, however much various individuals might contend that this practice detracted from the prestige of the Navy and of those officers on those ships so guided.

There are records indicating that, prior to the establishment of this practice, officers in command of U.S. Navy ships often paid for the services of local pilots out of their own pockets, rather than risk the ships under their command in certain dangerous waters and weather conditions. One who did not do so, undoubtedly, was the commander of the *U.S.S. Ossipee*, which ran aground at Cape Henry, at the entrance to Chesapeake Bay, at considerable expense to the government.

Subsequent records seem to indicate that the navy encouraged and even ordered ship commanders to hire local pilots — at government expense — when and where there would seem to be a need for their services, and there is a report about how a battleship commander, whose ship got aground off Charleston, was court-martialed for not employing a pilot at the time. The story of this happening is told in the book, *History of Compulsory Pilotage*, by Captain J. Edward O'Brien, as follows:

> ...the battleship Raleigh grounded off Charleston, and its commander, Captain Coghlan, was court-martialed for not

> employing a branch pilot, or bar pilot. Admiral Remy, in his report of the case, said: "Considering the Raleigh's draft, he (the captain) should have employed a licensed local pilot before entering the harbor of Charleston."

These and other instances of U.S. Navy vessels getting aground or getting wrecked or sunk as they entered or left seaports without professional pilots on board assisting them all tended to enhance the reputations of the traditional, local, professional, "state" pilots. The happenings brought more of government officialdom over into their camp and helped immeasurably in frustrating those who would abolish the state pilotage system entirely, in favor of one in which the greater part of the exercise of this important function would be carried on by itinerant, irresponsible, untrained "federal" pilots and tugboat captains.

One of the main factors in the losing battle being fought by the anti-pilotage forces was their disposition to emphasize chiefly business and monetary considerations, with scarcely any references to the many services—patriotic, charitable, guardian, humanitarian—that the traditional old-time pilots performed as a matter of course under the compulsory pilotage system. In contending so vigorously for reciprocity from the Southern states with regard to pilotage fees, the New England ship operators showed that they were motivated almost wholly by a desire to save money and to bring steam tugs into the picture for purely economic or mercenary reasons. This oversight and this attitude were scarcely conducive to enlisting sympathizers and supporters for their cause.

On the other hand, supporters of the traditional state pilotage system, in their speeches and written statements, de-emphasized the profit motive and gave expansive accounts of the many and varied services performed by the old-timer local port pilots—as part of their jobs or not. For illustration, there is this excerpt from the "*Supplemental Note of Argument Filed by Counsel for the American Pilots' Association Against the Abolishment of Compulsory Pilotage before the Senate Committee on Commerce, March 8, 1892*:

> The law requires that pilot boats shall be cruising day in and day out, month in and month out, year in and year out, at sea; watchful sentinels at all times, in all kinds of weather, as long as the best sea boats can live, compelled by law, and never shrinking from the task, to render aid and assistance to vessels seeking or requiring it, riding upon the storm for days, at times without the reward of one dollar, periling and sometimes losing their lives in the performance of this duty; at all times at the call of those desiring a pilot, and often in bad weather guiding them to safety; a sure and certain restraint

> upon tugboats and others who would exact exorbitant charges for services to masters of vessels, because the state pilots' charges are fixed by law; bound to succor them if their crews are sick or their vessels disabled from any cause; a living and ever-present safeguard to master, owner, and insurance companies; and, lastly, quarantine officers to the adjacent ports, and life-saving stations to wretched, wornout, ships' crews.

This portion of that "*Supplemental Note of Argument*" did much to refute the contention of the opposition that pilots in the Southern states were collecting pilotage fees without performing any service. The known fact of these pilots being on duty, on station, on their pilot boats, on the open sea, on call, on the alert, at principal port entrances, 24 hours of every day in the year—all of which is likewise the customary activity of the state pilots of today—was ample service performed, as this report and other similar ones have pointed out.

As for the tugboats, the argument for tugs as substitutes for port pilots never was a very convincing one, but the vociferous advocates of an enforced, federal, national, non-compulsory pilotage system continued to stand on the premise that coastwose sailing vessels towed by tugs in entering and leaving seaports had no need for the local or so-called state pilot. The tugboat and barge interests of the Northern states found it feasible and profitable to support this contention. It seems that all were willing to accept the obvious risks—of course realizing that it would be the insurance companies, to whom somebody's good money was being paid in policy premiums, who would pay the costs of all maritime disasters. The marine insurance companies in general had continued to be unalterably opposed to any tampering with the state pilotage system as it then existed.

The argument for tugs as replacements for pilots could not and did not hold water, for it was demonstrated before the assembled Congress that many sailing vessels pulled in long tows behind tugs got fouled up in Southern waters, getting aground, capsizing, striking obstructions, and even sinking. Examples were given of tugboats with an 8-foot draft attempting to tow ships with a 30-foot draft in rough seas, with a dangerous situation thus created, not only for the ships and their cargoes, crews, and passengers, but also for the tugs themselves. It was demonstrated also that tugs in general were not built to operate in heavy weather and rough seas, and they were liable to capsize, thus leaving their tows or prospective tows in a helpless, dangerous state. For this reason, tugboats could not be expected to venture very far offshore in stormy weather to assist vessels in distress or in need of a pilot.

In spite of all this and other adverse testimony given to Congress in this controversy, the anti-pilotage forces and the tugboat interests persisted in their efforts to modify or obliterate the existing state pilotage system through federal legislation, introducing the same old bills, re-tailored and re-worded, in various new guises. As late as 1906, one of these bills, a particularly objectionable one, found its way into a session of the 59th Congress.

It was of course another "Maine" bill, H.R. 5281, introduced by Representative Charles E. Littlefield of Maine. It sought the same damaging effects that would have resulted from passage of any of the Dingley bills, presented periodically for a period of over 20 years. It provided for federal licensing, *by the inspectors of hulls and boilers*, of all pilots operating on sailing vessels. *It exempted such pilots from all state or municipal maritime laws*. and it prohibitied the levying of any charges by state or local governments upon sailing vessels towed into and out of United States ports by tugboats. It was the same old story, the same old conflict between the Northern and Southern shipping interests, the same old axe to be laid to the root of the tree.

The bill was considered and discussed by the Merchant Marine and Fisheries Committee of the House of Representatives and then was introduced on the floor. In the ensuing House debate on it, the case of the traditional state pilots versus the tugboats was ably and eloquently presented by Congressman Stephen M. Sparkman of Florida—in part, as follows:

> ...it is said local pilots are unnecessary, as the tow boats can do the work, and crude though this measure is, provision is herein made for this class of boats, not by requiring them to have a skilled bar pilot on board, for that would not suit the purposes of this bill, but one of those inspectors-created pilots is to do the work. It is a well-known fact, however, that these tugboats, even with a skilled pilot aboard, cannot take the place of the pilot at all times, if it can do so at any time. They are not constructed for rough weather, and when the storm comes and the waves run high, they still will be compelled to seek shelter, while the unfortunate ship with her crew and cargo will be obliged to remain outside and ride out the storm, with the danger of being driven and wrecked upon the shore.

Again the grim spectacle of mammoth U.S. Navy ships lying hard aground and helpless at seaport entrances must be brought into the picture as Congressman Sparkmen, continuing his speech, has more to say about the inadequacy of tugboats and the imperative need for local, trained, experienced, professional port pilots—as follows:

> Furthermore, there should always be a skilled bar pilot on the vessel being towed, for a knowledge of the bottom and the currents is

> essential. Being usually towed in the rear of a towboat by a long hawser, she is constantly in danger, in shoal waters where the currents are swift, of sheering to one side or the other and grounding upon the banks or upon a recently-formed bar. This often happens, and it is just what happened to the battleships *Kearsage* and *Kentucky* in New York Harbor last January. There was a pilot on the flagship *Maine*, the leader of the fleet, but none on the *Kearsarge* and the *Kentucky*, which were following, with a distance of only about 400 yards between each ship. The flagship went out easily, while the other ships mentioned suddenly sheered to one side and grounded, partly because the sailing master, as was found, so it is said by the board of inquiry, thought the current was setting in one direction when it was actually running in another—a mistake a bar pilot familiar with the harbor, shoals, and currents would not have made.
>
> The *Rhode Island* in May last, also without a bar pilot, grounded on York Spit at the entrance to the York River in Virginia, the sailing master evidently not knowing what a pilot would have known, that is, that the bar was there. A pilot had tendered his services while the ship was outside but the same were refused, the commander thinking, no doubt, that he could go in without one.
>
> These vessels were all subsequently floated. But think what might have been the consequences if they had not been gotten off, costing as they did many millions of dollars in their constructions, to say nothing of the cost of their removal as wrecks and the inevitable injury to the channel.

Further along in his oratory, Congressman Sparkman very shrewdly came to the defense of the Navy officers involed in all such groundings of Navy ships, expressing sympathy and understanding. In doing so, he made capital for the cause of the state pilots and to state pilotage system, to wit:

> Mr. Chairman, some criticism of the naval officials has been indulged in on account of these and other similar accidents, the claim being that they showed incompetency on the part of those in charge of the vessels. But the trouble is not there, as the naval officers are as highly skilled in the duties rightfully expected of them as any other similar class of experts in the world. The trouble is that they are often expected to perform the duties of a pilot, for which they have no training other than that possessed generally by American sailing masters, which does not enable them to take vessels into our Southern harbors, with their treacherous channels and shifting sands.

Twenty-One

More of Stephen M. Sparkman

It has been said that this speech by Congressman Sparkman, of which only random portions have been given here thus far, was the greatest in United States history on behalf of the compulsory pilotage system and that his able opposition to the enactment of that proposed adverse piece of legislation was the biggest factor in its eventual defeat. However, that masterpiece of oratory and elucidation had and still has other excellent qualities. It explains. It expounds. It tells the story. At least, it tells the greater part of the story—for us as well as for those statesmen of long ago—the story of the benignant and worthwhile profession of piloting. It would seem to be appropriate then, aside from the fact of the eloquence involved, to give the remainder of that speech here:

> It will thus be seen that the bill proposes to create pilots out of the masters and mates of coastwise sailing vessels at the option of such masters and mates and the inspectors of hulls and boilers, and to substitute them for the regular pilots by prohibiting, as it does, the enforcement of any State or municipal requirement to take or pay for any State pilot by any coastwise vessel piloted by its captain or mate or towed by any boat under the command of a pilot, *so licensed*, which, as I shall show presently, will practically put the pilots at a large majority if not *all* the ports in the states mentioned out of business.
>
> Mr. Chairman, I shall take but little time in showing the importance of an efficient pilot system to our maritime commerce at each port in this country. Indeed I should consume no time at all in such an effort but for the suggestion made by the mere introduction of this bill here that its advocates and friends do not consider such a system to be worthy of consideration or of preservation.
>
> But, Sir, the experience of the world condemns such an idea. For

hundreds of years, the pilot has been considered an important adjunct to maritime commerce. In fact, the system had its origin in the necessities of the sailing vessel when the demands of commerce for the first time sent her from her own harbor to distant lands and unfamiliar waters, for the purpose of distributing the products of the earth to the consumer. And from then until now, the skill of the local pilot has been considered necessary, at least to the sailing ship entering or leaving a port.

The Supreme Court of the United States, presided over by the ablest and most enlightened men produced by our civilization, said in the case of *exparte* McNeil (13 Wall) that 'the pilot is as much a part of the merchant marine as the hull of a ship or the helm by which it is guided;' and the learned justices might well have added: 'as indispensable to the successful voyage as either,' for if dangers are found in the dashing billows and the hurricane's sweep far out at sea, perils also lurk in the hidden rock and the shifting sands near the coast. The trained pilot may alone be trusted to guard against the one, while the skilled navigator can alone cope with the other.

Men are trained for both positions and may, *indeed must*, have a general knowledge of the duties of the other. The navigator is trained aboard the ship and at sea, the pilot mostly in the harbor and on the bar where he is expected to follow his vocation. At least, that is the way it should be and as it is under the systems in all the maritime states of this country. Under them, the pilot is controlled by the States or, rather by local boards created by State legislation and composed of men living in the communities immediately bordering on the harbor to be served by the pilot and who are hence familiar with all the necessities of such a harbor. This has ever been the practice of the maritime world, and rightfully so too, as all pilot matters can be much better controlled by local authorities near a given harbor or bar then by an authority remote from such pilotage grounds.

The Supreme Court of the United States, in discussing this very feature of pilotage, says, 'It is local and not national, and it is likely to be best provided for, not by one system or plan of regulation, but by as many as the legislative discretion of the several states deems applicable to the local peculiarities of the ports within their limits.

The conditions at no two harbors are the same, Mr. Chairman, and especially is this true of the harbors in the section of the country to which it is intended this bill shall apply. The harbor at Tampa and that at Pensacola are not alike, but are essentially different as to conditions, and the same is true of Key West and Jacksonville, as it is in all the other harbors in that section. Courses and distances, currents and channels, the bars and the banks are different. In many, the bottoms are constantly changing, a bar perhaps forming today where none existed yesterday, currents setting in one direction now and in another direction a little later on, requiring constant and daily watching on the part of the pilot, in order for him to be fitted to conduct ships safely over the bar and through the harbor.

Now, sir, the States in their control of pilotage undertake to guard against these dangers. Under the present State systems, a pilot must serve a long apprenticeship, from four to eight years, not on a dozen or even *two* bars, but on *the one bar* on currents, the nature of the bottom, taking soundings, piloting vessels, familiarizing himself with the courses and distances; and in-between-times, he must go to sea, spending several months on a sailing vessel, until he shall have thoroughly learned how to handle all classes of ships. Then he is examined by a local board of pilot commissioners or port wardens, at least one of whom is an expert pilot for that particular bar. Having been thus examined and found competent by this expert board, he is given a license to pilot only on that bar alone and no other, and there he must live and work to the day of his death, unless he leaves the business or in like manner qualifies himself to pilot at some other port.

That, sir, is what the States require for the safety of life and property. What does this bill propose to give us? Why, sir, under its provisions the pilot need never have *seen* the harbor in which he is to perform his service or have taken a ship across its bar; nor is he required to possess any of the qualifications of a pilot except such of those that he may have gathered as a seaman. All that is necessary under the provisions of this bill for the creation of a full-fledged pilot is for the captain or mate of a coastwise sailing vessel to appear before the inspectors of hulls and boilers anywhere in the country, maybe hundreds—yes, thousands—of miles away from a particular harbor in which he wishes to act as pilot *and*, knowing nothing perhaps about its condition or the requisite qualifications of a pilot there, *claim* to be a skillful pilot, and offer himself for a license—when it shall become the duty of these same inspectors to examine his proof, and if they are satisfied from such personal examination that he is qualified, to grant him a license to pilot *within the limits mentioned in the license*, which might embrace not only that one harbor, but the whole Atlantic and Gulf coasts as well.

And this, Mr. Chairman, is the system that is to take the place of that now in existence in the States south of the Potomac, and under which our commerce has been builded up to its present proportions.

There followed a rather dull and monotonous recital of the names of various organizations, commercial, fraternal, and labor union, that publicly had voiced opposition to any and all attempts to abolish compulsory pilotage. These included the New York Board of Marine Underwriters, the Marine Underwriters of Boston, the New Orleans Board of Underwriters, the American Pilots Association, the American Association of Masters and Mates of Steam Vessels, the International Seamen's Union, the Knights of Labor, the American Federation of Labor, the entire body of marine underwriters of the United States, quarantine officers, and leading commercial bodies of the South Atlantic and gulf ports. Then came the Congressman's concluding remarks, as follows:

> So, Mr. Chairman, we have arrayed against this bill these great industrial forces, speaking not only in the interest of the pilot, but also in favor of life and property and the continued growth of our maritime commerce, now developing more rapidly than ever before in the history of the country.
>
> Then, sir, why strike this blow at American commerce when the States themselves can be trusted to act? Why make so much haste in the direction of the centralization of all powers in the hands of the Federal Government, when at least this one can be better left with the States?
>
> The pilots themselves merit a better fate, for there is no class of people more deserving. No skilled vocation or profession performs so much and obtains so little from the great interests they serve. Facing danger, often beyond the hope of relief, risking their lives for the cause they serve, they are ever at the post of duty, and they should not be destroyed in order that avarice may increase its gains or monopoly, its power.

It is recorded that loud applause followed this conclusion of this important speech, masterfully telling the pilotage story, in the U.S. House of Representatives on Thursday, June 28, 1906.

Twenty-Two

Pilots as Gate Keepers

Dangers are always present at the entrances to our seaports and safe harbors—physical, nature-caused, and man-made dangers, to ships, pilot boats, cargoes, passengers, crews, pilots; but there is another danger there that is far greater than all of these put together. It is the danger of plague and pestilence and the contamination of our cities and towns and the health of our people-by the millions!—through the introduction of deadly contagious diseases coming by ships from places all over the world and entering the United States by way of those same harbor entrances, the water gates to our country.

There was a time, long ago in our history, when nothing or nothing much was done, officially and otherwise, to avert or eliminate that danger. During that time, the Ports of New Orleans, Memphis, Savannah, Charleston, and Norfolk and Portsmouth in Virginia, all were contaminated by infectious diseases, such as cholera and yellow fever, the spread of which soon reached epidemic proportions, killing thousands. In 1855, the steamship *Ben Franklin* put in at the Port of Norfolk and Portsmouth with yellow fever on board. It infected these two cities and a veritable plague resulted. Out of 20,000 inhabitants, some 5000 died and another 10,000 fled the city.

Since that long-ago time, and not very long afterward, it was found that there *was* something that could be done about averting and eliminating that ever-present danger of ship-borne contagion. That something was to require those steadfast, reliable, responsible port pilots, already involved intricately in the manifold activities concerned with the safety of lives and property aboard ship, to act as watch dogs or gate keepers in this matter and to direct all ships coming from suspected or known disease-infested ports to proper quarantine facilities set up outside the port, thus providing a control and a preventive.

From that time on, port pilots have performed that duty diligently, even when it was not required by law, continually going aboard disease-carrying ships to con them into quarantine stations, without regard to their own safety and welfare. During the last quarter of the last century, the various coastal states made this a mandatory thing in their pilotage laws.

In that long-lasting conflict over the retention of the State Pilotage system and compulsory pilotage, the State Pilotage forces made sure to keep calling attention to this phase of the port pilot's work (which was in truth a quasi-public service) and the zeal and fidelity with which it was carried out. They also called attention to the possibility of its not being carried out at all ever again if the State Pilotage System were abolished and "federal pilots" got themselves installed at the various ports. These and other pertinent matters were called to the attention of the Congress—effectively—in 1886 in that previously mentioned *Statement in Behalf of the American Pilots' Association*, as follows:

> The present system of pilotage offers better protection and more safeguards against yellow fever and cholera than all the other agencies employed by the state and national governments.
>
> The pilot laws of all the states require the pilots to stop all infected vessels and vessels from infected ports, carry them to quarantine, and at once report them to the health officer of the port. The pilots have never shirked this duty, although its performance is attended with great danger. In one summer, five of the Delaware Bay pilots died from disease contracted in this way, beside many members of their families to whom it was communicated.
>
> These pilots are the pickets that stand watch night and day over the lives of American people, a chain of ever-watchful sentinels belting our coast from Boston to Galveston. Not their own interests, but the prosperity of their port, and the lives of their wives and children, are the guerdon of their vigilance.
>
> Will the Congress of the United States, at the instance of a few selfish ship owners and ship brokers seeking to save a few paltry dollars, pass these laws for the abolition of compulsory pilotage, dismiss these faithful sentinels, and put the lives of the population of our sea coasts in the hands of transient masters or mates having no interest in the ports—who would be only too glad to get rid of a case of yellow fever on board by running in and landing him at the nearest port? Can the country afford to dispense with the services of one thousand pilots who are now standing guard at the gates of their own homes? There is not a year that would not witness the introduction of epidemic disease in most of the ports of our country, were it not for these pilots!"

Some of this was strong medicine, but all of it was based on stark reality, and the opponents of the State Pilotage System and compulsory pilotage could not prevail against it. That Congress, the 49th, was persuaded. Unfortunately and wastefully, later Congresses had to be persuaded anew, over and over again. In the persuasive efforts, the danger and horror of contagious diseases coming into our country through our seaports was brought up again of course, and some of the efforts, besides dwelling on the painful illnesses and the loss of human life, told about the commercial bankruptcy that inevitably follows in a city that has been invaded by an epidemic.

The American Pilots' Association soon became the accepted leader of the State Pilotage forces in their long-continuing fight to preserve a *status quo* that had been proven efficient and fair dealing throughout many long years. In defending the essentiality of the compulsory pilotage concept and furthering its cause, the association took care to enlist the attention and sympathies of the general public, the business community, and government officials of every sort.

In one part of that impressive *Statement* of 1886, it made clear-cut and pointed references to "the public welfare," "the welfare of the state," and "the highest interest of the state." Since the welfare of the state was known to be a composite of the welfare of all its citizens and the needs of the one to be relatedly the needs of the other, these remarks were appropriate—and efficaceous. That part of the statement is given here, mainly because it is an educative and adequate summary of the story of professional piloting *then and now*:

> The commercial prosperity of a coastal state largely depends upon the condition of her bays, rivers, and harbors. They are the highways which connect her with the ocean and the outside world, and they hold the same relation to her foreign commerce that her railroads, canals, and turnpikes do to her internal trade. They are as much her property—subject to the right delegated by the Constitution to Congress 'to regulate commerce'—as the lands which lie upon their banks. To keep this property in the highest state of excellence, to render these highways safe and convenient for travel, is to invite commerce and all its attendant advantages. To neglect them and allow them to become unsafe and inconvenient of access, is to forfeit that commerce and all its profits. It is therefore in the highest interests of the state that her waters should be: 1st, free of wrecks and obstructions of any kind and 2nd, provided with skillful and competent pilots, who know their lights, buoys, wharves, docks, et cetera.
>
> A perfect knowledge of these can be obtained and retained only by constant inspection, great vigilance, and daily experience.

Recognizing these truths, the Atlantic and Gulf states, from Massachusetts to Texas, have provided themselves with pilots for every port who, by long years of observation and experience, have made themselves perfectly familiar with the waters of their several localities.

In nearly all of these states, the laws require a long and laborious apprenticeship on board a pilot boat before the prosepctive pilot is allowed a license or 'branch.' In New York, it is five years; in Pennsylvania and Delaware, it is six years; in Virginia, five years; and so on! And after such apprenticeship, they are subject to a most thorough examination as to character and capacity before they can receive their branch.

Surely the states would not subject their own citizens to such arduous conditions, did not the public welfare demand it. In many of these ports, the sinking of one large vessel on the edge of the channels might obstruct and perhaps terminate navigation for months and possibly years. In the Southern states, whose coasts present, from Cape Hatteras to the Florida Keys, a succession of breakers and bars and shoals whose shifting sands, borne by currents hither and thither, are continually filling up the old channels and opening new ones, it is absolutely necessary that pilotage there should be confined to those only who, by daily contact and constant observation and that practical skill which familiarity alone can give, are able to ensure safety to the incoming or outgoing vessel. As an evidence of this, it may be stated that the Board of Harbor Commissioners of Charleston, South Carolina, require every pilot to make soundings of the bar at least twice a month. If this be necessary for the pilots who have spent their lives there, how would it be possible for the pilot who visits it once in six months or a year to bring a vessel into that port safely, if compulsory pilotage were abolished?

As the law now stands, these pilots are familiar with their several localities. If the channels change, they know it. If a storm extinguishes a light or carries away a buoy, they know it. If a recent wreck obstructs the channel, they know it. But how can the man who is absent at sea when these things happen be cognizant of them? He may leave the harbor all right but when he comes back a month or six months later, he runs afoul of a wreck or steers by the misplaced buoy, or stands on, looking for the extinguished light, until he runs his ship ashore. Again, it is made the duty of the resident pilots to report all these matters, and their own interests, bound up with the welfare of the port, impels them to do so.

Twenty-Three

The Fading Fight

During the period from 1886 to 1917, at which time the United States entered World War I, the anti-pilotage bills introduced in the national Congress were very numerous *but not very different* one from the other. Some were just carry-overs from previous legislative sessions, while others were supposedly new bills with such little innovation in their phrasing as to be almost identical to previous ones.

Almost every session saw one or more of them introduced, and the major portion of them were sponsored by legislators from the State of Maine. All were framed on the same basic pattern, and all were after the same result, the elimination of compulsory pilotage and its requirement for the enforced payment of pilotage fees in the southern Atlantic and Gulf seaports. The chief supporters and backers of these bills were New England sailing ship interests and seagoing barge owners, and to clarify the picture, it should be pointed out that what they sought to abolish was *compulsory pilotage under state laws* — hence the need to induce the federal government to take action in the matter.

It would be repetitious and pointless to tell about each and every one of those bills in chronological order. Some of the more significant ones, notably those sponsored by Congressman Dingley of Maine, already have been dealt with, along with the battles that brought about their defeat.

It would be repetitious and pointless also to give the exact wording of these bills, since the same intents and purposes were inherent in all of them. However, it would be germane to the full comprehension of the lop-sidedness of this conflict to give instances of the constant use of misleading titles and the device of submerging language of sinister import within the context of certain legislative proposals, the whole of which appeared to be directed toward other more innocent purposes. This practice was censured very positively by Captain J. Edward O'Brien in his book, *History of Compulsory Pilotage*, as follows:

> The most remarkable feature of this whole controversy consists of the misleading titles of the bills before Congress on the subject of pilotage. In 1873, the title of one was simply 'A Bill Concerning Pilots' Fees.' In 1875, it was 'A Bill to Relieve Certain Ships and Vessels from Compulsory Pilotage.' Afterward, when the term *compulsory pilotage* came to be understood as nothing more than pilotage under local laws designed to prevent recklessness in navigation, the titles were again changed and became such as these: 'A Bill to Exempt American Sailing Vessels from the Obligation to Pay Pilots for Services Not Rendered,' and 'A Bill to Remove Discrimination Against American Sailing Vessels.' ...The true aim of all these bills, from the beginning to the end, has been one and the same. Their only object has been what it was honestly and bluntly declared to be by the title of the first Hale bill in 1875, 'A Bill to Abolish Compulsory Pilotage Under State Laws.'

At another place in his book, Captain O'Brien cites a typical example of such deception, in the title and context of one more bill, Senate Bill 2162, introduced in the first session of the 54th Congress in 1896. It was introduced by Senator Frye—of Maine, of course—and it purported to apply principally to steam vessels. Writing about it years later, Captain O'Brien states:

> To my utter astonishment, I found upon examination of this innocent-looking bill that it contained the following provision relating, not to steam vessels, but to sailing vessels, designed to abrogate totally all State laws providing for compulsory pilotage.

The objectionable provision is given here in part:

> Any person employed as master or chief mate on sailing vessels not sailing under register may, upon application, be licensed by the local inspectors as master or mate of such vessels, and may be licensed to act in the dual capacity of master and pilot or chief mate and pilot, upon waters upon which they have been qulaified so to act; and when so licensed and so acting, shall be exempt from all State pilotage laws; and they shall have all the rights and privileges on such sailing vessels as are granted to steamboat pilots under this title. Before granting such licenses, however, the inspectors shall make diligent inquiry as to the character of the applicant and shall carefully examine him as to ... etc.... etc.... etc....

If this bill had become law, it would have effected the total and complete accomplishment of all the results sought by the New England shipping interests ever since the first Dingley bill was introduced in 1874. It would have authorized the creation of hordes of federally-licensed pseudo pilots who would act in the dual capacity of pilots and masters or mates of their coastwise sailing vessels, and it would have exempted them and their ships from all State pilotage laws.

This would have meant, practically, the complete elimination of the established State pilotage system and the traditional compulsory pilotage principle from the coastwise trade. From there, it could have been only a step to the elimination of both from the foreign trade, although there was at the time complete support for compulsory pilotage on all vessels engaged in foreign trade, both sail and steam, regardless of their nationality or flag. It was therefore essentially a sectional struggle, between the Northerners and the Southerners on our Atlantic seaboard, a civil war—if you please!—and this time it would turn out to be the Southerners who would win.

There was a very scanty minimum of the anti-pilotage bills that did not follow the same old line and repetitious nature of the majority, and one of these was a new departure. It was introduced in the 53rd Congress by Senator Joseph N. Dolph—of Maine of course. It proposed that all pilots and pilotage matters be placed under the control of the Secretary of the Treasury. Due to the alertness of the American Pilots' Association officials, who were quick to see the harm in it and voice the organization's dissatisfaction to the Secretary of the Treasury and other cabinet officials, the bill was not permitted to come to a vote.

Another such bill, HR 5462, non-conforming and away from the established trend, was introduced in the House of Representatives in 1900 by Congressman William P. Daly of New Jersey. It was similar in a way to the Dolph bill just mentioned. It provided that the licensing and control of all pilots operating throughout the United States in harbors, bays, sounds, inlets, passes, rivers, and all seaports would be placed under the jurisdiction of the United States Steamboat Insepction Service and that the *United States Revised Statutes* would be the code of laws governing all pilots formerly under State Pilotage laws. It was titled simply—and deceitfully—"A Bill Regulating Pilots." In effect, it provided for the abolishment of all State Pilotage systems.

This bill was opposed, successfully, by the American Pilots' Association, representing all of the member port groups and all of the pilots, but they were not alone in the fight. Nationwide, prominent business, merchant, and shipping interests, and particularly the marine insurance companies, who saw threats to their prosperity in the abolishment of the state pilotage system, responded with alacrity and urged their opposition upon the liegislators. The marine insurance companies of New York, as a group, sent a report, which showed the strength of their opposition to any meddling with the *status quo* of the system, to the *Merchant Marine and Fisheries Committee* of the House of Representatives on January 17, 1900. This report, because of its high informational content, and regardless of its tending to be somewhat long-winded, is given here:

> The undersigned marine insurance companies of this city and others interested in the shipping trade and representing a large proportion of the vessels engaged in the foreign commerce at the Port of New York, respectfully protest against the passage of the bill HR 5462, entitled 'A Bill Regulating Pilots,' which has been referred to your honorable committee, for the following reasons:
>
> This is the most important port in the United States, the values of the vessels and cargoes entering and leaving it being more than 60% of the entire foreign commerce of the United States. Its aids to navigation and commerce, and especially its pilotage service, should be of the highest class and should be conducted with an accuracy and certainty precluding any failure or mistake.
>
> The steamers trading between New York and foreign ports are of the largest class, their drafts varying from 26 feet to 32½ feet, with a gradual but constant increase made imperative by the demands of commerce. When fully laden, these vessels pass through the channels with only one or two feet between their keels and the bottom, sometimes even less, and they therefore at all times require skillful handling. These large vessels arrive and depart at stated dates, almost with the precision of ferryboats, and with a degree of immunity from accident in the approaches of this harbor not exceeded in any port in the world; which, taking into consideration their extreme length and depth, their immense weight and momentum, and the many vessels moving in the waters of the port, is very high testimony to the efficiency of the present pilotage system.
>
> This pilotage system has been controlled for nearly 50 years, under the laws of the state, by a board selected by the persons most interested in the safety and prosperity of shipping, that is, the owners of the ships and cargoes and the marine underwriters, upon the latter of whom most of the losses eventually fall. From a crude and unreliable service, it has been brought to a high degree of efficiency, the character of its personnel has been raised, the methods of cruising and boarding vessels have been improved, and in fact a service which is highly satisfactory has been created.
>
> The bill HR 5462 proposes arbitrarily and unnecessarily to destroy this system and to take the control of this important service out of the hands of those most interested in its efficiency, those by whom it has been brought to its present satisfactory condition, and to confide it to those who, whatever ability they may have in other respects,

cannot be said with certainty to have had any experience whatever with the duties and requirements of the service.

The result will be that the carefully trained expert pilot, whose life is devoted to the specialty of safely handling large vessels under difficult circumstances, will ultimately be replaced by men of less ability who are wanting in the special training and knowledge that is insured in the present pilotage system, the good name of the port for safety and convenience will be injured and its business will suffer as a consequence; for which change no demand has been made by those who are most vitally and deeply interested and who now most earnestly urge that no such radical change be permitted or made in this at present satisfactory and most valuable marine service.

Twenty-Four

The Conflict Comes to an End

There were many reasons why this pilotage conflict, which lasted approximately 50 years, at long last should come to an end in those very first years of the 20th century. One cogent reason is suggested in a certain remark made by Congressman Daly of New Jersey after his bill, that odious HR 5462 described in the previous chapter, was defeated. In the minutes of one of the American Pilots' Association meetings of that period, we find this paragraph, referring to the State Pilots' victory over the proponents of that bill:

> Our friends in Congress stood by us to a man, and I refer to those especially who were members of the Committee on Merchant Marine and Fisheries, all of whom I believe felt friendly toward us, except possibly Mr. Daly, who however at the end of the session expressed his friendship *and regretted very much that he was deceived by the parties who prompted him to introduce the bill.*

Therein lies evidence that members of Congress were becoming more and more aware of the repetitious nature of the steady stream of anti-pilotage bills and their tired, time-worn innovative aims, their one-sideness, and the futility and wastefulness of their being presented over and over again in different guises. Legislators had become wary and resistant.

Nevertheless, die-hards continued to introduce more of the same, though most of these attempts were feeble and were summarily defeated. There was of course that Littlefield bill presented to the 59th Congress, and already told about in an earlier chapter. There is no record of any such bill's having been introduced in the 60th Congress (1907–1909). However, in January of 1911, during the third session of the 61st Congress, there came another one, introduced by Congressman John P. Swasey—of Maine of course. It was titled: 'A Bill to Provide for

Further Federal Regulation of Pilots,' and in the eyes of the traditional accredited pilots, it was the most obnoxious that had come along thus far.

It proposed that any and all pilots be incorporated into a federal pilotage system and be examined, classified, appointed, and licensed by the U.S. Steamboat Inspection Service. Thereafter, all of these new "federal pilots" were to be divided up into four grades, depending on the amount of the yearly tonnage entering specific ports, and this gradation would determine and set each pilot's pay, which would be on a yearly salary basis. The Steamboat Inspection Service would decide on the total number of pilots to be licensed, and the Secretary of Commerce and Labor would buy all the equipment and supplies, including the pilot boats. The government, in other words, would be "taking over" the pilot boats already in use (paying for them of course), and if the various port groups did not like the prices paid, there would be an appraisal board to whom they could go for redress; (but the appraisal board alone would determine the final and incontrovertible price).

Pilotage rates were to be established by law for vessels in the foreign trade for all of our seaports, and the fees were to be collected by the principal customs officers of each port. There was even a provision for imposing legal liens on vessels that did not pay up. All moneys collected were to be deposited in the Federal Treasury and would constitute a "pilotage fund"—*definitely not to be confused with a pilots' fund*, such as port groups traditionally have maintained—out of which the new "federal" pilots *would not* get remuneration for their services on a profit-sharing basis, as pilots formerly had been remunerated. Their compensation would be on a yearly fixed-salary basis, and that was one provision that the pilotage fraternity knew for sure that they could not stomach.

The bill was so blatantly obnoxious that there was little anxiety over it and scarcely any doubt about its impending defeat. However, since it was introduced only a month and a few days before Congress adjourned, with insufficient time for proper study, debate, and coming to a vote, there was reason to believe that its introduction was merely a maneuver—to help set the stage for new, similar, legislation to be introduced in the next Congress.

In the next Congress, the 62nd, which met from April 4, 1911 to March 3, 1913, a very similar bill—sure enough!—was introduced in the senate. It even had the same title, "A Bill to Provide Further Federal Regulation of Pilotage." It was handed to the Senate Committee on Commerce for study and discussion, and then it was sent to the Secretary of Commerce, Hon. Charles Nagel, with a request for his opinion of it. His written commentary, dated December 19, 1912, completely disapproved of the bill, and his announcement that "the legislation is unnecessary" was a landmark decision in the pilots' long struggle to preserve the integrity of their system and their profession. It marked the end of that struggle, essentially, for there was only one more feeble attempt, in 1915, to abolish compulsory pilotage.

The Secretary's commentary reads, in part, as follows:

> A careful analysis of the bill suggests that its effect will be to take from the several states the authority which they have exercised since 1789 of regulating their pilotage systems and place this authority under the jurisdiction of the Federal Government....
>
> Under these state laws, the pilotage system has been maintained at a high standard of efficiency, rates have been kept down to a reasonable figure consistent with good service, and the maintenance of the equipment is assured by stringent regulations respecting the number and character of pilot boats, extent of cruising grounds, location of stations, et cetera.
>
> Efforts have been made from time to time by vessel owners to have Congress enact legislation affecting the State Pilotage systems by exempting certain vessels from compulsory pilotage, by reducing rates, and by placing the service under Federal jurisdiction, et cetera, but so far these efforts have been unavailing from the fact that it could not be shown that such changes were either necessary or beneficial to commercial interests ... it would seem that the various commercial bodies of the ports ... do not think the present pilotage system is embarrassing or onerous.
>
> The bill in its present form is so vague that, even were it enacted, there is no possibility of its execution. No provision is made for the supervision of the service after the change from the old and the creation of the new conditions, no appropriation from which to meet expenses, and no provision whatever for the general administration of the law.
>
> In my opinion the legislation is unnecessary, and I believe that the regulation of the pilotage system should be left with the several states. I therefore cannot approve the bill.

Here in this commentary, accepted and approved by so many lawmakers and their constituents, was clear evidence that the traditional pilotage system and those who made it work well at long last were receiving the support of the executive branch of the government, another good reason for the conflict to be coming to an end.

Still another reason, and probably the most powerful one, was the big decline in the use of sailing vessels in commerce, coincident with the rapid rise in the number and tonnage of steam vessels in use. This decline was conspicuous in the coastwise trade—where the conflict had originated in the first place. Since coastwise steam vessels had been exempted from State Pilotage laws ince 1871 and sailing ship interests had then begun the fight seeking the same exemption for coastwise sailing vessels, the rapid disasppearance of sailing vessels from the coastwise trade made the fight no longer necessary.

In addition to the wariness of members of Congress, the strong support of compulsory pilotage by the labor organizations, the marine insurance companies, chambers of commerce, the general press, leaders in industry, and the public at large, caused interest in the abolition of compulsory pilotage to lag.

Although some states, as sovereign states, had abolished compulsory pilotage within their territorial limits, most of them eventually reinstated it. Maryland abolished it in 1852 and reinstated it only a year later. Marylanders soon found out that the elimination of this mandatory facet of the ship guidance service had had such adverse results, such as the loss of trade to the Port of Baltimore and the making of excessive charges for pilotage services—in other words, *gouging*—that the very merchants and shipmasters who had been the cause of the abolishment sought and obtained a reversal of the decision of the legislature and a new pilotage law, still in existence, giving approval to the compulsory pilotage principle.

Twenty-Five

Pilots in the First World War

Even before America's entry as a combatant in the First World War, the State Pilotage system, with its well-trained personnel, was proving to be a great asset to the government, a government still on the sidelines but nevertheless deeply involved and actually on the brink. At first, when war in Europe was declared in 1914, the immediate effect on foreign shipping in United States ports was a sharp decline. This was due to the fact that, for a time in the beginning, foreign ships tended to flee our ports abruptly and return to their home countries to help sustain the war effort there. This of course had a depreciating effect on pilotage services and pilots' earnings.

In the weeks that followed, however, as 15 nations one after another became involved in the conflict, it became evident that the economic needs and the need for war equipment and materials would have to be supplied in large measure by the neutral nations, and belligerents on both sides turned to America for much of these supplies. Although the neutral position of the United States called for an avoidance of any act or actions that might involve us in the war, there was a big increase in maritime commerce, that permitted by its neutrality policies. This resulted in a convergence of many ships of many nations upon its seaports and in much extra service to be performed by the port pilots, who performed it very creditably, as history relates.

Also, many of the belligerent nations suddenly became engaged in extended ship-building programs essential to their war efforts. This meant more and more ships manned by newly trained officers and crewmen who were completely unfamiliar with the American coast and its seaports. Also, the blockading tactics of the belligerents sent many battle-damaged and unseaworthy ships into American ports. In the book *State Pilotage in America*, we find this reference to that situation:

> Bringing such crippled ships with newly-trained crews over the

> bars and shoals and through narrow channels in all types of weather was indeed an assignment which could only be fulfilled by experienced pilots acquainted with local conditions. It is clear that in such circumstances the state pilotage system was most invaluable and its services imperative. It is inconceivable what harm might have obtained during this period if state pilotage had been permitted to decline under the pressure of anti-pilotage efforts in the late 19th century. This most surely would have happened, had not the Congress sustained it through the long struggle over coastal sailing vessels through the turn of the century....

When the United States entered the war on April 6, 1917 and immediately launched a tremendous ship building and ship operational program, the pilotage services and problems rapidly increased and soon were multitudinous and diversified out of all proportion to those of peace times. In addition to the great number of United States navy and merchant marine ships to be guided in and out of the ports recurrently, there were also the many foreign ships that came to American shores for materials and munitions to be used in the war efforts of their individual countries. The most numerous of course were the American merchant vessels which had been requisitioned or taken over by the federal government. Added to these were some 87 foreign ships seized or chartered by the United States Government.

As of September 1, 1918, there were 2614 ships (other than United States Navy and other military ships) owned or controlled under some form of contract by the federal government. Of these, 1656 were steam vessels other than tankers, 772 were sailing vessels, and 186 were tankers. All of them were vessels of 500 gross tons or over. Their total dead-weight tonnage was 10,334, 196 tons. These statistics are from a 1918 "*Second Annual Report of the United States Shipping Board*," the semi-emergency federal agency established by law on September 7, 1916 to carry out a program of re-vitalizing and expanding the merchant marine. It was emphasized in the enactment of the law that all of this would be for peaceful purposes.

It is easy to see how and why this great increase in ships and shipping at American ports tended to make the work of the pilots more difficult, demanding, and dangerous. Congested ports became all the more congested. New-type and newly-designed experimental vessels, American as well as foreign, manned by newly-trained officers and green crewmen, entered into the picture and cluttered the port seaways and approaches. Convoys in long strings came and went precariously. Battle-torn ships limped in laboriously.

Because of this, more and more pilots were needed and were recruited. These came from the ranks of the apprentices and the pilot boat operators undoubtedly. Since the apprenticeship programs of most port groups were rigidly demanding ones requiring years of strict training before the would-be pilot got his "branch," there can be little doubt that these newly-made pilots readily filled the bill. At one time during the war, there were 140 pilots operating at the Port of New York alone, and some of them could have been these novice pilots, which certainly did not mean that they were "new at the game."

Although the authority of that United States Shipping Board was limited at the start, with all of its operations ostensibly being carried on for peaceful purposes only, all of this changed dramatically after the United States declared war. Far greater powers were given to it under the *Urgent Deficiencies Act* of June 15, 1917, wherein emergency authority was given to the President to requisition, construct, and operate ships, this authority and power to be exercised through any agencies that he might select. By executive order on July 11, 1917, he delegated all his authority for the construction of ships to the newly-formed Emergency Fleet Corporation and his authority for the acquisition and operation of ships to the United States Shipping Board.

This delegation of this authority to the United States Shipping Board encompassed practically all maritime activities of any kind, including the taking over and operating of the entire merchant marine, the seizing of interned enemy vessels, the chartering of domestic and foreign vessels, and other maritime matters.

One would think that, in line with all this expansion of power an in view of the concentrated attention demanded by the overtaxed port facilities, the Shipping Board would want to assume complete control of the state pilotage system. However, this was not considered necessary, then or ever, neither by the executive or the legislative branches of government. This fact was and is a great tribute to the state pilotage system. In that war and in every other national emergency, the port pilots came forward promptly and eagerly to offer their services and assistance to the nation in its peril.

In every instance, they have co-operated with government authorities and have adapted their lfestyle and their work system to stated wartime needs, while still retaining, practically unchanged, the peacetime organizational structure. In this war, World War I, the bulk of the pilots operated on much the same plan followed in peacetime, except for the differences involved with the complex problems created by the many ship convoys entering and leaving American ports. The over-all operation of the system remained under state control, and the rates charged for the service were practically the same as peacetime rates. It was a system working just about as well as it worked under normal conditions.

Naturally, at the end of the war in November of 1918, the state pilotage system moved swiftly and easily back to its peacetime status, unlike shipping in general, which had to undergo long-drawn-out readjustments. The merchant marine remained under government control and operation for quite a long time after the war, the while its individual, private functions and operations were being re-established in the world of international commerce.

There followed a period of tranquility — in the pilot ranks and on the legislative seas — that lasted until World War II. There were no new laws affecting pilotage until 1933, when a new law, affecting pilotage only very moderately, was enacted merely to revise the terminology of an existing law and re-define the term "steam vessels" in the interests of inspection and pilotage needs.

Since this existing law, which exempted coastwise engine-powered vessels from compulsory pilotage laws, was enacted in 1871, when there were no such things as diesel engines or gasoline engines, and decreed only that "every coast-wise *steam* vessel" was to be exempt, there was no provision therein for exempting the great number of coastwise vessels powered by mechanical means other than steam engines. Most of these ships carried in their crews at least one man who was a licensed "federal" pilot, and although it was generally assumed and tacitly agreed on all sides that they were entitled to this exemption, *the law did not say so*.

In this old law, the term *steam vessel* was defined, for inspection purposes, as follows: "Every vessel propelled in whole or in part by steam shall be considered a steam vessel within the meaning of this title." The new 1933 law extended the compass and signification of the term by redefining it thusly: "Every vessel subject to inspection propelled in whole or in part by steam or any other form of mechanical or electrical power shall be considered a steam vessel within the meaning of the term and subject to all the provisions of this act." Motorboats, ("all vessels propelled by machinery and not more than 65 feet in length except tugboats and towboats propelled by steam,") were exempted from the terms of this definition and of course exempted from the compulsory pilotage laws of the various states as well as from federal inspection by the Steamboat Inspection Service. This *Act of June 13, 1933* had scarcely any restricting effect on the activities of the state pilots, although it presumptively had the effect of decreasing the number of ships subject to state compulsory pilotage laws.

Concerning the long period of tranquility — for traditional, old-order pilots — between the two great wars, the historical outline, *State Pilotage in America*, has this to say:

> So far as pilotage was concerned, neither the post-war adjustment period nor the great depression of the 1930s brought any particular

> changes of significance, except that the number of ships entering and leaving harbors was obviously diminished for periods of time, thus depressing pilot incomes. Pilots therefore felt the weight of the depression, as did all other professional groups, but there were no outstanding events worthy of special notice.

That brings us to World War II and a consideration of its impact on the piloting profession.

Twenty-Six

American Pilots Go to War Again

It was wartime in the United States long before the Japanese attack on Pearl Harbor, chiefly because we were giving generous amounts of material support and encouragement to those nations caught up in the struggle against the aggressor "Axis Powers," and because it was realized that our neutral position in the world of warring nations was becoming increasingly precarious. Stockpiling of materials for the support of our own war-effort-to-come was going on apace and American militarists wanted no withholding of the material support for our soon-to-be allies.

Although the United States in 1939 made a neutrality proclamation that was loud and clear to all the world, we nevertheless continued to help the allied powers unstintingly. Later in that same year, an Act of Congress lifted the embargo on arms shipment to belligerents and placed all such commerce on a cash and carry basis. About a year later, when Great Britain was getting the worst of it and an invasion of England from the continent seemed imminent, the President of the United States called for aid to Britain in every reasonable manner short of war, declaring the United States to be "An arsenal of democracy." A few months later, in March of 1941, the *Lend-Lease* law was enacted, and following Hitler's attack on Russia, we pledged our all-out help and support for Russia.

Thus, since about 1937, when President Roosevelt made his famous "Quarantine of Aggressors" speech in Chicago, events and activities with intimations of war had been multiplying rapidly and accumulatively. It was wartime especially at our seaports—on their seaward approaches, in their harbors, and along their waterfronts and docks—during this period. There was congestion, confusion, hurry, excitement, and avalanches of activity, all of it precipitated by the steadily increasing number of ship and cargo movements in and out of the ports from day to day and night after night.

Early in the period, it was realized in maritime circles that the help of trained, experienced, and competent port pilots would be sorely—desperately!—needed in the months ahead. As in the First World War, the organized port pilot groups, the state pilots, came forward promptly and zealously as one man to give of their knowledge and services unstintingly in alleviating the distressful conditions. The so-called "federal" pilots were still around, as they are still "around" today, but their status as lonewolf, free-lance itinerants, lacking needed equipment such as pilot boats on station on the open sea and in the harbor, prevented their being of much help. It was the state pilots who "handled the rush," as they had done very creditably in World War I, and government remembered!

Months before Pearl Harbor, pilot representatives had been attending conferences held in Washington for the express purpose of enabling the federal government to avail itself of the services of the state pilots on the highest levels. Out of these consultations came the decision that, if and when war came, not only would the help of the entire body of pilots be enlisted in an all-out war, but the pilots themselves would be enlisted in a branch of the armed forces and given a military status. During World War I, the lack of such military status for the pilots had been felt and very deeply deplored.

Helping to bring all this about was the American Pilots' Association, representing the various port groups. Its president at the time was Captain John S. Delano of Maryland. On July 8, 1941, just five months before Pearl Harbor, he sent the following letter, which became an important document in the annals of the association, to the United States Maritime Commission:

> Gentlemen:
>
> On behalf of the American Pilots' Association, which encompasses all the state pilots serving ships engaged in foreign commerce in and out of the 33 ports of the 20 seaboard states of the Atlantic, Pacific, and Gulf coasts, I respectfully wish to submit this brief for your matured consideration in the National Welfare and for the furtherance of public safety during the existing emergency, as a supplement to the hearing given us by the Commission on this subject:
>
> 1. As essential as is the pilot service in normal times, it becomes infinitely more so during crises of national emergency, when the usual navigational aids may, of necessity, be curtailed or extinguished. It then becomes imperative that a trained and informed personnel be ready to maintain the service at the highest standard of efficiency.
>
> 2. Under authority given by the First Congress in 1789, the several

states have exercised complete control in regulating, policing, and disciplining pilots, and maintained rigid standards of character, training, and loyalty to duty, considered unexcelled by any pilot service in the world.

3. Our membership is composed of American seafarers, descendants of several generations in the service in many instances.

4. Our equipment is always under searching scrutiny. It must be seaworthy and manned by peculiarly and expertly trained pilots on stations covering our 6000 miles of seacoast, as guardians of commerce, rendering a most essential service 24 hours a day under all weather conditions.

5. The cost of present equipment maintained by the service exceeds 4 million dollars, and the annual operating expense is in excess of 2 million dollars. These financial outlays are assumed by the pilots without federal, state, or municipal subsidies of any nature whatsoever.

6. Our personnel have voluntarily requested and acquired a file of birth certificates, FBI fingerprinting, and efficiency and service records, to be submitted to any and all appropriate parties upon request.

7. More than 100,000 vessels were handled during the year 1940, including many publicly-owned and naval vessels, with the astounding record of only 1/25th of 1% of them incurring accidents, these being mostly minor groundings.

8. We have traditionally operated as a semi-public body, through complete co-operation in every possible manner with the Navy, Coast Guard, Public Health Service, Customs, Lighthouse, and the U.S. Engineers Departments.

9. During past emergencies, we have been consulted about and entrusted with highly confidential military and naval secrets concerning the placing of mines and submarine nets, etc. in our respective areas.

10. Never has a single state pilot ever attempted to go out on strike or to refuse to answer the call to duty in the century and a half of our existence.

11. The record of the saving of lives and property at sea by pilot boats on their stations is noteworthy.

We cherish an inherent confidence in the admiration for our form of government, which to us seafarers means mostly those branches with which we are usually identified, the Navy, Coast Guard, U.S. Maritime Commission, and the other legislative and administrative maritime bodies. We have the deepest conviction that they desire to accept and support the services of a national institution whose patriotism, loyalty, and efficiency have been recognized since the infancy of our nation, and we respectfully ask that consideration be given to the selection of members of this organization for the task of piloting all public vessels in and out of our great American ports, when such service is required.

We believe that the public interest and safety, national defense, and aid to those nations opposing the Axis powers can best be served by reducing the fifth-column activities, sabotage, and the sinking of vessels through incompetence or design in any of our great ports (which could very easily retard the whole defense program by tieing up an entire defense area) by the employment of these pilots holding both Federal and State licenses, men who are bonded and vouched for by the respective states in which they were created. They are the only organized and dependable group capable of rendering complete and uninterrupted service to shipping.

The free-lance or irregular pilots maintain no equipment, nor are they regulated or controlled by any Federal or State authority. Being unorganized, they offer none of the advantages of the groups of State pilots, who are constantly informed of port conditions as to movements of vessels in foggy or adverse weather, through the medium of radio-telephone equipment and other sources of information available only to these state pilots. The nonexistence of these advantages, in addition to the lack of experience of the free-lance as a result of irregular employment, makes it impossible for them to maintain the high standards of service which are traditional with the organized State Pilots.

We are not concerned with, nor do we include in our criticism, those pilots of a ship's company or regularly employed pilots chosen from among a corporation's ship masters and held ashore just for that purpose. Our criticism is directed against those not included in a regular ship's personnel who practice unfair and completely irresponsible competition at rates commensurate with their inferior services.

The members of the American Pilots' Association hold the Federal Government's endorsement, in addition to possessing the safeguard of the State Pilot license, the prerequisites for which are infinitely higher than those required for obtaining the federal license.

In conclusion, we believe that, because of the pilot's inability to assume financial responsibility for damage, it becomes imperative in the interest of sound and reasonable business expediency to employ the services of only the most capable pilots in reducing accidents to a minimum.

The pilots join me in expressing our sincere appreciation for the confidence given us. We trust that this statement of facts will receive favorable consideration.

The statement did receive favorable consideration, by the United States Maritime Commission and by the United States Navy Department as well. The Secretary of the Navy, Frank Knox, mindful of the fact that the United States Coast Guard becomes an arm of the United States Navy in wartime and that there would be multitudinous needs and problems arising from the greater use of near-coastal and estuarine or "inside" waters, directed the Commandant of the Coast Guard, on August 18, 1942, to make a survey of those needs and problems and the over-all pilotage situation, for the purpose of having an advance plan for taking care of these exigencies competently and efficiently.

He particularly directed the Commandant to make a study of the various problems that would be inherent in a government plan to organize, control, and supervise the activities of American pilots, to confer with other affected agencies, governmental and otherwise, and to initiate procedures designed to bring about executive orders or legislation necessary to implement the plan. The Coast Guard immediately instituted the survey and eventually came up with a mass of pertinent and important information. In making a count of available qualified pilots, they found it expedient to categorize them as follows:

1) Pilots operating under state laws, i.e., the State Pilots.
2) Federally licensed pilots not members of ships' crews operating in coastal waters, i.e., the "federal," unorganized pilots operating as lone wolf itinerants in most cases.
3) Federally licensed pilots who were members of ships' crews.
4) Docking pilots.
5) Accredited pilots, i.e., those given special government accreditation for specific navigational areas.

In spite of all precautions taken by the military and all agencies of the federal government to avoid and avert provocative incidents and gestures during this period, the actual fighting war came to us nevertheless when Japan suddenly attacked Pearl Harbor, with disastrous results for us, on December 7, 1941. The next day, both the United States and Great Britain declared war on Japan. Three days later, Germany and Italy declared war on the United States and, on the same day, the United States declared war on both of them and we were in it up to our necks.

Twenty-Seven

The Pilots and the U.S. Coast Guard

Immediately after those declarations of war, the United States government embarked upon a massive, far-reaching, crash program of ship building, aircraft production, munitions making, and the rapid supplying of these and other materials of war to our armed forces and the forces of our allies overseas, with the economy of the entire nation geared to the urgency and tempo of the program. As these manifold materials of war converged on our seaports "wanting out," to put it succinctly, congestion, confusion, and consternation resulted naturally.

In spite of and because of that morass of confusion and congestion, the state pilots "went to war" immediately, without waiting for any official relationship with the government to be established, to help send the ships and the materials safely and quickly on their way. That official relationship did not come about until nearly a year later, though there was on hand a cordial and co-operative relationship, based on mutal confidence and trust, that had been in existence for some time and now was flourishing all the more.

It had become, earlier, quite apparent—to the government, to the military machine, and to the merchant marine—that great and absolute reliance was going to have to be place on the well-organized state pilotage system throughout the war. As the war progressed, it became increasingly evident that this confidence was justified. Almost a full year after Pearl Harbor, it was stated publicly by Admiral E.S. Land, administrator of the War Shipping Administration that "no serious delays have come to the attention of the War Shipping Administration as a result of the inefficiency or non-availability of pilots, with the possible exception of Alaska. The state pilotage system was not operative in Alaska at that time, and piloting there in general could have been a somewhat hit-and-miss affair.

During almost all of that first year of the war, the powers that be, such as the War Shipping Administration, the Maritime Commission, the Navy, and the Coast Guard, had been conferring and working toward the adoption of a feasible liaison plan that would fuse the entire body of civilian pilots with some branch of the armed forces. From the very first discussions and indications, it became apparent that this segment would be the United States Coast Guard.

It was the contention of Coast Guard officials that certain wartime needs and inevitabilities would forbid permitting piloting procedures to go on exactly as they had been going on in peacetime and would necessitate the making of special rules and regulations for the duration of the emergency. The pilots on the whole were cognizant of this necessity, and they expressed their willingness to co-operate in bringing about certain modifications of their conventional methods of performing their guidance services.

One special consideration was in the area of rates charged for the piloting services. The government stipulated that it would not countenance any profiteering or gouging, or as one official communication mellifluently expressed it, "excess earnings." In this connection, government officials had in mind not only the inordinate number of foreign and domestic ships that would be entering and leaving our ports in aid of the war effort but also the many ships that would be coming into our bays and harbors for shelter and refuge from enemy attacks. The government deemed it essential that rates should be reduced for these latter vessels and that standard fair rates should be set and maintained for all of the others. The government also contended that it should exercise some control over the qualifying and assignments of individual pilots and over the available supply of accredited pilots.

Following one of these conferences, in the office of the Commandant of the Coast Guard on August 21, 1942, further study of the pilotage situation was made by the War Shipping Administration. Then, on October 30, 1942, Admiral Land sent a communication embodying the findings of that study to the Coast Guard Commandant. In it, he stated, among other things, the following:

> "Generally speaking, we feel that a rate reduction of at least 50 percent is warranted for vessels entering port entirely for shelter, but this reduction also may depend on the volume of service rendered. Some procedure might be worked out to guard against excess earnings, by the establishment of a standard rate with a recapture provision, though such a course would present difficult administrative problems. We believe the more desirable method would be to set fair rates for the services performed and leave it to the stronger associations to aid the weaker. The War Shipping Administration recognizes the high standard of service performed by the pilots over a long period of years and is anxious that no steps be taken which, at the

> end of the war, will prevent the pilots and their associations from resuming the status they held at the beginning of the war. We do believe however that some control is necessary over the qualifications of individual pilots, the available supply, and rates. We urge, however, that no long-term standards be set in the latter cases, but that provision be made for re-examination at frequent intervals.

It will be seen from this that the WSA was cognizant of the fact that, with the setting of standard fair rates, there would be inequities and deprivations, as far as pilots were concerned. Some of the smaller Southern ports had little or no prospect of getting anywhere near the large volume of shipping and commerce that the larger Northern ports were getting. Also, it is conceivable that the commerce and shipping of these small Southern ports *took a sharp drop because of the war effort*.

Therefore, since according to the traditional organizational set-up, a pilot's pay was his share of what was left in his association's pilots' fund after all of the association's operating expenses were paid out of it, the pay, in relation to his high professional standing and the take-home pay of some of those Northern pilots, could be considered to be quite low.

In addition to these recommendations in this communication of the WSA, the War Shipping Administration also made the following ones:

> 1. That all pilots be accredited by the U.S. Coast Guard, excepting those who were ships' officers actually serving aboard a vessel and who, from such service, may be assumed to have been accredited.
> 2. That existing pilotage rates shall prevail, except for concessions given to ships entering port for shelter.
> 3. That rates of 50 percent of the commercial rates shall be established for all vessels entering ports for shelter, "entrance for shelter" to be defined officially.
> 4. That periodical reports of the earnings of each port associàtion shall be submitted to the United States Coast Guard and that the amounts of the pilotage fees shall be reviewed periodically.
> 5. That rates for pilotage by independent federally-licensed pilots who are not serving as officers of vessels shall be subject to review by an appropriate government agency or representative, with the idea of keeping those rates at a reasonably low level.
> 6. That a pool of pilots for Alaskan service be established and some means of relief be provided at Cape Spencer so as to eliminate any need for through or round trips by pilots.
> 7. That every effort be made to presserve existing pilots' associations, to the end that, after the war, they may resume their operation

> as at present and that, so far as is practicable in any control exercised by the Navy and Coast guard, the services of various qualified officers and members of the pilots' organizations shall be utilized.
> 8. That, should it be decided to enroll pilots as members of the Navy or Coast Guard, it shall be made clear that such members, in rendering pilot service, shall not transgress the authority of the masters of vessels, who remain always in command.

The Coast Guard found these recommendations acceptable and came up with some additionable recommendations of its own. Some of these were based on some rather acute problems that had arisen in the Cape Cod and Chesapeake and Delaware canals at the beginning of the war. These were due to traffic congestion and frequent accidents.

It was decided officially then that, since the skill of the local pilots and their knowledge of local port and harbor conditions were so essential to the war effort, the first step in alleviating troublesome port conditions and solving ship movement problems necessarily would be the bringing of the main body of these state pilots into an over-all pilotage control system as soon as possible. It thereupon seemed only natural that enlisting the pilots in the Coast Guard Reserve would be the most propitious way to effect that first step.

Consequently, on November 25, 1942, the Commandant of the Coast Guard, Vice-Admiral R.R. Waesche, sent a lengthy and well-prepared statement embodying this and other pilot recommendations to the Secretary of the Navy. This report had been previously approved by all of the port pilot associations and by all government agencies concerned with pilotage. The Secretary of the Navy stated his approval two days later. The recommendations in this report produced the government policy for wartime pilotage control. These recommendations and some of Admiral Waesche's comments concerning them are given here:

> 1. That steps be taken, the initial ones preferably by the state pilot associations and the state pilot commissioners, to place into effect immediately the rate reductions (for vessels entering ports only for shelter) recommended by the War Shipping Administration and that reports of earnings be submitted regularly by the state pilots' associations. A vessel "entering for shelter" is defined, insofar as this recommendation is concerned, as a vessel which enters or passes through a port or place solely as a result of military orders or routing instructions designed to protect the vessel from enemy action and which does not enter for the purpose of trade or commerce with the port or place.
> 2. That all eligible members of the state pilot associations of the American Pilots' Association...shall be enrolled as temporary

members of the Coast Guard Reserve for limited duty in connection with pilotage for the duration of the emergency, without government pay, and with commissioned rank commensurate with their age, duties and responsibilities.

3. That each group of state pilots in the Coast Guard Reserve be under the command of the Senior Coast Guard Reserve officer of that group, who would be responsible to the District Coast Guard Officer concerned with the efficient working of the organization in his charge.

4. That the president of the American Pilots' Association, upon enrollment in the Coast Guard Reserve as heretofore recommended, shall be assigned to duty at Headquarters in connection with pilotage control.

5. That all pilot vessels of the State pilots' associations which can be used to advantage by the Coast Guard and which have not been enrolled in the Coast Guard Reserve, be so enrolled with their crews.

6. That the state pilots' associations take steps to have state regulations for pilotage require each state pilot to have a current federal pilot license covering all of the waters covered by his state license.

7. That the District Coast Guard Officer in each naval district shall be the representative of the Navy and Coast Guard responsible for all matters concerning control of pilotage in these districts.

8. That when it becomes necessary to set up special groups of pilots at a port or place as a wartime measure, the organization, administration, and operation of such groups shall be the obligation of the District Coast Guard Officer, who would be authorized to require, at his discretion, that the personnel of such groups shall be members of the Coast Guard Reserve and to require that, insofar as is practicable, pilots employed to augment the regular number of pilots at a port also shall be licensed by the respective states, preferably on a temporary basis.

9. That when control of pilotage in any areas beyond that covered in the preceding recommendations becomes necessary, regulations similar to the sample in the appendix of this report shall be promulgated.

Admiral Waesche's appertaining comments, with only minor deletions, are given here:

It will be noted that Recommendations one through six are based on the complete co-operation of the state pilots' associations. The object is to assure that the pilot arrives without delay aboard the vessel to be piloted, that he is professionally, physically, and morally qualified for the job, that he is militarily responsible for the vital

> war information daily entrusted to him, and finally that the fee for his service is reasonable.
>
> Recommendations one through six do not visualize in any way a replacement of the state pilotage system, but rather a regulation and co-ordination of the existing system in accordance with wartime requirements, and only for the duration of the emergency. They would not constitute a substitution of the command of any vessel being piloted, inasmuch as the legal relations and responsibilities of the master and the pilot would be unchanged. Since the pilots would receive no government pay, there would be no change in the methods for collection and distribution of pilotage fees, although these fees would be modified as recommended above.
>
> It is realized that the defiinition of 'entering for shelter' contained in Recommendation one involves more work for less pay for some pilot associations....
>
> Recommendations seven and eight are corollaries of the recommendations that precede them, and they provide for the regulation and control of not only state-licensed but also of federally licensed pilots in the same manner. One officer in each naval district is made responsible for this regulation and control, and he is authorized to set up special groups of pilots where they are needed. The Alaska pilotage situation is an example of such a need.
>
> The measure indicated in Recommendation nine provides for drastic regulatory action in any area where the results of co-operation are inadequate.
>
> Appropriate action is now being taken by the Coast Guard in connection with the above recommendations.

It is noteworthy that the Commandant called attention to the fact that there was no recommendation to change "the legal relations and responsibilities" of shipmasters and pilots in any way, such as, particularly, requiring shipmasters to abrogate their commands in favor of the pilots aboard their ships. These finedrawn relations were traditional and were adhered to with iron-bound dedication, as they are steadfastly adhered to in modern times.

When a pilot is aboard a ship in the exercise of his profession, he has the status of an officer of that ship, and his orders as such must be obeyed by the crew. When the ship's captain is on board, the orders of the pilot are considered to be the orders of the captain. In the chain of command, the pilot is lower than the captain and the pilot is subject to the captain's orders and disciplinary action, but he is not subject to being given any work or duty except that of piloting. Once in charge of a vessel at sea, it is his prime duty to stay with the handling of the ship until it reaches its destination or some place of safety.

Twenty-Eight

Semper Paratus

After that prompt approval of that Coast Guard report by the Secretary of the Navy, organizational activities moved swiftly. The approval message came on November 27, 1942, and a week later, on December 4th, the Coast Guard issued its first directive to the pilotage fraternity. The key paragraph of that directive read as follows:

> It is intended that each association of state-licensed pilots shall operate as a group of temporary members of the Coast Guard Reserve, with the present president of each group acting for the duration as the Senior Coast Guard Reserve Officer attached and being responsible directly to the District Coast Guard Officer for the efficient operation of that group.

In certain cases, geographic location made it more feasible for the Senior CGR officer of the pilot group at work directly under the Captain of the Port, an emergency Coast Guard command operation installed, as a wartime measure at the various ports, rather than under the DCGO. The COP authority was always "right there" on the scene, while the DCGO headquarters could have been 50 or 100 miles away. The Captain of the Port, a Coast Guard authority, should not be confused with the *Port Director*, a U.S. Navy command operation.

No radical changes in the piloting procedures were called for, though Coast Guard officials did prescribe a minor change in the traditional rotation system of assigning pilots to ships, a system in which each pilot in an association "took his turn," according to his rating, regardless of the type or character of the ship that was to be conned. It was directed that this system was not to be rigidly adhered to and that the senior pilot officer should assign the more important ships and more difficult tasks to the most experienced and most competent men. This plan, besides making sure of utilizing the best skills at the most critical times and places, had the effect also of giving some military character to the port groups.

On December 11th, the first pilots were sworn in. This took place at the Port of Boston, and these pilots thereby became commissioned officers in the USCG Temporary Reserve, a new wartime branch of the service. It was the same branch in which were included the volunteer wartime aircraft spotters and beach patrollers. On December 15th, the New York Harbor pilots enlisted, and other port pilot groups followed suit almost instantaneously.

Only full-time pilots were enlisted. At many ports, in the South principally, commerce and shipping had dropped to such a low level, *because* of the war in most cases, that full-time pilots were not required, and therefore none were enlisted at these ports. Many of the part-time pilots held other jobs ashore.

In the larger major ports such as New York and Boston, the senior pilots or association presidents were given the rank of commander. The rest of the older pilots became lieutenant-commanders, and the younger men became lieutenants or lieutenants, junior grade. In the smaller ports where there were fewer pilots, the ranks were somewhat lower. All were commissioned for the duration only, to serve without pay, but all continued to receive their pilotage pay in the usual manner as though they were civilians. They could resign for cause. They could not be transferred from their home ports against their wishes. At one time near the war's end, there were 657 of them in the Temporary Reserve.

Pilot boats were enlisted also, along with their crews. The crewmen were taken into the *regular* Coast Guard Reserve for full-time active duty with pay. They were given petty officer ratings such as boatswain's mate and machinist's mate. Their ratings and pay were commensurate with the jobs they had held, their experience, and the pay they had received as civilians. The need for pilot boats of precise design, construction, and equipment was felt acutely and some 60 of them were requisitioned. They were called CGR vessels, and those letters always preceded their identifying number, painted on their sides or mentioned in oral or printed communications. They were manned and used only by designated military personnel and were "off limits" to civilians.

The first important operational order for the new coastguardsmen came out on December 23, 1942. It was issued by the District Coast Guard Officer of the First Naval District, which comprised the states of Maine, New Hampshire, Massachusetts, and other parts of New England, and it was published immediately as a routine *Notice to Mariners*. This meant that it would go to all seagoing personnel, Coast Guard, Navy, Merchant Marine, and others, in all naval districts, by mail or radio broadcast, and that its provisions would apply nationwide and at sea. It was important not only as an operational order, but also because it set forth some policywise statements regarding the status of the newly-assimilated state pilotage system. This *Notice to Mariners* read as follows:

> State pilots for the ports of Portland, Maine and of Boston and Cape Cod Canal, Massachusetts, respectively, are now members of the United States Coast Guard Reserve without pay from the government. This step is in the interest of port security, the safeguarding of vital war information, and the co-ordination of the existing state pilotage system in accordance with wartime requirements.
>
> Pilotage will continue as before. While actually piloting a vessel, the pilot is still acting as a state pilot, rather than as a Coast Guard officer. The state pilot's relationship to the master or commanding officer, the vessel, and the owner remains as established in maritime law. There is no substitution of command by reason of the membership of the pilot in the Coast Guard Reserve. Masters and commanding officers are still responsible for the navigation of their vessels and may relieve or supersede the pilot whenever in their judgment it is necessary, as heretofore. The United States Government is still not responsible for any negligence of the pilot.
>
> The pilot is still entitled to his fees as prescribed by the state, and these fees shall be collected in the usual manner.

Here was a virtual *Notice to Everybody*, everybody concerned, that is, especially the officers of foreign and domestic merchant ships—who could have been misled by the new Coast Guard uniforms of the new pilot-officers—that they were pilots and not much else officially.

The trust and confidence which the government unreservedly placed in the pilotage fraternity was a great tribute to their integrity and skill. They were made responsible in large measure for the security of the ports, especially as this referred to delays, congestation, accidents, and sabotage that could hamper ship movements by blocking seaward approaches and entering channels.

In accordance with statutory and wartime regulations, security measures were delegated to three co-ordinated offices, (1) the Captain of the Port (Coast Guard), (2) the Port Director (Navy), and (3) the Pilot Command (the newly commissioned officer-pilots). The Pilot Command worked in close co-operation with the other offices, maintained a special liason with the Port Director's office, obtained convoy information, and sat in at convoy conferences.

These convoy conferences always included the Port Director, the Captain of the Port, the masters and mates of the cargo ships in the con voy, the Navy officers in command of the escort vessels, and the pilot representatives of the Pilot Command. The pilots were given complete information, including precise time schedules, about convoys of ships that were scheduled to leave or enter the ports. They met incoming convoys out at sea, put men aboard each of the vessels, and conducted them one by one, across the bars and along meandering channels to quarantine and eventually to safe anchorages or dockside berths in the harbor.

They likewise conducted outgoing vessels to many a convoy rendezvous outside the port. According to official Coast Guard records, during the fiscal year ending June 30, 1945, they handled 120,000 piloting assignments in the 39 port areas of the Atlantic, Pacific, and Gulf coasts without one serious accident and with only a very small number of minor groundings.

Undoubtedly the greatest single undertaking and accomplishment of pilots in the war was that performed by the Hell Gate pilots of New York Harbor in taking more than 15,000 vessels through that dangerous narrow passage without the loss of a single ship, without one serious accident, and with only a few minor ones. This was an incredible feat, considering the heavy traffic incident to the war effort on this constricted waterway. By the "Hell Gate Pilots" are meant all those who operated there during the war emergency, including those extras who were brought in from other areas to assist the regular peacetime complement of pilots, only about five in number. Although these five were competent and knew the waters well, they were too few in number to handle the enormous traffic, and many Sandy Hook pilots were added to the operation.

Hell Gate channel, notoriously dangerous to ships because of its strong tidal currents, hidden rocks, and scanty maneuvering room, is a narrow part of the so-called East River, which is actually a sea-water strait, about 16 miles long connecting upper New York Bay with Long Island Sound. Both of these bodies of water are estuaries, or arms of the ocean. The passage separates the Borough of Manhattan, the heart and hub of the metropolis, from the Boroughs of Brooklyn and Queens on Long Island, both heavily industrial on their waterfronts. At one point, this waterway is only 600 feet wide from shore to shore.

In an official Coast Guard report issued about two years after the end of the war, there is this commentary on that Hell Gate situation:

> Upon being militarized and enrolled in the Temporary Reserve in December o 1942, these Hell Gate pilots faced the greatest undertaking in their history. Meeting problems of piloting through Hell Gate was all in the day's work for them normally. They were used to the currents pushing up the East River but not conforming to the river's course, to the up-river flow which set against the Brooklyn

> shore as far as the Williamsburg Bridge and then sheered over and set against the Manhattan shore; but the tremendous volume of waterborne traffic to come was to tax their abilities to the utmost. Tugs and tows going up-river could not follow the rule of keeping to the right, for their tows would have ended up in the Brooklyn Navy Yard. Instead, a short distance before reaching Corlear's Hook, they started pulling for the Manhattan shore, and on reaching the Hook, headed for the Brooklyn shore to even off. Aside from the narrow, confined channels, treacherous currents, and mid-stream rocky areas, *there were 22 changes of course in the 16-mile run*. Add to these factors the tremendous volume of wartime shipping through Hell Gate, and one can gain some appreciation of the task which faced these Temporary Reserve pilots.

These pilots battled the swift and swirling currents when convoy traffic was inordinately heavy and weather conditions were unusually hampering—winds, rain, cold, fog, poor visibility—for long periods without remission or let-up. While they were at it, they had to acquire a swift education in the complicated workings of new wartime warning signal systems for ship traffic, in the operation of new instruments and techniques for determining the exact location, speed, and type of area vessels that were not even visible, and in the safe guidance of ships of close formation with many others, avoiding collisions, through waters beset with many natural dangers. A number of the ships at times carried enough ammunition to destroy the city and its millions of people.

Pilots went aboard hundreds of ships that they had never seen before, with absolutely no prior knowledge of their underway characteristics—whether or not they were sluggish, cranky, responsive to bridge signals and ships's wheel, or scarcely able to get out of their own way. Often, too, a language barrier prevented any intelligent conversations with captains and crews.

Many leviathans—20,000 tons and over—were taken through the Hell Gate passage. If any of them had grounded or sunk, the passage would have been completely blocked to all but the very small craft. Cargo ships, tankers, and transports would have been compelled to take the outside, submarine-infested waters in a 200-mile detour around Long Island.

With the coming of peace, the successful accomplishment of this and other hazardous and demanding assignments by these pilot members of the U.S.C.G. Temporary Reserve was applauded by Coast Guard officials and those of many other agencies of government. All were lavish in their praise for the pilots' over-all contribution to the winning of the war.

The pilots had justified and validated, as never before, that making of that important decision of the first Congress of the United States, when our nation was in its infancy—the decision to leave pilotage and its regulation and control in the hands of the various states, where it still reposes. They had demonstrated their importance as an auxiliary arm of the nation's defense forces and had responded—to a man!—when their country's peril and duty called.

Their far-reaching knowledge of local harbor conditions—the hidden channels, the hidden obstructions, the sandbars, the shoals, the sets of the currents, the prevailing winds, the specific aids to navigation to make use of, the exact courses to steer—all of this had proved to be an essential and indispensable component part of the united war effort.

Twenty-Nine

Another Postwar Period

Just like the period immediately following World War I, this postwar period in America was one of enormous dislocation and painful readjustment, for the economy of the nation as a whole and for the maritime industry specifically. Neither could be converted overnight back to a normal-running, peacetime economy. The government had absorbed, not to say confiscated, the entire shipping industry, and now it was time to recondition the ships and give them back to their rightful owners in private business. This would take time, and it did take time—about 10 years, during which shipping companies slowly reestablished their normal relationships with former customers and ships gradually returned to old itineraries and schedules.

In the piloting fraternity, however, the readjustment was almost instantaneous. This was due undoubtedly to the government's wartime policy of leaving the state pilotage system intact and unaltered, except for some minor modifications and controls essential to the efficient progression of the war effort. It had been stipulated very positively that these modifications and controls would exist only for the duration of the war.

Pilots and pilot leaders who had been given special wartime commissions as officers in the military services readily shucked their military uniforms and commitments, and they easily and instantaneously assumed their former positions as full-time port pilots and members and officials of civilian pilot associations. The metamorphosis was swift and easy because their status as pilots had scarcely been disturbed when the federal government absorbed the state pilotage system at the beginning of the war. The pilot boats were returned to the various port associations, after having been renovated and refurbished, at government expense, to the point where they were in condition relatively as good as their condition when they were first taken over by the Coast Guard—with allowances for ordinary wear and tear of course.

Few, if any, peacetime civilian organizations were so readily adaptable to being converted to wartime activities and then back again to peacetime occupations. This adaptability, proven in two great wars, would seem to qualify the piloting fraternity as an always ready—*Semper Paratus*—auxiliary branch of the Coast Guard when war comes. Now that peace had broken out, they were ready again, immediately after the war ended, to take their places, aboard ships or standing by on station, ready to serve the pilotage needs of normal commerce and shipping with an indestructible system that not even a war could damage. It was mindful of that hectic period at the beginning of the war when they had been standing by together, ready to serve the needs of wartime commerce and shipping. During that time, the Commandant of the Coast Guard, in an address before the American Pilots' Association in Washington, D.C., had this to say concerning their availability and service:

> There is no doubt that the pilots do constitute a very large part in this war effort. Unless our merchant ships are kept moving rapidly and safely, we are not going to win the war. Merchant shipping is the bottleneck, and the pilots have an important responsibility.

To return to the postwar period, there is being given here the following excerpt from the book *State Pilotage in America*, which points out some significant facts relative to that period:

> With the gradual return of shipping to its more normal state, the pilots looked forward to the future with confidence. Foreign ship building was on the move with programs to replace their battered merchant fleets with new types of modern design and speed. The Federal Maritime Board and the American shipping companies, in the early 1950s, started a program for the replacement of all ships under subsidized operation. The large oil and ore carriers were planning ships in new dimensions. The increase in large vessels would affect navigation in the sharp turns of the more narrow channels. Greater drafts would require the application of careful pilotage operations in the more shallow harbors and docking areas. Roll on-roll-off ships were being laid out on the drafting boards, and many other interesting changes were in the process of development.
>
> In addition to all this, a whole new dimension in pilotage was in the offing on the Great Lakes, affecting not only ship navigation and operation, but the organizational features of pilotage as well.

This last was a reference to the proposed St. Lawrence Seaway, a stupendous project that had been gaining favor and momentum in the late 1940s just before the start of the war. The United States' and Canadian governments had been developing plans for this project for a long time. It called for the deepening, widening, and general improvement of the existing St. Lawrence—Great Lakes waterway, to the extent that it would accomodate more and larger ocean-going vessels and thus bring more overseas commerce to our seaports on the Great Lakes. That is what they would become in actuality. The ocean, in effect, would be brought more appreciably to the front doors of Cleveland, Detroit, Chicago, Milwaukee, Duluth and they would thus become genuine seaports, deep in the interior of our country.

Plans finally were completed and approved in May of 1954. They called for the construction of a modern waterway with a mean depth of no less than 27 feet, with manifold improvements in channel maintenance, and with new and improved dams and locks to facilitate ship movements.

A voluminous published survey of the entire project, *The New Billion-Dollar Story of the St. Lawrence Seaway Power Development*, put out in 1958, includes the following reference to the culmination of those seaway plans:

> The St. Lawrence Seaway legislation passed in the U.S. House of Representatives by a vote of 241 to 158, the following day the Senate approved it, and the Wiley-Dondero Act became Public Law 358 of the 83rd Congress. President Eisenhower signed the bill on May 13, 1954.
>
> On August 10, 1954, 411 years to the day after Jacques Cartier named the river, and 1700 years after Saint Lawrence had been martyred, ground was broken for the U.S.-Canadian St. Lawrence project, and the dream of hundreds of years bore fruit.

It soon became obvious, following the enactment of this law, that there were going to be many navigational and operational problems connected with this great new waterway, particularly where it ran through the Great Lakes within the territorial limits of the United States. It became evident also that many more problems were going to continue to arise and that pilotage would be at the heart and core of many of them.

Questions of jurisdiction, of interpretations and modifications of existing laws, and of reciprocity with Canada came to the forefront. There alwyas had been a robust and volatile maritime commerce on the Great Lakes, and it involved freighters, tankers, and ore carriers comparable in size to the average ocean-going merchant ship. Since these lakers never ventured out upon the so-called high seas, they were exempted from the compulsory pilotage law and were not subject to the solicitations of "state pilots." They used the services of federally-licensed pilots, members of their own crews in most cases, in accordance with the terms of the Act of 1871, which had exempted them, as well as coastwise steam vessels, from the requirements of the state pilotage system.

This law provided that "all coast-wise seagoing vessels and vessels navigating the Great Lakes shall be under the navigation laws of the United States when navigating within the jurisdiction thereof," and it further provided that "all vessels propelled in whole or in part by steam in such waters, not sailing under register, shall be under the control and direction, except when on the high seas, of pilots licensed by the U.S. Steamboat Inspection Service."

Inasmuch as the lakers were not engaged in foreign commerce that took them across the oceans of the world and into foreign ports, there was no need for them to be under register, and instead they were under enrollment or license merely. The purpose of registering a ship in official government maritime archives is to declare its nationality in foreign seas and foreign ports, whereas enrollment, applicable to American flag vessels engaged in the coastwise or domestic trade, enables them to obtain a coasting license, to obtain federal pilot licenses for their officers, and to be exempted from the obligation to hire resident port pilots when entering or leaving ports.

The lakers thus were entitled to be under enrollment and exempt from compulsory pilotage regulations. In fact, there never had been any state pilotage system or groups on the Great Lakes. The very small amount of foreign shipping on the Great Lakes—that is to say, the foreign flag ships and the United States flag ships sailing under register, did not warrant the establishment and development of a state pilotage program there.

Also, since the waters of four of the five Great Lakes were contiguous with the Canadian shores as well as our own, it was quite certain that, in the formation of any state pilotage program embodying the compulsory pilotage concept, special arrangements would have to be made with the Canadian authorities. Since the American Constitution forbids the individual states to make treaties with foreign powers, such arrangements would have been impossible. Even if such mutual arrangements had been permissible under the constitution, it would not have been practical or wise to have attempted making them, since there would have been eight individual states dealing separately with the Canadian government on a single common undertaking. The accompanying confusions can well be imagined.

Thirty

A System Tailored for the Great Lakes

Ever since the year 1909, in recognition of the internationality of the navigable waters of the Great Lakes, there had been a treaty between the United States and Canada regarding commerce and shipping on the Lakes. It provided, among other things, that the "navigation of all navigable boundary waters shall forever continue free and open for the purpose of commerce, to the inhabitants and to the ships, vessels, and boats of both countries equally, subject however to any laws and regulations of either country, within its own territory, not inconsistent with such privilege of free navigation and applying equally and without discrimination to the inhabitants, ships, vessels, and boats of both countries."

The treaty provided further that the same right of free navigation would apply to Lake Michigan, wholly within the United States and not a part of the boundary or border of the two countries, but nevertheless connected to Lake Huron, a part of the border, by a navigable strait. It also provided that that same right of free navigation would extend to any canals—"canals now existing or which may hereafter be constructed on either side of the line"—and that both countries might establish rules and regulations for the use of such canals within their territorial limits and might even charge tolls for such use, on the condition, however, that such rules, regulations, and tolls would be applicable to the citizens of both countries, equally and impartially.

It should be easy for anyone to comprehend the stern necessity for the inclusion of those equal treatment clauses in that treaty. The persistent need for the continued maintenance of cordial and equitable relations between the two peoples of the two nations made their inclusion imperative.

However, it became evident quite early in the development of the construction plans for the new Seaway that this tried-and-true treaty and its provisions now would not do the job, as far as piloting and cordial relations were concerned, once the seaway was completed and the expected log-jams of American and foreign ships from overseas began entering the Great Lakes—just as the Great Lakes "Rules of the Road," differing from the International Rules and the Inland Rules, now would not fit the conditions. For one thing, the passing whistle signals were different in each area, making for some dangerous confusion. Also, great numbers of locally stationed pilots, with their set lifestyle and method of operating, rather than the itinerant federal pilots then consorting and working on the Lakes haphazardly, would be needed there around the clock.

Pilotage regulations affecting all of the American, Canadian, and foreign ships using the Seaway would have to be established, the sizeable complement of new pilots would have to be indoctrinated, and appropriate legislation to implement all of these requirements would have to be developed and processed. It was considered absolutely necessary that any American pilotage system on the Seaway in the Great Lakes should be in parallel conformity with a regulated Canadian pilotage system. In developing the appropriate legislation, therefore, it was imperative that the views and proposals of both nations be considered impartially.

To this end, the American State Department, Department of Commerce, Coast Guard, and other interested and involved agencies carried on interdepartmental conferences. Some of these discussion groups included representative of the Canadian Government, notably members of its Department of Transportation. Since the American Secretary of Commerce had been made responsible for the supervision and control of the government-owned St. Lawrence Seaway Development Corporation, it was deemed logical and feasible to place Great Lakes pilotage control also in that department. Our Department of Commerce then would work with its counterpart in Canada under similar legislative authority to establish a smooth-working, bi-lateral pilotage system.

There were many problems to be solved and many administrative kinks to be ironed out. This was done in a series of legislative hearings, proposals, reports, and committee meetings that went on for several years, even after the Seaway had been completed and opened in 1959. The American Pilots' Association participated in many of these hearings. Also, at many of the hearings and committee meetings in both houses of Congress, the president of the association was there by request to give his opinion and advice on certain legislative proposals having to do with the operation of the Seaway.

The committees were particularly interested in adapting certain features of the American state pilotage system to the Seaway legislation that would be ultimately adopted. It was realized that, since these were international waters and the Canadians had their own pilotage fraternity operating in their own style, the American state pilotage system, with its autonomous port groups, could not be transferred intact and unmodified to the Lakes areas.

The American State Department, indubitably bound to be a party to all the negotiations, also recognized the need to adopt some of the features of the American state pilotage system. Although the Department of Commerce had been given broad supervisory powers over the American share of the Seaway operation, including the authority to enlist and register pilots, to limit the number of pilots made available, and to set fair rates and miscellaneous charges, any written arrangements between the Department of Commerce and Canadian authorities required the approbation of the Secretary of State, since the whole affair was an international affair, necessarily under the State Department's over-all jurisdiction.

In this regard, in February of 1960, a Deputy Assistant Secretary of State had this to say before a United States Senate sub-committee in support of Senate Bill 3019 regulating pilotage on the Seaway:

> In the development of the provisions of the bill with regard to the regulation of pilotage, we have had the benefit of expert information furnished by Captain Hilton Lowe, President of the American Pilots' Association. As a result of the material obtained from this and other sources, including our Canadian friends, provision had been made in S. 3019 for a regulated system which incorporates essential elements of some state pilotage systems.
>
> A basic pattern similar to that of the state pilotage systems and to elements of the Canadian pilotage system has been followed in the bill for the creation of a pool or pools by a voluntary association or associations of United States registered pilots to provide the arrangements and facilities necessary for the efficient dispatching of vessels and the rendering of pilotage services required by the bill. The Secretary of Commerce is empowered to authorize the formation of such pools, to make regulations for their operation, and to conduct inspections.

These pilotage pools were nothing more nor less than that same type of voluntary associations of qualified port pilots that constituted the organized port groups on the United States seacoast, existing mainly for the furtherance of efficiency and facility in the performance of pilotage services. It was recognized that certain delimited Seaway sectors, such as those containing locks, dams, and tortuous tricky channels, would need special pilotage arrangements. These authorized pools, groups of pilots working the same area day after day and amassing, individually and collectively, a great shore of knowledge concerning the waters and how best to bring ships safely across them, were expected to fulfill that need. Thus pilotage in those areas would take on some of the appearance and some of the characteristics of the state pilotage systems on the seacoasts.

This and many other elements of proposed legislation were discussed and debated in congressional committees and in conferences of agencies of the executive branch of government involved in the management of the Seaway project, and these discussions and debates dragged out through a long period of legislative activity. Some of the reasons for this long-winded and searching legislative activity are given in this committee report, Senate Report #1284, dated April 21, 1960:

> Opening of the St. Lawrence Seaway in 1959 has greatly complicated vessel safety problems on the Great Lakes by making possible entry into the Lakes of ocean vessels of higher tonnage and in far greater numbers than previously was the case. In addition to the 2,206 United States and Canadian vessels operating on the Lakes exclusively or in large part, some 1033 foreign vessels and 61 vessels under United States Registry made round-trip voyages in the Lakes in 1959. All indications are that this total, and foreign vessels particularly, will increase in the years ahead.
>
> The upsurge of foreign vessels navigating United States waters of the Great Lakes and the entry of United States ocean vessels into the area present a definite threat to safe navigation. There is presently statutory requirement for the use of qualified pilots on both United States and Canadian vessels navigating only on the Great Lakes. However, as evidenced by the reported accidents and near accidents during the first year's operation of the St. Lawrence Seaway, operation of the ocean-going vessels without skilled Lake pilots presents a threat of considerable magnitude, not only to the Lake vessels, but also to the ocean vessels, whose officers in some cases may not be sufficiently familiar with the Great Lakes Rules of the Road, the restricted waters, et cetera.
>
> It seems to be beyond question that certain general areas of United States waters in and adjoining the Great Lakes do require and will be designated for expert navigation in the interest of safety. These areas include the St. Lawrence River as far as St. Regis, the waters of western Lake Erie, and the Detroit, St. Clair, and St. Mary's Rivers and the waters adjacent thereto.

Senate Bill 3019 eventually was enacted, and its provisions, as amended and annotated, were put into effect forthwith. One provision gave authority to the President of the United States to designate certain areas as restricted areas in which special pilotage regulations would be in effect. Other areas not designated as restricted areas were considered to be open waters whereon other, ordinary regulations would apply.

For one thing, the freighters, tankers, and or carriers known as "lakers," which never ventured out on the open sea, were left to their *status quo*, not affected by the new legislation. This meant that their commerce would still be considered to be in the nature of a coastwise operation, that the essential piloting for them would continue to be done by federally licensed pilots who were permanent members of their crews, and that they would be exempt from any new compulsory state pilotage program that might be adopted on the lakes. Also, Canadian lakers, with officers properly licensed as pilots by the Canadian government, were to be permitted to navigate unmolested in United States waters, so long as our lakers, with officers properly licensed as pilots by our government, could navigate unmolested in Canadian waters.

In the designated restricted areas, a completely different set of rules would apply. American citizens serving as pilots for American registered (ocean-going) vessels and foreign vessels in these waters would have to be "United States registered pilots." This meant that an American pilot must *not* be a regular member of a ship's crew, that he must be "registered" by the United States Secretary of Commerce, and that he must also hold a valid "unlimited master's license authorizing navigation on the Great Lakes and suitably endorsed for pilotage on routes specified therein," this license to be issued by the United States Coast Guard.

Those same American registered vessels and foreign vessels, *when not operating in restricted designated areas*, were authorized to use the services of registered pilots who were regular members of their crews or other officers of their vessels qualified for navigation in those unrestricted areas. It was pointed out that such vessels might use the "qualified officer of the vessel" to a great extent in the interest of economy, but where no such qualified officers were in the ships' companies, local registered pilots must be employed in the dangerous areas.

The terms *registered pilot* and *pilots registered by the Secretary of Commerce*, brand-new in the pilotage profession, accentuate the differing nature of this Great Lakes pilotage system as compared with the traditional and standard State pilotage systems on the seacoasts. The Department of Commerce never had been in the pilotage picture before, and pilots never had been "registered" before. They formerly had been "licensed" and, during the war, "accredited," but they never had been "registered" before.

Another new and differing feature of the Great Lakes system was the federal government's designation of certain waterway areas as "restricted areas" where special innovative pilotage rules would apply.

Also there was that new element of reciprocity with the pilots and pilotage system of a foreign country, never encountered before, although reciprocity between pilots of two different states bordering on the same navigable body of water—Chesapeake Bay, for instance—was "old stuff" to American pilots.

Nevertheless, the American pilotage fraternity, as readily as it had adapted to the emergencies and disruptions of two world wars, adapted to these and other innovations and new dimensions, conceived only on account of the unique character of the Great Lakes-St. Lawrence Seaway project. They very ably demonstrated their capability of adjusting to drastically-changed conditions in the interest of the public welfare and the welfare of their country. The Great Lakes system still contained many operational and organizational features of the state pilotage system that had proved valid and efficient in meeting the ships guidance needs of the nation down through the years, and the American Pilots' Association had a lot to do with that.

The newly enacted Seaway law provided authority for the Secretary of Commerce to appoint an Advisory Committee of three public members experienced in the field of maritime operations to oversee the operation of the pilotage system on the Seaway. On September 12, 1960, the president of the American Pilots' Association was selected to be one of those members.

Thirty-One

Back to Sandy Hook

"New York is the greatest of all the great cities I have seen. To my mind, it has everything...the finest harbor and the most skillful pilots...."

Who said that? Who are those skillful pilots mentioned? What do they do to deserve such high praise?

That was said by no less a personage than Sir Ivan Thompson, former captain of the Cunard Line's *Queen Elizabeth*, the one-time world's largest ocean liner, in an article that he wrote for *The New Yorker* magazine. He was speaking of the Sandy Hook pilots.

The Sandy Hook pilots carefully guide ships of all sizes, shapes, and kinds, of all nationalities, in all kinds of weather, at all hours of the day or night, in and out of New York Harbor, from and back to safe deep water well out on the open sea. They take their turns in a well-organized rotation system controlled from a central pilotage headquarters on shore. This headquarters or base of operations is located at 24 State Street, a tall office building overlooking the major portion of New York Harbor. It is on the tip end of Manhattan Island, the hub of the city of New York. The building is tenanted mostly by shipping companies and those with some connection, however tenuous, with maritime commerce. The night office and base of operations is at Pier 19 on Staten Island, down the bay towards the open sea.

Captains of ships that constantly visit important seaports all over the world have said publicly that they take pilots aboard more quickly at New York than at any other port and are guided in to a safe anchorage or dockside berth with an ease and dispatch not encountered anywhere else. An important factor contributing to this expeditious handling of transient ships is the excellent equipment maintained by these Sandy Hook pilots. This equipment includes, besides two boarding launches, a multiplicity of expensive, modern, ship-to-shore radiotelephone accouterments.

The operation and maintenance of this essential equipment is a big job in itself and requires a large staff in addition to the pilots. This staff includes deck and engine room crews, cooks, and office personnel, about 85 persons in all. For the year 1970, the cost of this operation and maintenance was well over a million dollars.

Undoubtedly the biggest factor contributing to the safe and rapid handling of ships here is the individual and collective skill of the Sandy Hook pilots engendered by many long years of training and practical experience. The Sandy Hook pilots of today are the end product of a training system that began back in the year 1694, when this particular port pilots' association was founded. Since then, the system has been improved continually year after year until now the Sandy Hook pilotage service is considered to be the finest in the world.

If it were not for this assured and consummate skill of these Sandy Hook pilots, the accident rate at the port would go up, and this could result in the loss of many millions of dollars each year in lost time and costly ship repairs. As a consequence, the insurance rates would necessarily be increased, placing a tremendous financial burden on the shoulders of the ship owners and leading eventually to a great loss in prestige and popularity for the port—which of course would mean a great loss of shipping and commerce.

Conversely, whether in fair weather or foul and foggy weather, this expertise of these men expedites the movements of many ships from the open sea to the docks, where there are gangs of high-priced longshoremen waiting to work the ships, thus bringing about savings of many millions of dollars each year in *gained* time and *reduced* expenses. Waiting gangs could cost $1000 an hour and more. Thus, if only one out of every eight ships is saved only one hour when loading gangs are waiting at the dock, the savings to shippers would be equal in sum to the pilotage fees for a whole year. This constitutes a great inducement to shippers and ship owners to use the port as a terminus or port of call. It should be obvious to all that this consummate skill of those certain pilots has a lot to do with the continuing popularity and commercial success of the Port of New York—and along with the know-how, there is dependability.

At the Port of New York, qualified pilots are available to transient ships at all times without exception, at sea or ashore, aboard pilot boats on station off Sandy Hook (anchored or cruising), or waiting in shoreside official quarters adjacent to the New York City waterfront. They are on call 24 hours a day, 365 days a year. They observe no holidays and they make no overtime charges, neither for working on holidays nor for working hours in excess of the standard eight-hour work day. They never go out on strike.

There is always a pilot boat or two on station at the harbor entrance with several ready, willing, and able pilots aboard them. Of the three large station pilot boats, two are steamers and one is a sailing schooner with auxiliary engine. The schooner is used mostly as a tender or supply ship. The four boarding launches (motorboats, in other words) are used to ferry pilots from the station boats to incoming ships and to pick up pilots disembarking from outward-bound ships.

Prior to 1885, in a time when the New York pilots were not fully organized, it was the custom for groups of pilots, usually six in each group, to own and operate boats co-operatively there. In consequence, there were at one time some 30 sailing vessels in the pilotage service there, and it was customary for the pilots to cruise great distances out to sea in order to be the first to "speak" an incoming vessel and be given the job of piloting her in.

When this swarming, congested, wasteful competition, commonly referred to as the "mad race to the sea," was finally eliminated through the organization of a tighter and more exclusive pilots' association, the number of pilot boats was reduced almost as a matter of course. One or two large steamships, with ample living quarters aboard, were put into service and stationed at a fixed spot off Sandy Hook. A goodly number of expert pilots were berthed aboard them, and the now highly-organized rotation system came into being.

Nowadays the pilot boats on station in that same general area have on board at all times pilots in sufficient numbers to accomodate any number of incoming ships likely to request pilotage service in quick succession. the pilots are rotated within their class of license or branch in conformity with the type of ship approaching the port in each case. The entire rotation system is controlled from the pilotage headquarters on shore with the help of an efficient ship-to-shore radio-telephone communications system.

When an outward-bound ship reaches the safe open water there in the vicinity of the station boats and completes the slowdown maneuver of "dropping the pilot," as it has been called for hundreds of years, the pilot is picked up by one of the small motorboats and taken to a large pilot boat on station, there to await his turn for an assignment on an inbound ship. Once ashore again, he will begin awaiting his turn for an assignment on an outward-bound ship. And so it goes, over and over again, throughout the year.

If it were not for the availabililty and usefulness of those station pilot boats and the other "tools of the trade," the boarding motorboats, and electronic communications equipments, et cetera, pilotage at the Port of New York would not be such an efficient and smooth-running affair; and if it were not for the fact that these tools of the trade are owned collectively by the pilots themselves, according to tradition and the law, these tools of the trade undoubtedly would not be provided and maintained with such a high degree of efficiency and expertness. To provide and maintain such tools of the trade is a specified obligation of the port pilots' associations throughout the nation.

Today's pilot boats are kept in first-class condition. They are provided with good food, good working, living, and sleeping quarters, and ample ships' stores and safety devices such as fire extinguishers, life jackets, life rafts, flares, signaling instruments, et cetera. By reason of their being modern vessels substituted for the old-order sailing vessels, it is possible for them and their pilot passengers to remain on station for long periods of time under very adverse conditions of wind and weather and disturbed sea.

In the field of signaling devices, there are of course those that must be used, according to law, to inform the officers of incoming ships—at night as well as in the daytime—of the pilot boat's identity and the availability of a resident, local pilot who knows the waters well. This predicates the use by the incoming ships of standardized signaling sevices to request a pilot. These are several in type and style.

In the daytime, a pilot may be summoned to an incoming ship by the display of either the International Code Flag Signals letter *G*, or by the letters *P.T.*, or simply by the letter *P*, the flag known as the "pilot jack" and otherwise known as "The Blue Peter."

At night, a pilot is summoned to a ship by the display of a blue "pyrotechnic" light or flare every 15 minutes, or by a bright white light flashed or shown just a little way above the main deck at short frequent intervals for about a minute at a time, or by the letters *P.T.* sent in Morse code by a flashing light beamed at the pilot vessel.

The pilot boat on station is required to display the pilot flag in the daytime and a certain specific arrangement of lights at night. According to both the International Rules and the Rules of the Road, "A steam vessel, when engaged on her station on pilotage duty in waters of the United States, *and at anchor*, shall carry a white light at the masthead visible all around the horizon and of such a character as to be visible on a dark night with a clear atmosphere at a distance of at least two miles...and shall carry at a distance of eight feet below her white masthead light a red light, visible all around the horizon and of such a character as to be visible on a dark night at a distance of at least two miles... and shall also exhibit a flare-up light or flare-up lights at short intervals which shall never exceed fifteen minutes."

When such steam pilot vessels (those propelled in whole or in part by steam or by any other form of mechanical or electrical power) are not at anchor, they are required to carry, additionally, the standard red and green port and starboard running lights.

In addition to the International and Inland Rules, there are many other regulations affecting the operation and maintenance of the

Sandy Hook pilot boats. These are those mandated by the New York Board of Pilot Commissioners and those in the by-laws of the local port group, the United New York-New Jersey Sandy Hook Pilots' Association.

First and foremost are the rules governing the number of boats permitted and required to be on station at all times, along with specific rules for their operation, maintenance, inspection, and minimum requirements. A rigid rule decrees that log books must be kept on all boats and kept up-to-date at all times. This rule applies to those boats that spend most of their time moored alongshore as well as to those on station offshore.

In addition to the usual chronological running accounts of daily activity aboard, the log books must contain vital statistics of everyone on board at any given time—each officer, pilot, crewman, guest, or passenger. These statistics will include their names, ages, home addresses, telephone numbers, names of next of kin, and certain other information required by the commissioners and the association. The logs also must show the times of arrival and departure of station pilot boats, the names of pilots taken off or put aboard ships, the names of the ships, the exact times of these contacts, and accounts of the services rendered.

The economy of the New York Metropolitan Area, which includes certain large areas outside the city limits and areas in other states than New York, is dependent in very large measure on the water-born commerce at the Port of New York. This is of such magnitude that the livelihood of one out of every four persons living in the area is provided by it.

A study made by the Port of New York Authority shows that commerce in the New York-New Jersey port district creates 430,000 jobs in an average year. These jobs provide wages of $2,100,000,000 per year as the result of the movement of 140,000,000 tons of commerce into, out of, and through the port each year. These are jobs that would not exist in the Metropolitan area were it not for the prestige and popularity of that port as a terminus.

The fine service and excellent safety record of the Sandy Hook pilots greatly enhances that prestige and popularity. During one recent five-year period, they handled over 123,000 ocean-going ships with an accident rate of 89/1000ths of 1%; *and* 88% of this infinitesimally small number were of a minor nature. *Every* year the total value of the ships and cargoes handled by the Sandy Hook pilots is well over *one hundred billion dollars.* How important then must be that safety record of the Sandy Hook pilots!

Thirty-Two

The Making of a Pilot

Pilots at the Port of New York are licensed by the New York State Board of Commissioners of Pilots after having gone through rigorous training in an apprenticeship program that stretches out to 15 years before the coveted "full branch" license, entitling an individual to pilot *any ship* of *any* size or importance, is granted. Many years ago, the state's lawmakers, in their wisdom, created this board in order to provide for the continued well-being of this highly-regarded pilotage system, to support the continuity of the guild principle heretofore operative in this and other pilots' associations, to supply a guiding and protective hand in the background and behind the scenes, and thus to help maintain the supremacy of the Port of New York over all others in the world.

It does indeed take 15 years to become a full branch Sandy Hook pilot, qualified to pilot *any* ship entering or leaving the busy Port of New York. The first eight years are spent working on the pilot boats, riding big ships in and out of the harbor in the company of licensed pilots doing their jobs, and acquiring a fund of first-hand knowledge, experience, and know-how. A young rookie or fledgling pilot is first assigned to the boats as "the spare boy," and his duties are just what the name implies. He does all the "odd" jobs, the deck swabbing, the brass polishing, the trash removing, the errand running, the "dirty" work. At this time he is a probationary or junior apprentice.

He studies basic seamanship and acquires practical experience as a member of a pilot boat crew, becoming in turn a deckhand, a boatswain, and a motorboat operator. After two years, if he measures up, he may be promoted to the grade of "boatkeeper." In the olden days, this rating made the apprentice eligible to become the captain of a sailing pilot vessel. Nowadays, whenever granted, it means that he is eligible to become the captain or mate of a modern pilot boat propelled by steam or other mechanical means.

During this eight-year period, the apprentice must pass a long list of examinations that give him an able seaman's papers, a motor boat operator's license, a radio telephone operator's license, his papers as master of a pilot boat, and finally his *federal* license as a first class pilot, not to be confused with the highly-prized and much more prestigious *state* pilot's license. At the conclusion of this eight-year period, he is examined by the New York State Board of Commissioners of Pilots and, if successful in the comprehensive oral and written examinations, he is granted a state license as a deputy pilot.

All of this is only the first phase or half-way-along for the new pilot. He is still considered to be an apprentice in need of further training, and the next seven years are spent in on-the-job training, during which he learns a great deal more about ship handling. At the end of the first of those seven years, he again appears before the pilot commissioners to be examined and to have his record reviewed. If his progress has been satisfactory, his license is renewed for another year, in a higher bracket enabling him to pilot larger ships of deeper draft.

Likewise, at the end of all the succeeding years in that seven-year period, he is promoted, if eligible, to higher grades enabling him to pilot progressively larger vessels, until he reaches the ultimate goal of becoming a full branch pilot authorized to guide the world's largest ships in and out of the Port of New York.

The gradation of pilot licenses according to ship size is a stern necessity at most of the larger ports, due to problems of traffic, prevalent shoals, and constant adverse winds and stormy weather. At the Port of New York, this gradation is rather more elaborate than elsewhere. The present six grades of Sandy Hook pilot licenses were established by regulations promulgated in April of 1959 by the New York State Board of Commissioners of Pilots. The following verbatim excerpt from those regulations will serve to explain this grading system:

Sandy Hook Pilot Licenses

A...The board hereby establishes the following grades of pilot licenses for Sandy Hook pilots, the said grades being based on draft of vessels served and their tonnage:

Sixth Grade: Draft not to exceed 20 feet of water, and the gross registered tonnage not to exceed 8,500 tons.

Fifth Grade: Draft not to exceed 24 feet of water, and the gross registered tonnage not to exceed 11,500 tons.

Fourth Grade: Draft not to exceed 28 feet of water, and the gross registered tonnage not to exceed 18,000 tons.

Third Grade: Draft not to exceed 32 feet of water, and the gross registered tonnage not to exceed 33,000 tons.

Second Grade: Draft *unlimited*, and the gross registered tonnage not to exceed 35,000 tons.

First Grade: Draft *unlimited*, and tonnage *unlimited*.

B...A pilot, upon first being declared qualified by the commissioners to be a pilot, shall be entitled to a license of the sixth grade, and thereafter, if such pilot is considered by the commissioners to be in all respects fitted for advancement, entitled to be advanced in grade as follows:

On completion of one year's service, to the fifth grade

On completion of two years' service, to the fourth grade.

On completion of three years' service, to the third grade.

On completion of *two years service in the third grade*, to the second grade.

On completion of *two years service in the second grade*, to the first grade.

Suspension and revocation of Sandy Hook pilot licenses can and does happen, as a penalty for pilots' having failed to abide by regulations, either wilfully or through careless negligence, and as a postlude to conduct, afloat or ashore, that brings discredit to the profession. Less severe penalties are prescribed for the lesser infractions.

A few samples out of the miscellany of likely wrongdoings that incur penalties of one kind or another are given here:

> Wilfully or negligently causing unnecessary delays of arriving or departing vessels while boarding or leaving them.
>
> Being absent from duty over and above the alloted free time period, for any cause whatsoever, without reporting to the association and the commissioners.
>
> Failing to report vessels in distress, new waterway obstructions, misplaced buoys, and other deficiencies in the regular aids to navigation.
>
> Failing to obey promptly all orders given out by the pilots' association or the Board of Commissioners of Pilots.
>
> Refusing to accept assignments under the rotation system without just cause or adequate reason.
>
> Being intoxicated while on duty.

The reporting requirements are very strict, demanding that completely accurate records of all pilotage activities be kept at all times. Pilots must report each and every assignment to the office of the commissioners, and each of these reports must include the name of the piloted vessel, its draft, nationality, hailing port, destination, the time it was boarded inbound and outward bound, the length of time the pilot was detained on board at quarantine and elsewhere, and the number and kind of services performed for it. Also, vessels that refuse the pilot's offer to service must be reported to both the pilot commissioners and the port association officials.

Along with proficiency and dedication to duty, another paramount requirement of the profession, especially at New York, is proper social conduct. Under this heading, sobriety is emphasized and demanded by the regulations of the state pilots' association and the state pilotage authority. Also, pilots are directed to live within their means and to refrain from incurring debts beyond their ability to pay easily.

Aside from the requisite qualifications with regard to training, knowledge, experience, skill, health, social behavior, et cetera, American pilots must have still another important qualification—an all-embracing attitude of genuine concern and responsibility for the welfare of the nations and the general public. By its very nature, pilotage under the state pilotage system tends to be a quasi-public service. While many of the basic features of the private enterprise concept are inherent in its structure and operation, its authorization and certain of its controls are by public legislation. It operates under individual sets of relevant state and national laws, is supervised by a state government board of commissioners, is mandatory upon commercial shipping interests and indirectly upon the general public, and must be responsive to the demands of the public, as it serves their commercial needs.

Thirty-Three

The Apprenticeship Programs

In many states, there are no maximum or minimum restrictions by statute on the number of pilots that may be appointed for the various seaports. The determination of the number of pilots to be accredited at each port is left to the pilotage authority at those ports. In some states, both a maximum and a minimum number are prescribed by law, while in other coastal states only a maximum *or* a minimum number is specified.

In every one of our coastal states, however, the principal and primary qualification decreed by law to be necessary to a person's being licensed as a pilot is the fact of his having accumulated a fund of actual experience in piloting ships at a given port. How does he get that experience without the sanction of that required license? One may get it by becoming an apprentice attached to a port pilots' association, of which there are some 52 or more all over the United States, and many more throughout the world.

The apprenticeship programs of the present-day pilots' associations retain the principal features of the apprentice programs of the medieval guilds, for, as has been pointed out, the guild pattern has been adopted and followed almost universally down through the years in the organizing and operating of these pilots' associations. Historians have noted that the apprenticeship programs seemed to be the very heart of the guild system of long ago, in that it satisfied a constant demand for skilled labor on the part of the masters, guaranteed a sufficiency of skilled workmen in the craft or service, and provided for ready replacements for guild members retiring or dropping out for various reasons.

The craft and service guilds, different and distinct from the merchant guilds, were composed of autonomous groups of artisans and skilled workers classified, in each group, as masters, journeymen, and apprentices, according to their experience and competence. They imposed upon themselved rigid high standards of workmanship, social behavior, and economic stability. All of this enhanced their ability as groups, to gain prestige and potency, and their chief virtues were to be found in the strong sense of responsibility, dignity, and independance thus engendered in the minds and hearts of all the members.

Apprentices in those times had a hard life filled, apparently, with austerity and drudgery. Their entire social and economic existence was circumscribed by the regulations of the guilds without mercy or favoritism. They worked long hours, as much as 12 hours a day regularly, and did all of the "dirty work." Their conduct, industriousness, and competence were under surveillance at all times. It was harsh and hard going, but it was worth it all in the end. They received an excellent education and training providing them with the skills and know-how enabling them to make a good living and become respected, worthwhile citizens. It has been said that no more effective system of professional training was ever conceived.

It was the custom then for the sons of master craftsmen to follow in the father's footsteps and learn his trade. This did not mean that they were accorded any special consideration or permissiveness, nor did it mean that non-relative outsiders were excluded, if they were bright, ambitious, clean-cut young men serious about learning the trade or craft. Relatives and nonrelatives, both, had to measure up to the same rigid code in order to remain in the guild and be upgraded slowly but surely. All of these standards were and are inherent in the present-day pilots' associations.

The masters and the by-laws of those old-time guilds did a thorough job of regulating the business affairs of the groups and the activities of their members. They helped to settle disputes between members and customers, and they penalized poor workmanship and fraudulent practices. They encouraged a proper respect for the consumer's requirements, and they discouraged self-seeking and greed as primary incentives for working at the craft. They prohibited shoddy workmanship for the sake of quick profits or easy money, and they guaranteed the high quality of each and every product of the guild. They arranged for an equitable division of profits and promoted programs of "fringe benefits." They brought about a solidarity of common purpose and an abiding fellowship, internally as well as with members of other guilds in other crafts. All of this constituted a new social force that brought dignity and geniality to many otherwise humble and grueling occupations.

As in the pilotage systems of today however, with parts of their control and regulation coming from within and part from outside by government authorities, the relationships between masters, journeymen, and apprentices were supervised in part by the early governments, by super-imposing certain apprenticeship regulations. This was due to the expanded commerce and increased guild activity of the times, which undoubtedly was productive of certain abuses and unwarranted hardships in the apprentice ranks.

A typical set of such regulations was the "Statute of Apprentices," enacted in England in 1563 during the reign of Queen Elizabeth. This code, similar to a "Statute of Laborers" enacted 200 years earlier, was in effect for 250 years, and under its provisions, the governments authority was supreme in the matter of relationships between masters, journeymen, and apprentices. It set the standards for working conditions and, every year, the pay scale, through justices-of-the-peace in the various areas where the guilds operated.

Apprentices were required to serve as apprentices for seven years, working as much as 12 hours a day or, in the wintertime during all of the daylight hours. The work was hard, often grueling and torturous, and the pay was small and by-the-year rather than on a weekly or monthly basis. Six months' notice was required as a condition to terminating the employment arrangement. This sovereign authority and the regulations imposed by the guilds themselves maintained the rigidity of the discipline without let-up or leniency.

Down through the years, the discipline of the modern-day pilot guilds, especially with regard to the apprentice training, has been no less rigid and demanding. This has been so undoubtedly because of the extreme rigors and harsh physical and mental demands of the occupation, which require the utmost in health, strength, sobriety, good judgement, and all-around competence. The acknowledged great need for the vigilant, unfaltering protection of life and property in those special areas just a little way offshore dictates these requirements.

Apprentices in the pilotage systems nearly always have had just about as hard a life as those in the guilds of long ago, except that the march of time and innovations in social customs have eliminated many of the restricting aspects of the apprentice's lot. For example, at one time in our history, apprentices were not allowed to get married during the first five years of their apprenticeship.

Harsh and rigid as the regulations were and are, this rigidity has always been considered a stern necessity in the apprenticeship programs. It was conceived in order to set a pattern for the lives of the would-be pilots and pre-ordain the style of their behavior throughout their entire professional careers.

Thirty-Four

A Time for Learning

There is one difference, not very great, between the modern and the medieval apprenticeship programs. This is in the area of age requirements. In the medieval and renaissance periods, there was little official demarcation of the age limits applying to those seeking admission to the apprenticeship programs of the various guilds and scarcely any uniformity in the stipulated age limits that did exist. These minimum age requirements varied, presumably, in accordance with the types and locations of the guilds. This was true of the pilotage guilds as well as the others and the variety in the requirements undoubtedly stemmed from the variousness of the locations, types, and sizes of the port groups and the ports they served.

Today in the United States, the age requirements for novice apprentices are clearly delimited in all of the states, though they do vary from state to state, and they are stipulated by law. Some states have age ranges from 17 to 21; other from 17 to 22; and still others from 17 to 22 and from 18 to 26. Many others have only a maximum age limit and no minimum and no spread. All of the legal limiations on age are aimed at starting young men off on piloting careers in their early youth—mainly for two reasons: to help them achieve a maximum of proficiency early in their careers and to help also in the molding of their characters.

In many cases, particularly in the Pacific Coast states, the recruitment of novice pilots does not necessarily come through a formal apprenticeship program. It may come and often does come, in considerable measure, from the ranks of mature, experienced seafaring persons, masters and mates of ocean-going vessels who already hold valid "federal" pilot licenses authorizing them to conduct their own ships in and out of seaports. Even in such cases however, a period of training and a demonstration of competency is required, if they are to become accredited port pilots authorized to conduct all sorts and sizes of foreign and domestic trans-oceanic ships in and out of various ports.

The length of time an apprentice must abide in that status before being authorized to pilot ships on his own initiative and all by himself usually is controlled by state law, and when state control is absent, by the port pilots' associations. On the average, this is a period of four years, though some states require more or less time in the learning period.

In some states, would-be pilots are graded as junior and senior apprentices, and the novice is required to go through a preliminary junior term, during which time his indoctrination and basic training will by effected. Once through the junior stage, he becomes a senior apprentice scheduled to go through the more advanced training that bears directly on the mechanics of the piloting job.

A good example of the rigid requirements essential to an apprenticeship program tailored especially for one of the larger ports are those in effect at the Port of New York, as laid down by the "Regulations of the Board of Commissioners of Pilots of the States of New York and New Jersey." They read as follows:

Sandy Hook Pilot Apprentices

A. There may be such number of Sandy Hook pilot apprentices as the commissioners may deem necessary. No person shall be accepted as apprentice unless he shall have established to the satisfaction of the commissioners that he (1) is a citizen of the United States not less than 18 years of age, (2) holds a certificate of graduation from a secondary school or a license as deck officer, issued under the laws of the United States, for vessels of 500 gross tons or over, (3) is physically and mentally sound, normal as to visual acuity and color perception, normal as to hearing, and free from impediment in speech, and (4) is of good character and temperamentally suited to meet the demands of the pilot service.

B. Apprentices shall be graded as *junior apprentices* and *boatkeepers*. Beginning with the date of his acceptance as an apprentice, and for not less than two years thereafter, an apprentice shall be graded as a junior apprentice. During the 30 days next preceding his completion of two years of service in the grade of junior apprentice, an apprentice may appear at a meeting of the board to apply for promotion to the grade of boatkeeper. If found by the board to be acceptable as to physical condition, including eyesight, and a fit and proper person qualified for such advancement, an apprentice so applying may be promoted to the grade boatkeeper, effective upon the date of the beginning of the third year of his apprenticeship. Every apprenticeship shall be served in the pilot boats of the Sandy Hook pilots, except for such portion of such apprenticeship as may be required by these regulations to be spent in company with the pilots of vessels.

C. From the beginning of the 43rd month of his apprenticeship, and during not less than six months thereafter, each apprentice shall be taken on board of inward and outward bound vessels and carefully instructed in the method of handling them, particularly in the use of steering apparatus, engine room signals, compass and other navigational instruments, and in the manner of berthing and unberthing vessels. He shall be given careful instruction in the tides, currents, soundings, and bearings and distances of the several shoals, rocks, bars, points of land, buoys, beacons, and lights, and he shall familiarize himself with the publications of the United States Government such as charts, Coast Pilots, and other books, tide tables, and current diagrams relating thereto. Such apprentice shall familiarize himself with the records of the United States Weather Bureau with respect to New York and adjacent territory and the effect of winds upon the handling of vessels within the waters for which he may be licensed. In no case shall any apprentice be licensed as a pilot until he shall have accompanied the pilots of vessels on not less than 150 trips, either inward or outward, and shall have furnished the commissioners with a record, sworn or affirmed by him to be correct, containing, with respect to each trip, the name and draft of vessel, the point of departure, the destination, and the name of the pilot, and shall have satisfied the commissioners that he is qualified in accordance with Section 92 of the navigation law and this regulation.

Several other states have apprenticeship regulations similar to those of New York but they are modified to meet the needs of their individual ports. Nearly all of them are just about as strict and as rigid, and in nearly all of them, the strictness and rigidity does not end with the completion of the apprenticeship period of service, but continues on throughout the pilot's lifetime of service.

All of the regulations demand a continuing self-disciplinary good behavior and a continuing adaptation to ever-changing conditions such as new or altered channels, new reefs and shoals, new navigational instruments and devices, a "new look" to the shoreline. Scarcely any other job in the field of commercial transportation demands such a high decree of expertness, physical fitness, mental alertness, and good social conduct as that required in piloting. That this was recognized and acknowledged early in our history is evidenced by the content and style of this New York State pilot license, the first one ever issued:

The people of the State of New York, by the Grace of God free and

> independant, to Zachary Rufler, mariner, greeting:
>
> Know ye that we, being well assured of the ability, skill and care and circumspection of said Zachary Rufler, have nominated, constituted, and appointed, and by these presents do nominate, constitute, and appoint you, the said Zachary Rufler, to be one of the branch pilots of the Port of New York to and from Sandy Hook from and to the said port. You, the said Zachary Rufler, truly behaving yourself in all things, as becometh in the service and station of a pilot, and observing, doing, fulfilling, keeping, and performing, all and singular, those things which, on your part and behalf as a pilot aforesaid, are and ought to be observed, done, fulfilled, and kept, and that in and by all things according to the directions, true intent, and meaning of an Act of the Legislature of our said State of New York, passed on the 14th day of April, 1784, entitled an *Act for the Regulation of Pilots and Pilotage for the Port of New York and for Other Purposes Herein Mentioned*, are to have and to hold the said office of branch pilot for the Port of New York together with the fees, salaries, perquisites, and advantages thereunto.
>
> In witness whereof, we have caused these our letters to be made patent and the Great Seal of our state to be hereunto affixed. Witness our great and well-beloved George Clinton, Esquire, Governor of our said state, Commander-in Chief of all the Militia, and Admiral of the Navy of the same, by and with the advice and consent of our Council of Appointment of our City of New York, the 22nd Day of April, in the year of our Lord one thousand seven hundred and eighty-four and of our independence the eighth.

There is an amusing anecdote concerning a prospective pilot who was being examined by the commissioners of a certain district and was being interrogated during the final, oral phase of the testing. They were inquiring into his specific knowledge of the waters at the port where he would be performing his services if appointed.

"Do you know where all the sandbars are?" he was asked.

"No, I don't" was the unexpected and startling reply.

"*What! — you don't!* Well, how in the world do you expect to do any piloting there?"

"Because I know where they ain't," was the confident reply.

P.S. — He got the job. It is very probable that the man was highly qualified and very probably had served a full, supervised apprenticeship as required by law at most of our ports.

The rigid standards of conduct for apprentices, with all of their restrictions and requirements, were present in the pilotage guild system more so than in any other craft or guild system, in the Old World *and* the New World. This undoubtedly was true because the extreme rigors and demands of the profession, involving as they did the protection of human life and valuable cargo constantly, required sobriety, level-headedness and a high degree of competence at all times. These demands and this responsibility set this guild and this profession apart from all others. How could it ever be classed in the same category with such things as the printing, tailoring, shoemaking guilds.

A good example of this iron-bound rigidity in the standards of conduct set for apprentice pilots, which have not changed very much down through the centuries, are these "Articles of Apprenticeship" subscribed to by one John Kelso, 16 years old, at New York on the "eighth day of August in the year of our Lord one thousand eight hundred and one:"

> Witnesseth, that John Kelso, now aged sixteen years, hath put himself and by these presents by and with the consent of Henry Kelso, his father, by his sealing and delivering, hath put himself and by these presents doth voluntarily and of his own free will and accord put himself apprentice to John Funck of the City of New York, to learn the art, trade, and mystery of a pilot, for the piloting of vessels to and from the City of New York by Sandy Hook, and after the manner of an apprentice to serve from the day of the date hereof, for and during and until the full end and term of five years next ensuing, during which term the said apprentice his master faithfully shall serve, his secrets keep, his lawful commands everywhere readily obey; he shall do no damage to his master, nor see it done by others without letting or giving notice to his said master.... he shall not commit matrimony within the said term...and at cards, dice, or any other unlawful game he shall not play, whereby his master shall have damage, neither with his own goods nor the goods of others, without license from his said master. He shall neither buy nor sell; he shall not absent himself day or night from his master's service without leave, nor haunt ale houses, taverns, or playhouses; but in all things shall behave himself as a faithful apprentice ought to do, within the said term. And said master shall use the utmost of his endeavour to teach or cause to be taught or instructed the said apprentice in the trade and mystery of a pilot for the piloting of vessels to and from the City of New York, by Sandy Hooke, and during the said term of five years shall pay to said apprentice the sum of seven dollars per month until the said apprentice shall be appointed boatkeeper, after which he shall pay him the wages usually allowed to boatkeepers, and for the true performance of all and singular the covenants and agreements aforesaid, said parties bind themselves each unto the other firmly by these presents. In witness whereof, the said parties have, interchangeably, set their

> hands and seals hereunto this eighth day of August in the twenty-fifth year of the independence of the United States of America and in the year of our Lord one thousand eight hundred and one.

It may be seen that this contractual agreement obligated the apprentice to perform a sizeable set of essential tasks and to refrain from engaging in a whole set of non-essential activities, many of which were off-the-job doings that one would have had to classify as part of his private life. His entire social and economic life was thus proscribed, so that he would have had scarcely any time or inclination to go about the business of committing matrimony, apparently a sort of misdemeanor in those days—for apprentice pilots, at any rate. It probably was placed in the same category with drinking, gambling, carousing, and being absent without permission.

It was a hard life all around and not very appealing to young men in quest of a career; and conditions have not changed very much down through the years, except that many of the socially restricting regulations have been abolished, to the extent that apprentices nowadays may and do commit matrimony, right out in the open, without fear of being censured for it. It seems that the rigid restrictions were deemed necessary at the time because it was honestly believed that no activity that diverted the attention of the apprentice from the full employment of his faculties in learning the serious business of piloting was to be sanctioned or tolerated.

The obligations of the master, as the wording of the agreement indicate, were only two in number: to help the apprentice to learn the profession of piloting by instructing or teaching him, and to pay him the wages due.

Thirty-Five

The Measure of Compensation

Pilots make good money. Most of them earn from $15,000 to $25,000 per year. These monies do not come from earned salaries or wages. They come, rather, from shared profits. The pilotage fees, paid by the ship owners or charterers, are collected by the individual port pilots' associations and deposited in their individual treasuries, out of which all the expenses of the association are paid, prior to the residue being divided up among the members. These expenses are those involved in the upkeep and operation of the pilot boats, the offices, the communications systems, et cetera.

This division of the profits is not an equal, share-and share-alike division, though it is an equitable one. In accordance with the favored guild principle, the concept upon which the port pilots' associations exist and operate, the net incomes or shares of the various pilot-members are determined by a number of factors specified in the by-laws of each group. These determinations would take into consideration such things as: the grade or class of license held, the total number of vessels piloted by each, the number of days worked by each, and the extent of special services rendered.

A big and enduring expense to be deducted before any sharing takes place is that incurred by the wage and subsistence needs of the pilot boat crews and the apprentices. Another expense item is the specified percentage of the pilotage fees that must be paid to the government's local pilotage authority to help maintain this supervisory body—and this facet of the profession is worthy of special note. It would be difficult, if not impossible, to point out or even trace down any other American quasi public utility or public service in which the workers themselves contribute a part of their earnings to help pay for the maintenance and operation of the government authority regulating them.

Pilotage costs are borne entirely by those who utilize the service—the commercial and transportation interests, the ship owners and charterers, the general public—and not by federal, state, and local governments. Fees are based on a vessel's draft or depth in the water—so much for each foot of draft. At one time in the recent past, the going rate at the larger ports was six dollars a foot, This meant that a ship that drew 30 feet paid $180 to be piloted in or out of the harbor.

This established measure of compensation is a heritage of the profession that has been handed down from the sea laws and ordinances of ancient and medieval times. In the *Sea Laws for France*, established by King Louis XIV in 1681, there is for instance this ArticleXI, reading as follows:

> The Master of the Ship shall be oblig'd, as soon as the Pilot gets aboard, to tell him how much his Vessels draws, under Pain of five and twenty Livres Fine, to the Benefit of the Pilot, for every Foot concealed.

It was only natural and eminently appropriate that a vessel's depth in the water should have become the measure of compensation. It must be obvious that the deeper the draft of a vessel, the great her "tons burden" or registered tonnage and over-all size, and the greater the difficulty in guiding her through the hazardous waters at harbor entrances and the more demands made upon a pilot's skill, ingenuity, and stamina. A positive knowledge of a vessel's size and draft, coupled with a familiarity of the varying water depths, the obstructions, the prevailing currents and winds, and the peculiar characteristics of channels and harbor floors is the prime essential of safe, efficient piloting.

This method of assessing charges for a pilot's services has served adequately down through the years, and the process has been modified only sparingly from time to time. The modifications did not alter or curtail the method. Rather, they expanded it and added to the amounts of the pilotage fees by providing for additional, incidental charges. For example, pilotage fees at some ports are based on the draft *and* the registered tonnage of each vessel, a combination method. In other ports, this combination method is similarly in use, except that it is not applicable to vessels of a size under a set minimum tonnage. Also, at most ports, additional charges are made for the performance of extra man-hours of work and additional services such as swinging ship to calibrate compass or direction-finder, standing by with a pilot boat for an inordinate period of time, being detained in quarantine for an unusually long period, being carried far out to sea against one's wishes, conducting ships from one berth to another within a harbor, and other activities not directly concerned with bringing a ship in or out of a port. At no time, however, is there any departure from the basic so-much-a-foot-of-draft principle. The extra charges merely supplement it.

Pilotage rates in general are set by statute in the various states. In some cases, the actual establishment is done by the state's Board of Pilot Commissioners, while in others the individual "Port Authority" will perform this function. In rare instances, rates are set by the judges of the superior courts at the ports. In some states, also, different rates are charged for different sections of rivers, bays, and estuaries, and the rate varies mainly with the separate distances involved, a situation resulting from conditions at ports where the service requires extended trips up and down long, winding rivers or across wide bays, sounds, and lagoons. Chesapeake Bay, New Orleans, and Tampa, Florida (where the pilotage run from the Tampa waterfront to the safe deep water of the Gulf of Mexico is 40 miles one-way) are cases in point.

It will be seen then that, because local conditions vary so diffusely, pilotage needs are of different dimensions everywhere on our seacoasts and, because of the complexity, no uniform practice regarding fees and other matters can be applied nationwide or even state-wide. Since nature, in forming our continents and seacoasts eons ago, paid no attention to uniformity or consistency of design, no two seaports are alike, neither in the topography of their harbor entrance bottoms nor the depths, widths, and windings of their navigable channels; and the sandbars, reefs, ridges, shoals, and deeps of a given port's close approaches are distinctly peculiar to it.

Local pilots, trained and experienced locally, are the only persons who can be trusted to have a full and up-to-date knowledge of such conditions, and their perception and comprehension are kept attuned to the conditions at all times. That is the essence of proficiency in the art and science of pilotage and the main reason for the survival and longevity of that special element of local autonomy still existent in the organize port groups. Without that local autonomy, it would be extremely difficult to adjust local pilotage activities to meet local transportation needs, at the Port of New York or anywhere else. That local autonomy principle and the state pilotage system as a whole have stood the test of time in serving the needs of commerce and the general public.

Thirty-Six

Back to Boston

We have seen how accredited pilots were on the scene at the Port of Boston as early as 1633 and how a good deal of the later pilotage activity in Boston Bay centered around the famous old Boston Light, first lit in 1716, with the first lighthouse keeper also acting as a pilot collecting fees from ships that he guided in and out of the port.

In 1742, an association of sea captains was formed there. It was named *The Fellowship Club*, and it was a guild in actuality. It became the progenitor of later organizations that developed into the Massachusetts state pilotage system, in which voluntary associations of private citizens worked together with government to mold a stable, reliable pilotage program under government sponsorship. Its name later was changed to *The Marine Society*, and it was chartered as such by King George II of England in 1754.

Its purpose was to add to the store of knowledge concerning the coastline and the bay bottoms by various sounding and charting operations and to assist in the disemination of that knowledge, all in the interest of safer ship handling alongshore. There also were some social and welfare benefits for the members. At one time it controlled all the pilotage operations in Boston Harbor, and from 1783 to 1836, its trustees acted as a board of pilot commissioners for the port, with the authority to examine and license prosepctive new pilots. In 1809 its name was changed again. It became the *Boston Marine Society*, and it became a corporation at that time. A regular pilots' association of the modern style evolved from it years later.

Here was a good example of that previously-mentioned, fruitful evolutionary process — from old-time guild to modern-day pilots' association — in which governmental authority at first tapped the resources of a private institution (not yet a pilots' association as we now know them) to begin bringing about an efficient ship guiding system in the interest of the public good. Thereafter and thus, private enterprise and government worked together to bring this about. It was inevitable that a prototype pilots' association should emerge from this set of circumstances.

In general, the initiative for forming these pilot groups came from the pilots, but they were supported wholeheartedly by the commercial and shipping interests *and* the government. A report on pilotage by the U.S. Department of Commerce, issued many years ago, substantiates this. It reads, in part, as follows:

> From the evidence at hand, it would appear that the shipping interests as well as the insurance and commercial interests of the ports encouraged the pilots in the formation of these associations. The advantages of a well-organized pilotage system were as apparent to these interests as to the pilots themselves, for the commerce of the ports was not only facilitated and expedited but made much safer by reason of the better organization resulting from the elimination of competition.
>
> Since associations have been formed along the present lines, pilotage grounds have been established, usually at the bar. These grounds are well known to mariners, who may safely count on finding there at practically all times and in all conditions of weather a pilot boat with a sufficient number of pilots aboard to accommodate any reasonable number of vessels that may come. There is little chance nowadays that a vessel will fail to find a pilot when needed.
>
> Instead of six or eight pilots owning a small pilot boat, the whole body of pilots of a port will own one or two large boats, generally steamers specially constructed to withstand unusual stresses of wind and weather.
>
> Still another advantage of the present organization of pilotage systems is that it permits the maintenance of a central office which is in constant touch with the pilot boats and arranges for the rotation of pilots. The association generally employs an agent to look after the routine business of the office.

Thus, it will be seen, the birth and development of the modern pilotage system with its self-governing pilots' associations came not only from the port pilot groups themselves but also from the industry they served. Its success over the years can be attributed a common interest in its development and a conglomerate awareness of the essentiality of these well-organized pilot groups. Shipping companies, marine insurance companies, exporting and importing merchants, government agencies, and other groups interested in ocean commerce were in favor of its development.

All of this should be borne in mind when certain random references to pilots' associations are found to be of a derogatory nature.

There seems to be a continued widespread tendency to regard them as super-exclusive locals of a powerful labor union, existing only to maintain a job monopoly and put out propaganda conducive to the retention of special privileges for them. It is of course well known and indisputable that these local port groups are indeed very exclusive—for very good reasons.

Pilots have long hours and irregular working periods. They are forced to spend much of their time between individual piloting assignments away from their homes, on pilot boats on station offshore and in association-owned houses and shelters on land, in the company of their fellow pilots. It is small wonder then that they tend to make their associations exclusive and in general rather "choosy." They cannot be blamed for desiring that *all* of their fellow pilots measure up to certain standards, of decency, congeniality, compatibility, and competence. The most important of these is competence. You have to "know your stuff" if you want to belong. The maintenance of a monopoly and the retention of special privileges must not be regarded as the prime motivating factors behind this exclusiveness aspect.

Thirty-Seven

The Boston Marine Society

No chronicles of pilotage, at the Port of Boston or in the nation at large, would be complete or comprehensive without studied references to this maritime organization and its manifold activities on behalf of safe ship handling in the approaches to the port.

At first it was a voluntary association of sea captains, named *The Fellowship Club*, organized in 1742, and a form of guild, as previously stated, dedicated to fostering social and welfare benefits for its members and to the gathering and dissemination of nautical knowledge and know-how. Twelve years later, its name was changed to *The Marine Society*. It had evolved by then into an embryo pilots' association. Its charter stated that its principal purposes were:

> To improve the knowledge of this coast by its several members upon their arrival from sea, communicating their observations inwards and outwards, of the variations of the needle, the soundings, courses, and distances, and all other remarkable things about it in writing, to be lodged with the Society for the making of the navigation more safe; and also to relieve one another and their families in poverty and other adverse accidents in life.

A little over 50 years later, in 1809, its name again was changed—to its present name, *Boston Marine Society*—by an act of the General Court of the Commonwealth of Massachusetts.

Membership in the original *Fellowship Club* at first had been restricted, according to its "Rules and Orders," to "such persons only who are now, or have been, Commanders of Vessels." Monthly meetings were held in certain pubs and taverns around Boston. The records show that some of these meeting places were taverns known as *The Sun*, *The Crown*, and *The Bunch of Grapes* as well as the *British*, the *American*, and the *Exchange* coffee houses. *The Bunch of Grapes* was located at the corner of King Street and Mackerel Lane, now the corner of State Street and Kilby Street, where a bank building now stands.

In due course, however, notably after that first change in the name of the association, shipping company executives and reputable persons especially interested in maritime affairs were admitted to membership, swelling the ranks and increasing the power and prestige of the society. Of the many influential persons admitted to it in those very early days, the most notable perhaps was John Adams, who later became the second president of the United States. His great and unflagging interest in the development of a strong Navy for our new nation was the basis for his eligibility. Another President who became a member was Franklin Delano Roosevelt, who was admitted in 1933 on the basis of his long experience in sailing. Many prominent New England personages—merchants, bankers, lawyers, public officials, sportsmen—were elected to honorary membership in the society.

In 1836, the Trustees of the Society, who had been acting as a board of pilot commissioners for over 50 years without compensation and at the Society's expense, asked to be relieved of this duty. In response, the Massachusetts legislature enacted a law making the Trustees a third party sitting with two appointed pilot commissioners to form a board for the control and regulation of pilotage at the Port of Boston. This arrangement lasted for nearly twenty years.

In 1855, the Society, once again desiring to be relieved of the burden and responsibility of any regulatory control of pilotage, abdicated its official position. Total control then was placed in the hands of the governor and the Council. After a seven year trial, this arrangement was found to be unsatisfactory. In 1862, at the collective behest of merchants, underwriters, ship owners, ship masters, and pilots, supervision of pilotage was put back into the hands of the Trustees of the Society, where it has remained ever since.

At the present time, the two pilot commissioners for the Port of Boston are *nominated* by the Trustees of the Society and then *appointed* by the Governor and the Council. This arrangement was made for the appointment of well-qualified mariners as pilot commissioners—men who have been pilots and/or ship masters using the services of pilots in ports all over the world. Another favorable result of this plan has been the creation of a solid core of pilots considered to be one of the finest and most efficient in the entire world.

No history of the Society or its predecessor organization, *The Fellowship Club*, would be complete without a report on "the Box." "*The Box*," a brass-bound, wood-and leather chest still in existence after more than 200 years of elapsed time since it first was put into service, is a cherished memento of the Society's beginnings and its early endeavors for the good and welfare of the mariner fraternity in general. Also, it has a kind of historical significance for all of us, seafarers or landlubbers. The next few paragraphs will tend to affirm this.

A particular rule of the original *Rules and Orders*, upon which the present by-laws of the Society are based, made certain provisions, as follows:

> Such Member or Members as shall go a Voyage to sea and shall Return Successful, without being Cast-away, taken by the Enemy, or meeting with any other Misfortune shall pay Six Pence Sterling into the Box for the use of the Society for each and every Month he shall have been absent.

The rule went on to state that if, on the other hand, such member or members did suffer any of the terrible misfortunes mentioned, he would be excused from paying the sixpence per month assessment and, in addition, he would be eligible to receive financial help from the box "according to the Nature of his Misfortune and the Ability of the Box."

Those end-of-the-voyage payments were dutifully dropped into the chest, forever referred to as "the Box" and still preserved to this day. Many an unfortunate ship master received a worthwhile financial lift from the fund in the box.

It might appear to some of us in these times that this beneficent arrangement could have been in truth a social security program strikingly similar to our present-day social security and unemployment insurance programs. It could have been the genesis and origin of the marine insurance business in America as well.

Year after year, down to the present day, the Society has been ever watchful over the welfare of the Port of Boston and its maritime facilities; and "the making of the navigation more safe" in Boston Bay and Massachusetts Bay has continued to be the Society's main objective. At the end of the Revolutionary War, during which, Boston Light, the first lighthouse erected in America, had been destroyed, the Society crusaded perseveringly for the building of a new one and for "the establishment of a regular, skillful System of Pilotage" for the port. As a result of this and other crusading by other interested parties, the light was re-built and restored to service late in 1783, with an accredited Port of Boston pilot, Thomas Knox, as keeper.

When George Washington visited Boston in October of 1789, during his first year as the first president of the new nation, there was a grand parade in his honor, and the Marine Society had a prominent part in this ceremony. In the official line of march or "Order of the Procession," as it was called, the Society's contingent was given a place of honor well up front. They carried "a banner with a strange device"—well, not really. It was an out-size oil painting, done on cloth, a seascape of the bay showing the lighthouse, an incoming ship, and a pilot boat heading toward the ship. A hand-lettered inscription on the banner read: "*A Ship passing the Lighthouse and a Boat going to her*."

According to selected printed items of the times, the Society also had a part in the preliminary arrangements for the big event. One newspaper announcement stated that all masters of vessels within the "Town of Boston" were invited:

> To meet at the *Bunch of Grapes* tavern on the morning of the arrival of the Presdient, there to form and fall into the procession immediately after the Marine Society, agreeable to the Request of the Town.

An item in the printed bulletin of instructions for participants in the parade went thusly:

> The Marine Society is desired to appoint some person to arrange and accompany the seamen.

This appointment was made, and this follow-up newspaper *Notice* appeared:

> The mates and seamen are desired to assemble on board the *Massachusetts Indiaman* at the Governor's Wharf; there the Captains Job Prince and Allen Hallet will attend to arrange them, agreeable to a vote of the Marine Society.

Bostonians, New Englanders, and perhaps all Americans owe a debt of gratitude to the Boston Marine Society. To this day, it continues with its work for its prime objectives: the best, most, and safest possible ship movements for the Port of Boston, and the most beneficent services affordable for deserving members of the mariner fraternity.

Thirty-Eight

A Long Line of Schooners

> Our ingenious friends, the Americans, have contrived a set of pilot boats which are the delight of every sailor.... They are truly 'water witches,' for while they look so delicate and fragile that one feels at first as if the most moderate breeze must brush them from the face of the ocean and scatter to the winds all of their gay drapery, they can and do defy, as a matter of habit and choice, the most furious gales with which the rugged seaboard of America is visited in February and March.

Who said that? Which Americans and what pilot boats?

That little eulogy came from an Englishman, an officer in the Royal Navy, in tribute to the Port of Boston pilot boats, which had evoked his admiration by reason of their symmetrical shapes, their weatherliness, their maneuverability, and their ruggedness. The quotation is from "King's Handbook of Boston Harbor," published in 1889 by M.F. Sweetser, and the lavish praise is of course for the pilot boats of those times and earlier.

These were schooners almost entirely, sailing ships exclusively, with no auxiliary power of any kind. As for their sizes, this will have to be given as it was given in those times and for many years prior to that time, merely by stating their tonnage or "tons burden." It had not become the custom as yet to describe a vessel by giving the measurements of her length, beam, draft, masts, and sail areas, including her length at the water line (l.w.l.) and her length over all (l.o.a.), et cetera. A knowledge of the tonnage was supposed to give, and did give, to persons with maritime know-how a good idea of the size of a vessel.

As a matter of historic fact, the measurement word *ton* itself derives from this practice, as it existed in medieval times. A *tun* was a huge wooden wine barrel of standard size and shape. When full of wine, it weighed about 2000 pounds. The size of a ship was made known, colloquially and otherwise, by stating what was known as her "tuns burden," that is to say, the number of these full tuns of wine that could be carried in her cargo holds. What could be more facile and natural!

These schooners averaged from 50 to 80 tons in size, though some were smaller and a few were larger. This tonnage rating very probably did not refer to their *cargo* tonnage, as it did in earlier times. By that time, most ships, especially naval vessels, were rated by their *displacement* tonnage, the actual weight of the water they displaced. Also, there was *registered* tonnage, an arbitrary and confusing cubic foot measurement. Having a good idea of any one of these tonnages, however, one is able to make an educated guess which tells one that these pilot boats averaged 70 to 100 feet at the water line. A detailed report of each of them and their exploits, from the 1830s to the 1900s, would make an interesting but rather long story, long enough to make a complete, separate book.

Another published "eulogy" is indicated here. This one appeared in a magazine, "Ballou's Pictorial," in 1889, as follows:

> These boats are well built, of exquisite model, and crack sailors; and they are manned by as fine a set of men as ever trod a deck or handled a sheet. They ride the waves like sea ducks and, with their hardy crews, are constantly exposed to the roughest weather...are the trimmest craft in our waters, and they are handled with a dexterity which only long professional experience can give. They are decked over, and in a heavy seaway their decks are constantly wet. In good hands, they are perfect lifeboats and are capable of making a voyage around the world. The skill of the best builders has been taxed to render them perfect in every respect.

This paean of praise was part of the text written around a woodcut marine illustration showing five of the six pilot boats which comprised the fleet operating at the Port of Boston at the time. These vessels, all schooners of fair size, were the *Syren* 1, the *Coquette* 2, the *Friend* 3, the *Bouquet* 4, the *Phantom* 5, and the *William Starkey* 6. The *Bouquet* was missing from the picture. It is noteworthy that all of these boats had been given a number along with its name and that the numbers were displayed prominently on one or another of each vessel's sails, for quick and positive identification undoubtedly. This was another custom peculiar to the Port of Boston.

It is worthy of note also that these Boston pilot boats on station during that era carried their own particular pilot flag, the signal flag that announced the boat's identity to incoming ships and offered them the services of a pilot. This was a blue-and-white flag, one-half blue and the other half white, displayed with the white half next to the mast or stay on which it was set flying.

The predominance of schooners in the pilotage service at Boston has continued down to the present day, though latterly of course they have been sailing vessels equipped with engine-driven propellers at their sterns, with neither method of propulsion being basically auxiliary to or dependent on the other. At the present time—or perhaps it would be better to say until very recently—there were only two pilot boats in service at Boston, and both of them were auxiliary schooners, so-called. They were the *Pilot* 1 and the *Roseway* 2.

The *Pilot* was a twin-screw, spoon-bowed schooner equipped with twin diesel engines of 165 horsepower each. She measured 98 feet at the waterline and 121 feet over all. She had a beam of 25 feet and a draft of 14 feet 5 inches. She had been designed, especially for the pilotage service, by a famous Massachusetts yacht designer, W. Sterling Burgess, son of a famous naval architect, Edward Burgess, and she was built in 1924 at the J.F. James shipyard at Essex, Massachusetts.

The *Roseway*, a clipper-bowed schooner equipped with the same twin diesels was built in 1926 at the same J.F. James shipyard. She was built stoutly, of oak mostly, and was capable of withstanding the ruinous onslaughts of heavy seas and obstreperous storms. She measured 94 feet at the waterline and 100 feet over all. She had a 25-foot beam and a 13-foot draft. She was *not* built especially for the pilotage service, but she found her way into it at the age of 15 years in 1941, when she was purchased as a replacement for the *Northern Light*, which had been taken over by the government for special service in World War II. The *Northern Light* was a superbly-designed, rugged schooner, modeled and named after another *Northern Light* of 100 years earlier in the history of the Port of Boston.

Both the *Roseway* and the *Pilot* were "decorated" for meritorious service in World War II by the U.S. Coast Guard. Each vessel proudly carries a bronze plaque engraved in this manner:

In Recognition of
The Valuable Service
Performed by
Roseway
During World War II
U.S. Coast Guard

During the war, the *Pilot* was the CG811, and the *Roseway* was the CG812. The Boston pilots regularly attached to them had a rough time of it, since now, like so many other pilots throughout the coastal states, they had to carry a double load. In addition to coping with abominable weather conditions, rough seas, and others of nature's constant hazards existing in wartime as well as in peacetime, they also had to deal with complicated mine fields, anti-submarine nets with narrow openings, and an exasperating absence of lighted marker buoys and beacons. They acquitted themselves nobly, however, and not one of the many hundreds of ships, loaded with troops and war equipment, that entered and left the Port of Boston was delayed because of the unavailability or ineptness of a pilot.

During World War I also, the pilots of Boston volunteered their services in the nation's defense, and these services were speedily accepted by a grateful government, though the pilots were not actually taken into any branch of the armed forces. Nevertheless, they really "went to war," in a body, under the jurisdiction of the U.S. Navy. The station pilot boats were equipped with guns and searchlights and had regular navy men on board as additional crew members. The boats were kept on patrol far outside the port, and all vessels approaching the entrance channels were required to report to them and give the password before being allowed to enter. If a vessel failed to stop and report, a shot was fired across her bow to bring her to attention. Many coastwise vessels, especially commercial fishing boats, were boarded and searched—for unusually large supplies of such things as fuel, food, fresh water, *to be delivered to enemy submarines for a price*.

Pilot boats #2 and #3, the *Louise* and the *Liberty*, under the command of U.S. Navy Ensigns, rendered distinguished service throughout the duration of the war. Each was given a commendation and a commemorative bronze plaque. These plaques are now in the headquarters of the Pilots of Boston association as mementoes. All pilotage of U.S. Navy vessels during the war was performed free of charge, for which official appreciation was officially expressed.

During the Spanish-American War as well, the Boston pilots volunteered their services to the nation and served it well and faithfully.

As for the War of 1812, a history book published in 1889, "A History of American Privateers" by Edgar S. Maclay, tells us that, during this war, pilot boats were among the first privateers to go to sea "to burn, sink, and destroy" vessels of the enemy. They carried crews of 50 to 60 men and were armed to the teeth, many of them mounting the famous "Long Tom" cannon amidships and carrying ample supplies of other arms that included muskets, pistols, cutlasses, and boarding pikes, all of which were put to good use on more than one occasion. The Boston pilots and pilot boats of that time most certainly must have been in on this.

Immediately after war had been declared, a speedy American pilot boat ran the British blockade and hurried across the Atlantic to Gothenburg, Sweden, to spread the word and warn American merchant ships then in the ports of Sweden, Denmark, Holland, Germany, Russia, and other European countries, thus enabling them to take action to avoid being captured or destroyed. It was a Sandy Hook pilot boat. The course of American history might have been altered very drastically if that pilot boat had failed in her mission.

In July of 1918, when German submarines were creating havoc with shipping off Cape Cod and George's Bank, several fishing schooners were sunk in the latter area. A Boston pilot boat picked up a dory containing ten survivors from one of the sunken fishermen and landed them safely in Boston.

Thirty-Nine

The "Canoes" and the "Yawls"

There is good reason for the quotation marks in that chapter heading—to avert misunderstandings and arguments and to fend off confusion in the minds of some readers. In telling about the small boats used to ferry pilots back and forth between pilot boats on station and ships underway outside Boston Harbor, there must first be an explanation regarding the name by which they are called, and have been called for many years, a name peculiar to this port and its environs. They are called "yawls" almost universally.

At one time, about 75 years ago, they were called "canoes—even in official records and in the pilotage Rules and Regulations—but that appellation eventually faded out of the picture in favor of a mass disposition to call them "yawls." The custom became a tradition handed down to the present day.

They are small open "pulling boats," to use navy terminology, without engines and propellers or masts and sails. Many people bluntly call them "rowboats." Actually they are a form of dory similar to the codfishermen's dories sent out from mother ships far out at sea, though they are built somewhat stouter and heavier than those very seaworthy boats. They are 14-footers especially designed and constructed to withstand the rough treatment they must undergo day after day. A hidebound tradition, perhaps, coupled with a steadfast reliance on their indomitable seaworthiness in the hands of a couple of husky young boatmen, has kept them on the scene all these years (while other pilot groups have been using motorboats exclusively for this work) and has kept the name *yawl* for them.

For the average recreational boatman and professional deepwater sailorman, this definitely is a misnomer—a big mistake. To them, the label *yawl* means only one thing: a two masted sailing vessel, either deep-keel or shallow-draft-with centerboard, with fore-and-aft sails including one or more triangular headsails commonly called "jibs," with its mainmast stepped further forward than a sloop's mast, and with its jigger or mizzenmast stepped far aft, usually abaft the rudder post in fact. They know that it is this rig that makes it a yawl and not the shape of its hull, its underway characteristics, or the kind of work or service it performs. To them, a yawl is nothing else and nothing else properly may be called a "yawl."

This conviction is not entirely valid, however, and there *is* something else that *may* be and *is* being called a "yawl"—properly—in these very times. For a hundred years and longer, the accredited pilots of the Port of Boston have been using this small open boat without power or sail as their "ship's boat" for carrying pilots to and fro between ships underway and the pilot boats on station far outside the harbor, and these little boats have been called "yawls", consistently and without abashment, for the past 75 years approximately. In prior times, they were called "canoes," an appellation probably picked up from the American Indians.

As in the case of the nautical term *sloop*, there was a time long ago when the name *yawl* did *not* designate a particular type of sailing rig, and like *sloop*, *yawl* derives from a Dutch word bandied about in the mariner fraternity of middle Europe at the time. The word is *jol*, pronounced "yawl," and it designated a type of small "ship's boat" then in use for ferrying men and materials between ship and shore and from ship to ship, according to lexicographers in general, and this boat is matched or paired with the so-called "jolly-boat" by them. The German version of the Dutch word *jol* is *jolle*, from which we certainly must have got *jolly-boat*, also defined in dictionaries—like *yawl*—as "a small ship's boat."

It takes no great stretch of the imagination to reach the valid conclusion that *yawl* was the old-time English seaman's phonetic rendtion of *jol*, just as in the case of the Dutch word *jagt*, pronounced "yacht" and meaning "chase" or "hunt," rendered into the familiar English word *yacht*. Also, it is easy to see that the yawl and the jolly-boat most certainly must have been one and the same.

At the present time, however, there seems to be no available documentation, neither in the great new all-inclusive dictionaries nor in the lore of the sea, as to where *jol* and *jolle* originally came from and why these names were given to that ship's boat. Even the eminent *Concise Oxford Dictionary*, in defining *yawl* and relating it etymologically to *jol* and *jolle*, sees fit to append the notation "origin unknown" to its mention of this relationship.

It would appear then that, technically or theoretically, since the appellation *yawl* long ago originally and continuously denoted a small ship's boat without power or sail, there is no need for explanations or quotation marks in spoken or written references to these yawls of the

Boston pilotage fraternity, but both undoubtedly will continue to abound, as in the past, to avert misunderstandings in the minds of outsiders. By "outsiders" is meant all "non-Bostonians" unacquainted with the manners and customs of this confraternity.

For some of those outsiders, who might very well be insiders, as far as an acquaintance with boats and ships and the sea is concerned, the misunderstandings will continue to exist, and those outsiders will continue to wonder out loud why in the name of good common sense these boats are not called by some such name as *skiff*, *dinghy*, *dory*, *punt*, *wherry*, or *jolly-boat*, all more indicative (to those outsiders) of their type and size and function than is *yawl*.

When an inbound ship reaches the pilotage grounds outside the Port of Boston and requests a pilot, the pilot boat's yawl, usually towed astern in a leisurely patrolling/drifting maneuver, is drawn up to the pilot boat and boarded by the assigned pilot and two apprentices who have acquired the rating of *boatkeeper* and have become skilled in handling the oars and maneuvering the yawl in all kinds of conditions.

The tow line is payed out again and the "three men in a boat" are towed astern as the pilot boat now heads toward the ship. They generally maneuver to leeward of the ship, and they generally find a Jacob's ladder already in place, hanging down from the deck on that side. When they get fairly close to the ship, the yawl is cast off and rowed to the Jacob's ladder, which the pilot must grab hold of and mount, often with considerable difficulty occasioned by much swing and sway and rock and roll on the part of the ship. In the meantime, the pilot boat has moved on out away from the ship, with the crew keeping an eye on the climbing pilot and the moving yawl. It finally maneuvers to pick up the yawl and take it in tow again, after its two passengers have come back aboard.

This procedure is gone through in all kinds of weather and at all hours of the day or night, without remission and without regard to fatigue or sleep factors that might enter in, and the Boston pilots have received many fine letters of commendation from grateful ship masters and shipping companies for their unswerving devotion to duty in the face of great and unusual dangers. Climbing a Jacob's ladder in a howling gale or when it is completely iced over in sub-zero weather is exemplary of those dangers.

In a 91-page brochure, "*Pilots and Pilot Boats of Boston Harbor*," written by Ralph M. Eastman, and published and distributed by the *Second Bank-State Street Trust Company* of Boston, one such letter is reproduced with some accuracy therein, and it deals with those very conditions mentioned. Much of the information contained in these pages has been obtained from this little booklet, and grateful acknowledgment is hereby expressed. The letter follows:

United States Lines
Pier 60, North River, New York, N.Y.

SS American Scout
Boston, Massachusetts

November 6, 1965

Boston Pilots
69 Long Wharf
Boston, Mass.

Gentlemen:

Our ship, "American Scout," United States Lines, took pilot off the Boston Lightship early in the morning of Saturday, November 5th. Weather was foul, a northeast gale was blowing, and a heavy sea was running. Three ships embarked pilots before us and all hands had a lively time, in fact it was a glowing hour for all concerned.

I shall not discuss the merits or the drawbacks of your facilities as opposed to, say, a powered launch. Rather than criticize, I wish to express my admiration and wonder at what I saw that morning.

The schooner was handled with nerve and skill, and the people in the dinghy elicited our admiration. You all gave yourselves to the job in hand, fired with the traditional pride that "the station must be manned." You did this knowing that at any moment your wives could be widowed.

I was grateful to see big Captain Eddy "hit that ladder," When he jumped for it and, blinking, hung on for a few seconds, he was "there." I had no worries after that.

Thank you for such devotion to duty. I am proud to know you all.

Sincerely and with
Best Wishes

(signed)

Archie Horka, Master
American Scout

The "big Captain Eddy" mentioned was Burton H. Eddy, who truly *was* a big man physically. At the time of this incident, he had been a commissioned pilot for more than 20 years.

Just about one year earlier, another such letter had been received at Boston. It came from the owners of the *SS Sagoland*, of the Swedish Orient Line, and it commended pilot James E. Frye very highly for his outstandingly fine performance in handling that ship in Boston Harbor, on August 31, 1954, at the height of hurricane Carol's onslaught against the Massachusetts coast. The ship's anchors would not hold, and pilot Frye had to jockey her about in a very confining area for over 3½ hours while the hurricane winds buffeted her, for there was absolutely no hope of being able to dock her during that blow. To quote Captain Rolfe Bauer, her master:

> It was only by the expert seamanship and skillful ship handling under extreme conditions, with heavy rain, low visibility, and wind gusts of 110 knots, that Captain Eddy kept the ship from being blown ashore.

When the hurricane winds finally abated, she was brought safely into her dockside berth.

In the annals of the Massachusetts state pilotage system, there are many more tales of heroism and hardiness and danger and damage, but space limitations will allow for only one more. Like so many other unusual happenings in the lively careers of the pilots of this area, this one involves severe cold, crippling ice, high winds, and shipwreck.

On February 2, 1859, the British schooner *Caroline of Dartmouth* was approaching the entrance to Boston Harbor when she struck on rocks and foundered. She was abandoned by her crew, but in accordance with the traditions of the sea, her captain chose to remain on board in the hope that eventually she might be saved. He was Captain James B. Apter of Brixham in Devon, England.

On the following morning, as the pilot boat *Friend* approached the shipwreck, Apter was discovered lashed to the side of the ship in immediate danger of dying from exposure to the elements. Captains James M. Dolliver and P.H. Chandler, the two pilots aboard the *Friend*, immediately embarked in the pilot boat's "canoe," as the yawls then were called, and managed to row through the choppy seas to the ship and Captain Apter, who was completely exhausted and nearly frozen to death by that time. They took him back to the *Friend*, where he soon got back on the road to recovery.

In Captain Apter's later report to local authorities, he gave the following graphic description of his predicament and his rescue:

> The efforts made for my salvation were of the most dangerous yet human nature, inasmuch as their course from the pilot boat to the vessel was in broken water nearly all the way ... and when I was lashed to the weather side of the vessel ... seeing them manage their little boat with such skill as every seaman must admire ... I was expecting every sea would fill their boat and dash them against the rocks ... and was very much concerned for their safety, as they afterwards told me they were for mine ... expecting I should be frozen to death, I being in that situation twenty-one hours ... when I was taken from the wreck.

For their gallantry and compassion, the British government awarded each of the pilots a gold medal bearing a likeness of Queen Victoria. Medals also were awarded to Judge Thomas Russell and his wife, both of whom had been aboard the *Friend* at the time, and to quote from official correspondence:

> ...not only gave striking proof of their courage and humanity by going in the pilot boat but also, by their encouragement and sympathy, afforded material aid to the pilots in the performance of their dangerous and gallant service.

Both pilots also were presented with silver medals by the Humane Society of Massachusetts for their bravery and persistence in saving Captain Apter's life.

The expression "crippling ice," as used just previously, may require some explication for some readers. Very often in the dead of winter in New England, crews of pilot boats, on station offshore or tied up at the dock in port, might go on deck some morning and find ropes and sheaves frozen in blocks, sails and halyards frozen to masts, anchors, chains, and coils of rope buried under mounds of solid ice, and yawls—bottoms up—frozen to the deck, solidly and immovably. Also, the water of the bays might be frozen over solidly, as has happened many times in the past.

In the famous "big freeze of Boston Harbor" in 1844, the great British liner, *Britannia*, was frozen in—imprisoned! Ice-breakers were called into service to set her free and cut a channel through the ice to the open sea. The task of laying out the correct course for the ice-breakers to follow fell to a Boston pilot, Captain William Carleton Fowler. He also *piloted* the *Britannia* on her way out. The entire action was considered to be a Herculean task, for which Fowler was given due credit, publicly and privately.

Forty

A Pilotage Headquarters

> The pilots of Boston shall keep an office in a central location on or near the waterfront, where all communications may be left for them and it shall be the duty of the pilots, when in Boston, to call at said office twice a day at least.

That was one of the "Rules and Regulations" established long ago by the pilot commissioners of the Port of Boston, and there is good reason to believe that a similar or identical rule has been embodied in the pilotage regulations of every major seaport in the world. This concept of maintaining a readily-accessible pilot headquarters or central office always has been considered to be an essential one never to be overlooked—for good reasons of course.

There must be a known, fixed place to which to send important communications regarding ship movements, particularly departures of outward-bound ships. There must be a definite, known place where pilots on shore will congregate, be a sort of labor pool, and be instantly available as needed. In the expansive, crowded, and complex maze of dockside moorings and harbor anchorages of the average port, the use of signal flags and signal lights to request a pilot is unworkable and out of the question. There must be a definite known place where pilots on shore may check on their placement in the rotation system and on upcoming assignments.

There must be a definite known place to which pilot boats on station *offshore* may *communicate* in an emergency, such as the imminent possibility of their being "manned out." Being "manned out" is a condition wherein a pilot boat on station, due to a heavy press of incoming traffic, has no more pilots left on board to accommodate any more incoming ships. This condition existed fairly often in bygone days—before the advent of wireless telegraphy, radio, and the two-way radio-telephone device; and in each case, it was possible for the condition to last for quite a long time before replacements came, because of the inadequacy of communications between ship and shore.

There is very little chance of this kind of thing happening nowadays however, since the central offices usually are in constant communication with the pilot boats by radio-telephone. They usually know when the supply of pilots offshore has become too low, and they are able to take immediate remedial steps, even to the extent of sending several pilots out to the pilotage grounds in a fast motorboat. Consequently, pilot groups at most major American ports can continue to make their continuing boast that no inbound ship arriving at their pilotage grounds ever fails to find an able, experienced, accredited pilot waiting to conduct them into a safe anchorage or mooring.

At Boston, and nearly everywhere on the New England coast for that matter, there are good reasons for this sort of constancy to exist. One of them is the "compulsory" factor. It is not only the *use* of the pilotage service that is compulsory. The duties of the pilots may be said to be compulsory as well. They are compelled to abide by certain relevant laws of the state and by the regulations of their association and the pilot commissioners.

Both sets of regulations place much emphasis on pilots being available day and night and in all kinds of weather, on their making their presence and availability known to incoming ships, and on their offering their services to any and all incoming ships without stint or discrimination. Even though a pilot boat, on station and displaying the required signals, is considered to be making an offer of pilotage service, it is up to the pilots to keep a sharp lookout for incoming ships and to expedite the transfer of a pilot if one is requested. Severe penalties, sometimes in the form of suspension or revocation of a pilot's commission, are prescribed for infractions of these rules.

Another reason for the steadfast adherence to the alertness requirement, at Boston and elsewhere, is the matter of increased income accruing to pilots' association's treasuries and to pilots. It is a standard rule at most ports that vessels which decline the offer of guidance service from pilot boats on station and proceed into the harbor on their own are liable for one-half the amount of the regular pilotage fee, to be paid to the local pilots' association for deposit in its members' pool. It stands to reason then that those aboard the station pilot boats should feel obliged to be alert to any and all ship movements in the approaches to their harbors. Adherence to this practice results in an increase in annual income for all hands without any increase in the work load.

At Boston, there is still one more authority and set of rules to which pilots must pay heed, though not with much concern however. This is the Harbor Master, who is a member of the Boston Police Department, which has jurisdiction over the harbor waters. It has its own set of Harbor Regulations but none of these have anything to do with the activities of pilots. Rather they are concerned mostly with the anchorage of vessels in the harbor—"the parking problem," so to speak—and with the observance of the regulations by shipmasters and crews. The Harbor Master sees to it that every ship from overseas is supplied with a copy of these regulations.

This marine division of the police department, originally established in 1853, now has a staff of 45 men and officers and five motorboats ranging in size from 16 to 60 feet in length. It has jurisdiction over 50 square miles of water extending out offshore to the three-mile limit and 46 square miles of land, mostly islands. The harbor is patrolled day and night to see that the regulations are being obeyed and that no vessels are anchored or underway in an improper or dangerous manner, as well as to move against criminal activity of any kind whatsoever.

To keep "the parking problem" under control, the Harbor Master may direct that certain ships be moved, and whenever compliance is not forthcoming in due time, he may himself cause their removal by hired tugboats at the expense of the captain or owners, an action reminiscent of the towing away of illegally-parked automobiles by city police.

The headquarters of the *Boston Pilots* (the association's official name) is on the waterfront naturally, on a pier, which Bostonians call ' "wharf." Every pier in Boston is called a "wharf," even the undistinguished ones. The distinguished ones have been given names—like *Long Wharf*, *Lewis Wharf*, *Commercial Whart*, *Gallup's Island Wharf*, et cetera. The *most* distinguished one, with a long and impressive history, is *Long Wharf*, on which the headquarters is located.

It was built in 1710, forming a sort of extension of King Street (now State Street) and reaching some 2000 feet out into the bay. In those days, it was considered to be a marvelous piece of construction engineering. Because of its great length, it always had a strategic military importance, and a shore battery stood on its outer end for many years. In 1768, British warships landed troops on it. Down through the years, ships of all sizes, shapes, and nationalities have tied up to it to load and unload cargo and people, who often were people of great importance or people in uniform in great numbers. One of Paul Revere's better known engravings is a marine scene showing the *Long Wharf* in all its glory, with a fleet of British warships deployed nearby.

Another time of quite some historical significance concerning this wharf is the fact that its owners, a corporation with a very unusual name, is one of the oldest business corporations in America. It was chartered in 1772 as "The Proprietors of Boston Pier or the Long Wharf," and it has operated continuously, under that same name, down to the present day.

The present location of the pilots' headquarters is on the fourth floor of a building labeled 69 Long Wharf, a 125-year old granite-block structure with a history all its own. It was erected in 1845 for the U.S. Government, to be used as a bonded warehouse, and it is said to be the first granite-block building in Boston. From the windows of the offices, the pilots get an excellent view of the harbor and its traffic. They have been there for 45 years at this writing.

Before that, they had been domiciled temporarily in the Harbor Building (now the Sheraton Building) on Atlantic Avenue. This had been an emergency roosting, lasting about a year, which resulted from their having been ousted from their permanent quarters at 74 Long Wharf because of the demands for more space by the United Fruit Company, the most important tenant of the wharf. The pilots had been there for 17 years.

Prior to that, for a matter of just 30 days or so, they had occupied temporary quarters at 67 Commercial Wharf, due to still another emergency. This was a fire in the middle of the night that burned out their quarters on Lewis Wharf, where they had been located *for at least 45 years and probably longer*. The earliest available records show that they were there on October 2, 1880, and various recorded items give reason to believe that they were there long before that. The fire destroyed most of their records, leaving one more of those gaps, previously mentioned, in the history of pilotage.

From a newspaper story in the *Boston Sunday Post of April 17, 1904*, we get the following good description of this headquarters on Lewis Wharf, as it was before the turn of the century:

> There were two rooms — the smaller one for washing up, changing clothes, or taking a nap between calls, and a large one where the pilots on the "shore watch" gathered while waiting for notice to take a ship out of the harbor. In those days, most of the older pilots wore beards, so they made quite a picturesque group as they relaxed in their easy chairs. The walls of the room were covered with sea pictures, drawings of notable sea captains, and pictures of early pilot boats, while marine glasses, charts, and compasses filled the window sills and shelves.
>
> At that time there were 34 pilots, who were divided into two watches. 17 went down to the harbor each Monday morning to board the four pilot boats. One cruised off Highland Light, another off Cape Ann, while the other two patrolled around Boston Light and the lightship. The pilots were ashore one week and at sea the next. After they had brought in ships, those on duty in the Bay took the first available outgoing craft, to be picked up by the "canoe" from the pilot boat to which they were attached.

This 1904 issue of this illustrious newspaper was made available to the public 50 years later by a man, Mr. Charles I. Lampee of Winchester, Massachusetts, whose two grandfathers were Boston pilots.

The present pilotage central office also is decorated with many photographs and paintings of pilot boats, pilots and marine scenes, along with souvenirs and mementoes such as plaques awarded for war service, letters of commendation, and treasured navigational instruments and parts of ships. Most of these are of comparatively recent history.

The most outstanding feature of this headquarters is one corner of a room that could be comparable to what is called a "ready room" in the air force. In this corner there is a giant-sized blackboard, a bulletin board, a big electric clock, a desk, a telephone, and a rack displaying the last names of all the pilots, each on its own, individual, narrow white stick or plaque placed horizontally one above the other in slotted brackets on the rack. Half of the names are in a group at the top, and the other half are in a group at the bottom.

The group at the top are the pilots on the "shore watch" at the office, while the group at the bottom are the pilots whose base of operations is on board the pilot boats on station offshore. When the pilot at the top of the upper group takes a ship out, his name stick is put at the bottom of his group and moves upward with each succeeding ship departure until it reaches the top again, at which time he very probably will be ashore again awaiting his turn, having conducted an arriving ship into the harbor. The movements of the pilots in the lower group are kept track of in the same way.

When a pilot is "dropped" from an outward-bound ship, he is picked up by a "yawl" and taken to a station pilot boat, there to await his turn to be assigned to an incoming ship. Thus, the rotation system, an "endless chain" procedure, is kept working afloat and ashore.

The giant-sized blackboard is divided into two equal sections, each about 4 feet wide and 5 feet high. The left-hand section is used for chalked-up information on expected arrivals of ships, while the section on the right carries information on the impending departures of ships. In this right-hand section, there are three vertical columns, one for the listing of the names of ships scheduled for departure, a second, to the right of this, a column listing their various locations, given in symbols or abbreviations, and thirdly, a column to the far right with the listings of the times of departure of each of the ships.

It is interesting to note that, for some reason not immediately apparent, this last, right-hand column works from the bottom up—that is to say, with the days of the week following each other from bottom to top. It is worthy of note also that the numerous question marks usually found in this column indicate the existence of an ever-present uncertainty as to the actual hour of departure of each ship. This column often would look like this, and actually *did* look *exactly* like this on February 3, 1956, according to a photograph taken in the office on that date:

Mon. ?
Mon. ?
Mon. P.M. ?
Mon. A.M.
Mon. P.M.
Mon. A.M.

Sun. Midnight
Sun. Midnight
Sun. P.M.
Sun. A.M. or P.M.

Sat. P.M.
Sat. P.M.
Sat. Noon
Sat. Noon
Sat. A.M. ?
Sat. 8 P.M.

Fri. Midnight ?

There is also another blackboard which lists the names of ships on which no fixed dates have been set for their time of departures.

Nowdays, because of the prevalent use of the radio-telephone afloat and ashore, instant communication regarding arrivals and departures is maintained constantly, and through the use of this modern facility, the number of available pilots on board the station boats is known at all times, so that there is little chance of their every being "manned out" completely. Also, advance information regarding incoming ships is transmitted to pilotage headquarters (and to the pilot boats) long before the ships actually enter the approaches to the port entrance. This information is transmitted, also, from the pilotage headquarters to steamship companies and agents, terminal operators, freight brokers, and other interested parties.

In the old days, at the Port of Boston, before there was any radio, or radio-telephone, or electric telegraph, news of the approach of incoming ships was transmitted from hilltop to hilltop by "visual telegraph," a system of signals. This accounts for the many "telegraph hills" along the Massachusetts coast from Martha's Vineyard to Boston. At one time, there were thirteen of these signal stations between West Chop, on the northernmost tip of Martha's Vineyard, where a lighthouse is located, and Dorchester Heights, close in to metropolitan

Boston. One of them is called just that—"Telegraph Hill." The others are: *Great Hill*, *Squirrel Hill*, *Baker Hill*, *Planters Hill*, *Hoop Pole HIll*, *Scituate Hill*, *Mann Hill*, *Prospect Hill*, *Booth Hill*, *Pine Hill*, *Parker Hill*, and *Monterey Hill*.

Forty-One

Pilots and Pirates

That Boston pilots in the latter half of the Ninteenth Century, incredibly, often had to contend with bloodthirsty, plundering pirates at the risk of their lives and often losing their lives, is positive historical fact and not compounded fantasy. However, these encounters did not take place outside the Port of Boston or anywhere else in American waters. They took place in China.

The period was an exciting era of enterprise for Boston ships and American seafarers, and they were known and respected in all major world seaports, including Shanghai. Boston pilots and pilot boats were known there too. It is reported by a reliable source that, during one period, from 1867 to 1932, there were pilots of eleven different nationalities holding pilot licenses at this once-international port. Britishers predominated, with 82 commissioned men, while the Americans rated second, with 33. This is not to say that all of these 115 were there at any one given time but, rather, that they numbered that many throughout the 65-year period.

The "reliable authority" reporting this is a document, *The Log of the Shanghai Pilot Service, 1831–1932*, compiled by Pilot Captain George Phil Philip, who received his commission as a pilot there in 1918. It found its way into the hands of the author of that brochure, "Pilots and Pilot boats of Boston Harbor," through the courtesy of Captain Horace Allen Arnold, a licensed pilot of the Port of Shanghai for many years. He was driven out by Japanese bombing planes during World War II, and he returned to his home town, Amityville, on the south shore of Long Island, where he lived until his death in 1949. This record does not cover any of the period after 1932 because that was the year in which Captain Philip, its compiler, retired from the pilotage service.

Although there were not any famous or popular Boston pilots at Shanghai, there were familiar Boston names among the American names on the pilot roster there and at least three pilot boats that had

Boston backgrounds. These were the *Daniel Webster*, and *Syren*, and the *Golden Gate*, all two-masted schooners.

The *Daniel Webster* was built at Chelsea. Massachusetts in 1851. In 1853, she left Boston on a voyage that took her around Cape Horn and up the Pacific coasts to San Francisco. Then in 1865, she left San Francisco and sailed for Shanghai to become a member of the pilot-boat fleet there. She operated in the service there until 1892, when she was driven ashore in a storm with three pilots on board. All hands were rescued, but the ship was lost.

An interesting anecdote concerning the *Daniel Webster* deals with a happening in 1852, before she set sail for the Pacific. That was the year in which Daniel Webster himself passed away. The pilots attached to the ship wanted to attend his funeral, which was to take place at his home in the town of Marshfield, in Plymouth County, about 15 miles southeast of metropolitan Boston. They started down there on the day of the funeral, but they unfortunately ran into a flat clam off-shore. Becalmed and dead in the water, they were too far out to row ashore in time for the funeral, and they were forced to pass it up, much to their chargrin.

"The *Golden Gate* was Boston-owned, and Boston, not San Francisco, was her "hailing port," her name notwithstanding. She arrived in Shanghai in 1865 and thus became the largest schooner operating there. She was lost in a typhoon in 1871.

The *Syren*, after having had several years of service as a pilot boat of the Port of Boston, was purchased by Robert Bennet Forbes, for himself and a few other pilots, expressly for service in China. This Forbes, a one-time yachtsman as well as a pilot, was the grandfather of the late Allan Forbes, a former president of the State Street Trust Company, who was instrumental in the publication of the bank's brochure on Boston pilots and pilot boats. The *Syren* served with renown at *Shanghai* until 1896, when she was run down by a schooner and sank. All hands but one were saved.

Grandfather Forbes once had owned the *Sylph*, a famous schooner yacht that also found its way into the pilotage service eventually. In 1835, shortly after her purchase by Forbes (at an incredibly low "distress" price) while she was still hard aground and damaged in Lone Rock Passage near Wood's Hole, she sailed in what is credited with having been the first recorded yacht race in America. This could have been called a "match race"—as in horse racing—since there were only two contestants, Forbes's *Sylph* and the *Wave*, owned and skippered by Commodore John C. Stevens.

The story of this race is the more interesting because of some odd sidelights. For one thing, it was an impromptu, spur-of-the-moment affair, instituted as a "trial of speed of Newport," when Forbes, underway on the refloated and reconditioned *Sylph*, spotted the *Wave* at anchor, hauled up for her, jumped aboard, and issued his challenge, called "an invitation" by him. Also, Forbes, the challenger, remained aboard the *Wave*, his opponent's boat, from start to finish of the race. His boat, *Sylph*, was skippered on this occasion by Captain William Carleton Fowler, previously mentioned, who soon afterward was commissioned a Boston pilot and served with dedication and renown, on at least eight well-known pilot boats *for 50 years*.

Only one yacht, the *Sylph*, made it to the finish. Although the *Wave* seemed to be the faster of the two in calm smooth water and at first bid fair to outrun the *Sylph*, she slowed after encountering rough weather and choppy seas in the open Long Island Sound, lost ground, handled with great difficulty, and finally was forced to bear away and head for a sheltered cove, forfeiting the race.

Exactly 100 years to the month from the time of that race, in August of 1935, it was commemorated by a "Centennial Race" held off Martha's Vineyard. This memorial race was sponsored by the *Southern Massachusetts Yacht Racing Association*, and it was run in the very same waters, along an almost identical course, at approximately the same time of day as that epochal race between the *Wave* and the *Sylph*.

The race was open to all cruising yachts, and they sailed in two divisions: from 30-feet to 45-foot over-all, and from 45-foot to 73-foot over-all. The descendants of Commodore Forbes and Commodore Stevens, the rival yachtsmen in the original race, presented handsome silver bowls as prizes for the winners; and a great grandson and namesake of Commodore Forbes took part in this anniversary race as a crewman on a Forbes family yacht.

In this book about pilots and piloting, this apparent preoccupation with yachts and yachting would seem to be divergent and irrelevant, but all of it is assuredly relevant and material. Yachts came into the piloting picture very conspicuously in the early competitive days when "the mad race to the sea" was a hard fact of life; and speed counted very much in the daily lives of pilots wresting a precarious living from the maritime commerce of the times. It was only natural that they should be forever darting favoring glances on speedy yachts that some day might be for sale and might be bought, perhaps by two or more pilots banding together, and put into the pilotage service.

This happened in the case of many fine yachts. At Boston, along with the *Sylph*, there were the *Coquette*, the first *Northern Light*, built around 1829, the second *Northern Light*, built just about 100 years later, and others. In those early 1830s, the *Sylph* and the first *Northern Light* were only American yachts of any renown. The *Northern Light* was owned by a Colonel W.P. Winchester.

The *Coquette*, one of the most admired of early American

yachts, appeared on the scene in the spring of 1846. She was graceful in contour and low in the water, with a clipper bow, resembling the famous racing yacht *America*. She was designed by Lewis Winde, celebrated yacht designer, who later turned his talents to designing vessels especially suited for the piloting service.

This famous yacht was designed and built originally for the family of James A. Perkins, a prominent young Bostonian with sporting instincts and lots of money to indulge them, by the firm of *Winde &Clinkard*, a partnership of that same yacht designer and Henry R. Clinkard, a highly-skilled shipwright. This had proved to be a fortuitous and profitable combination of talents. The *Coquette's* keel was laid down in their yard at Chelsea in the fall of 1845, and she was launched in the following Spring.

The *Coquette's* owner, Mr. Perkins, was invited to bring her to New York to take part in the second annual regatta of the New York Yacht Club. He did so and made a record run between Boston and New York, doing the 284 miles in 32 hours, averaging 9 knots, in heavy weather. When the *Coquette* arrived at New York, according to a contemporary report, "her model and indeed her entire appearance excited the greatest admiration."

Sad to say, in her first race, because of light winds prevailing, *Coquette* did not do well at all. However, in the run to Newport that followed, she came out with flying colors, along with the fast and weatherly *Northern Light*, also Winde-designed, against the armada of schooners that composed the club's fleet almost entirely. She sailed in many more races after that and dominated most of them.

She became a pilot boat in 1849, when Mr. Perkins decided to sell her, and she was bought by two fellow Boston pilots, Captain Elbridge Gerry Martin and Captain Samuel Colby. (Captain Martin had been her racing skipper for Mr. Perkins). She operated in the piloting service for 18 years, until she was sold, in 1867, to be a cargo carrier in the foreign trade.

While the subject under discussion is still yachts, it is relevant to note that the famous racing yacht *America*, the winner of the first international yacht race and the now famous America's Cup in 1851, was sailed by a Sandy Hook pilot, Captain Richard Brown of New Jersey. He took her across the Atlantic and raced her to the first of a long, unbroken succession of victories for United States yachts over those of Great Britain and other nations in this world-famous sports event.

It has been conceded generally, on both sides of the Atlantic, that a deciding factor in the winning of this first America's Cup, by an American ship skippered by an American harbor pilot, was her "gay drapery," that is to say, her sails, new and novel in cut and set to the British, and at first made fun of by them. They called them "flat-boards" because they were taut and flat, as opposed to British sails, which were loose and "baggy" up to that time.

When the *America* made some trial runs over there and out-ran some favorite British yachts, British eyes began to open wide and British mockery began to diminish. Then that historic first race took place, and the "flatboards" won the first one. There has been, in fact, a recent account of the race in the New England magazine *Yankee*, and it was titled just that, *Flat-Boards Won the First One*. Soon after the race, British opinion about American-style sails changed completely and the style began to be adopted throughout the British Isles.

To get back to Shanghai—it all began when the first foreign trading vessels arriving there in the early 1800s were either unable to obtain competent pilots or forced to rely on local Chinese pilots most of whom had a good knowledge of the adjacent coasts and the nearby Yangtze Kiang River, *along with a disposition to be in league with Chinese pirates for fun and profit*. They were adept at letting ships run aground in certain locations, supposedly by accident or miscalculation, so that the ships could be looted of their cargoes and stores by pirates lying in wait at those locations. Even after the arrival, accreditation, and "taking over" by British, American, and other non-Chinese pilots, there was great need to be constantly on the alert against pirate raids that could lead to personal injury and even death for pilots.

These raids were especially prevalent on the Yangtze River, the longest river in China and a major trade artery. It is navigable for over 1000 miles inland by the largest ocean liners. Its estuary and mouth are only a short distance from Shanghai proper, which actually is located on the Whangpoo, a much smaller river by compariosn. The many isolated bends of the Yangtze together with its many shoals and sandbars were conditions ideally suited for ambush and attack.

The Shanghai area also was the focal point of numerous pilotboat races, on which large sums of money were wagered. It also was the starting point of numerous long-distance tea-clipper races. Notable among these was the "Great Tea Race of 1872," between the famous square-rigger *Cutty Sark* and her long-time rival, *Thermopylae*. Shanghai pilots had a lot to do with the start of this race.

The race actually started miles up the Yangtze at Hongkew, a loading area, where flotillas of tea barges from inland clustered about the great cargo ships moored there, while coolie laborers on platforms rigged to the ships' sides passed chests of tea up to fellow workers on the ships' decks. The two rival tea clippers often loaded together there, and often left port within a few hours of each other bound for the same destination, London of course. It then became a hotly contested race, even though the rivals might seldom be in company with each other or even in sight of one another.

On this occasion, however, during the customary onshore race to be the first to get loaded and underway, the rivalry was especially keen, and everybody in the tea trade and most of the general public took notice and realized that this was going to be the race of the century, a true battle of the giants. The weather was threatening at this juncture. It was the monsoon season, hot and steamy, with irregular and uncertain onslaughts of wind, rain, and fog. Making sail was delayed to the very last minute.

The *Cutty Sark* was the first to finish loading, in the afternoon of June 17th, and she got underway at 7 P.M. that evening. The *Thermopylae* finished loading sometime after dark that same night and got underway several hours later. Both had pilots aboard of course. The following morning, it was seen that the *Cutty Sark* was in the lead, but not by very much, as both vessels dropped down the Yangtse and crossed the Woosung bar. Conditions appeared favorable for an auspicious start of an exciting, nip-and-tuck race, but the weather and the pilots had something to say about that. By nightfall, the fog had become so heavy that the pilots insisted on anchoring close to the lightship near the mouth of the Yangtse.

Around noon of the next day, it cleared enough for both clippers to be underway again, but not for long. They were able to drop down the river's estuary for only about six or seven miles, when the fog closed in again and hid all the essential landmarks and aids to navigation. Still mindful of their responsibility for the safety of the vessels and conscious of the authority vested in them, the pilots decreed another heaving to and anchoring.

The fog and the generally dirty weather lasted all through that night and the next morning, the 20th. The afternoon turned clear and both ships made sail, but only for about five hours. Before nightfall, both pilots saw fit to give orders to anchor again.

It was not until the morning of the 21, which was calm and clear, that the clippers were able to reach the open sea, drop the pilots, and get on with the business of racing, which, to both crews and both sets of officers, was more important than the business of delivering tea. Indeed, the tea cargoes were regarded by nearly all hands as ballast primarily, and in both cases, many thousands of pounds of the stuff were left ashore merely to trim ship in anticipation of the race.

However, fog came on heavy again in the middle of that day, the clippers lost sight of each other, and they did not see each other until the 26, when they were off Hong Kong. Here the race really did become nip-and-tuck, each vessel having turns at gradually drawing up on the other and gradually passing it, the weather taking turns at being fair and being dirty, and excitement on each vessel mounting to fever pitch.

On June 30, on account of course changes and not because of

fog, they lost sight of each other again, did not see each other until July 15 off Borneo, and again made it nip-and-tuck and exciting for all hands. And so it went for four long months, with mishaps and misadventures persistently dogging the wake of the *Cutty Sark*. The worst mishap of all befell her while she was in the lead somewhere in the Indian Ocean. She lost her rudder, lost a precious whole week while a jury rudder was being rigged, and consequently lost the race. The *Thermopylae* was the official winner, but the honors and the acclaim went to the *Cutty Sark*, still the favorite, since, in spite of her misfortunes, she arrived on the Thames not too far behind her rival.

The Shanghai pilots did not have a big hand in the running of this epic race, but there is much latitude for much speculating on how it might have started — and ended — if they had not had that big, decisive part in the beginning of it.

Forty-Two

The River Pilots

There are pilots who operate only on rivers, and there are some of these who never ever venture past the river mouths in plying their trade even though, for some of them, a good part of their rivers are veritable estuaries or arms of the sea because of the sea water flowing into and out of them day after day with the rise and fall of the tides. The St. Lawrence, the Hudson, the Thames, the Mississippi, the Yangtse, the Ganges, and many more throughout the world have this duality, being both rivers and estuaries. Just about all of them are navigable by giant trans-oceanic ships for a good part of their lengths, some of them for many hundreds of miles inland.

Why hire a pilot to guide one's ship up and down a river, of all places!

That, for many people, would seem to be a sensible observation. One simply steers one's ship straight down the middle where it is deepest and safest. That is all there is to it. Who needs a pilot!

Not so! It is not that simple! The "middle" often is shallow in places and it often is plentifully supplied with obstructions, both natural and man-made such as hidden rocks and sunken wrecks. Also, along with the flow of it mainstream, a river may have many adverse cross currents and counter currents. It may have winding channels that need to be followed assiduously in order to avoid groundings, and it may have an abundance of small "recreational" boats on its surface—anywhere at any given time. This in itself is a major hazard. Following restricted, narrow channels, it is almost impossible for a big ship to maneuver to avoid collisions with small boats without getting aground disastrously.

Only an experienced local river pilot can be trusted to have a complete and adequate knowledge of the channels, currents, shoals, and obstructions, and only he can be trusted with dealing effectively with the careless, reckless, and inept operation of small boats along the way. It has long been understood generally that the rivers and harbors of America are to be used with equal facility and non-restriction by both commercial and recreational vessels and that therefore the responsibility for safe passage in those waters must be equally divided between the commercial and the recreational operators and must be assumed voluntarily by both.

Unfortunately, the recreational boatmen too often shirk their responsibility in this, either through ignorance or waywardness, and thus put all of the burden on the pilots and ship captains. The pilots, consequently, must be interminably alert, not only to avert imminent collisions but also, in such attempts, to keep their giant vessels from grounding and being badly damaged. In such restricted, crowded waters, however, there is not much in the way of skillful ship handling that can be done to avert collisions with mishandled small boats.

Most operators of small boats in rivers and harbors do stick to the laid-down rules and common-sense procedures pertinent to safety aflloat, but many are reckless and irresponsible in their boat handling, while many others are merely ignorant or uninformed regarding safe boating concepts and procedures. This has resulted in a steadily increasing rise in the number of accidents involving big ships and small boats, and this situation has caused grave concern in maritime and piloting circles.

Pilots, who often must bear the brunt of the blame for such accidents, give freely of their time and energies to appear at yacht clubs and boating organizations to explain the problems involved in handling large ships on narrow rivers, trusting that a mutual understanding of the essential safety precautions to be taken mutually by all concerned will lead to the utilization of the full potential of our navigable rivers and harbors, both as commercial waterways and as recreational areas for the small-boat owner and his family and friends.

For the river pilot, then, in addition to the known physical hazards besetting his path along the river, there is that ever-present, ever-moving traffic that flows unpredictably in many directions at various speeds and a bit of indecision in ordering a change of course or speed could spell disaster. That is one of the things that make his work a "little different" from that of the seagoing "bar" pilots at the entrance to his river and cause the river pilots to band together, separate and aloof, in their own organizations.

This would seem to be a natural thing to do, and it is done throughout the world. For example, on the Columbia River, flowing into the Pacific Ocean between the states of Washington and Oregon, there are the Columbia River Bar Pilots, headquartered at Astoria, Oregon, near the coast, who guide ships in from sea and up the river as far as the city of Portland; and there are the Columbia River Pilots, headquartered at Portland, who take it from there and guide the ships further up the river.

At the Port of New York, there are of course the Sandy Hook Pilots who bring ships in from the open sea and the Hudson River Pilots comprised of those who guide ships up the Hudson River as far as Albany, approximately 125 miles north of Upper New York Bay. Ships bound up the river are boarded by the river pilots (via Jacob's ladder) in Upper New York Bay off the Staten Island quarantine station. Sometimes, in inclement weather, this can be as disturbing and perilous as boarding an incoming ship out on the open sea. The incoming Sandy Hook pilot is "dropped" at the same time.

Extended, long-range dredging operations have provided the Hudson River with a continuous channel having an average depth of not less than 32 feet. For most ships, the run to Albany, a matter of 10 to 16 hours, can be made without stopping, and this is done in most cases, giving the pilots extra long hours of duty. The larger, more cumbersome ships must avoid running at night to avoid getting into trouble due to ship handling and traffic problems, which makes it a two-day trip for the pilot.

At the Port of New Orleans, there are *three* separate and distinct pilot groups who do not compete with each other in any way. Rather, they assist and complement each other. They are the Associated Branch Pilots, who are the "bar" pilots that board ships at sea and guide them into the mouth of the Mississippi at the end of the delta, the Crescent River Port Pilots' Association, whose members guide ships up the delta to New Orleans, and the New Orleans-Baton Rouge Steamship Pilots' Association, whose members guide ships up and down the winding Mississippi to and from Baton Rouge and New Orleans.

The Associated Branch Pilots' organization happens to be a good example of the concept of "family dynasties of pilots." Some of its members are great great grandsons of members and organizers of the association of 140 years ago. It should not be construed, however, that blood relationships and family ties are the major criteria for membership, either in this pilots' association or in any others. Navigational and ship handling skills, together with integrity, common sense, good physical and mental health, and dependability, continue to be the most esteemed qualifications of all in the eyes of all concerned.

And so it goes throughout the world, with the separateness among groups at the same port not always being so cordial and cooperative. For instance, at certain ports in the British Isles, in Ireland particularly, the separateness often was an unfriendly and even hostile state of affairs at one time in history. At certain Irish ports, there were three distinct gradations of pilots: the "coasting pilots" (comparable to our "bar pilots,") the licensed "river pilots," and the "mud pilots." The mud pilots operated on the upper reaches of the rivers in areas not officially designated as "pilotage waters." Although they were considered to be legitimate pilots, there was no official recognition or licensing of them.

The coasting pilots considered themselves to be functionaries of much greater importance than the licensed river pilots, who let it be known at every opportunity that they had grave doubts about the existence of any such superiority. However, both most certainly regarded the mud pilots as creatures of immeasurably inferior rank, socially, intellectually, professionally.

The son of a coasting pilot or river pilot would not dream of contracting a *mésalliance* with the daughter of a mud pilot; nor would the son of a mud pilot be presumptuous enough, even when he had been drinking heavily, to aspire to the hand of the daughter of a river pilot or coasting pilot.

The mud pilot would ask you without abashment to buy him a drink, whereas you would have to use tact and diplomacy to get a river pilot or bar pilot to have a drink with you. Certainly these two would never ever be seen having a drink with a mud pilot.

It may be that the mud pilots were deserving, in the main, of such deprecatory behavior toward them. Most of them, none too tidy in dress and grooming, were not above a little skulduggery and hanky-panky as they practiced their profession. There is the story of one in particular who worked a stretch of river along with two rival mud pilots and did all in his power to damage their reputations, moral and professional, and get business away from them by fair means or foul.

On the average in fair weather, three or four ships a week went up the river in charge of one or another of these pilots, but occasionally bad weather and adverse winds would cause delays, and many ships from down river would be overdue. Later, when a favorable change occurred, these vessels would come up the river close together and crowd the anchorage, waiting for mud pilots to come aboard and conduct them to their final destination.

At such times, with a slew of cash customers on hand at the anchorage, this particular mud pilot, ordinarily quite skillful and adept, suddenly would become very unskillful and maladroit to all appearances, and two or three of his charges would find temporary homes stuck in the mud or on a sandbar halfway up the river. Of course there was method in his maladroitness. He would inform the captains and crews that they would have to lie there for a while until "high water" floated them off, and then he would scamper back to the anchorage and take charge of another waiting ship while his rivals were far up the river completing their initial assignments.

All of this was part of his cunning scheme to make extra money, and here is how the scheme worked, as told in his own words, after his tongue had been loosened—intentionally—at the local pub:

> Well, you see, if I can get done with my ship sooner than the other two fellows—and a bad lot they are too, I can tell you!—I can come back and take charge of a second ship before the other scoundrels are half over their journeys; so I manage to put one or two of the little vessels in a soft handy spot up the river. I am usually about three-quarters sprung before I can muster up courage for the job. Oh, I have a conscience, I can assure you, and I wouldn't let hurt nor harm come to anything in my charge—not for the world! They lay there nice and comfortable for a few days—just as safe as if they were in a drydock—until the spring tides float them off. I take charge of them for the remainder of the journey, when work is slack with me. I can make as much as the other two fellows put together, just by studying matters in this way. It goes to my heart though, if the tides are cutting and leave the poor lads in the mud a week or so; but then we manage to dig them out somehow, and there isn't a great deal of time lost after all. 'Twill be all the same a hundred years from now anyhow—Here's to your health!"

While we are in the British Isles, it might be fitting to tell the story of a certain redoubtable skipper, a Britisher, who was intolerant of the idea that any skipper worth his salt could not guide his ship safely in inshore waters without the help of a local pilot—"outside help," in his view. He was converted one very foggy afternoon, so they say, while his ship was slowly making its way in toward the west coast of England.

The fog stayed so thick that he had become more and more wary and was pacing the bridge, staring intently, trying to see through the gloom dead ahead and on both bows. He thought he saw a great dark shape looming up on their port bow and bearing down on them, and when he rushed over to the rail and leaned out staring, he made out the figure of a pipe-smoking man leaning against another rail only a few yards away.

"You there!" he yelled, "What do you think you're doing with your bloomin' ship! Don't you know the rules of the road!"

The man took the pipe out of his mouth and calmly replied: "This ain't no bloomin' ship, Guvnor! This 'ere's a lighthouse!"

The British Isles are important additionally in the story of piloting because of a certain memorable turning point in world history that took place there. It was brought about, to a great extent, by a lack of competent pilots. It was the defeat of the great Spanish Armada of 130 ships and 30,000 men that had set out to conquer England about 100 years after the discovery of America by Columbus.

It is recorded in the historical outline *State Pilotage in America* that the Armada, by pre-arrangement, was supposed to pick up a group of skilled pilots temporarily stationed on the continent at Dunkirk on the North Sea. For reasons not fully uncovered, they were unable to reach this port and therefore were unable to take aboard essential provisions, charts, and pilots, as well as an army of soldiers who were to be put ashore in the British Isles.

They then had to pursue their attempt at conquest without pilots or navigators or anyone else who was in any way familiar with the treacherous waters of the English Channel, the North Sea, the Irish Sea, and the foul, rocky west coast of Ireland on the Atlantic Ocean. It was here that they met their Waterloo and lost most of their ships, through storms and wrecks and defeats by the Irish. They were, at this stage, headed north with fair winds escaping from the English fleet, encountered in the channel off Plymouth. It was the wrong way home and the long way home, but it was their best choice under the circumstances. Only half of the fleet got back to Spain.

There is a story, true or not, concerning a cadet at the U.S. Naval Academy who, while giving an oral report on the Spanish Armada, asserted that the Armada was defeated because of the lack of three ships. When the professor chided him for this apparently erroneous statement and asked "What ships?", the cadet answered: "Leadership, marksmanship, and seamanship." Good seamanship undoubtedly was lacking to a great extent, and much of this lack probably was due to the lack of competent pilots.

Incredibly, along with the need for pilots to guide ships up and down rivers, there always has been a definite need for pilots to guide ships along and through man-made canals—notwithstanding the fact that canals generally are supposed to be dug deep and wide and obstructionless and made-to-order. The Panama, the Suez, the Erie, and others throughout the world have their regular groups of skilled pilots.

Canal pilots may be compared to river pilots, operate in much the same manner, and have much the same problems, except for the traffic problem. Traffic on canals seldom is haphazard or helterskelter. It generally is orderly, especially going through locks. This phase of piloting is chiefly mechanical and cut-and-dried, but it is a very necessary part of marine transportation.

Not all parts of all canals are man-made however. Some parts of some canals are "natural" waterways consisting of lakes, rivers, bays, and lagoons or certain sections of them. As such, they are liable to contain some of the same hazardous conditions as are found in the oceanic waters near seaports. These could be shoals, sandbars, submerged rocks, sunken wrecks, adverse currents, et cetera. Only local pilots can be trusted to know how to avoid them.

The Panama Canal run is a long one—a little over 50 miles from channel entrance to channel entrance. It usually takes from 7 to 8 hours on the average. The pilot goes aboard ships at one end or the other with his own scantling crew, men to be posted as lookouts on bow and stern and to handle mooring and towing lines. This is real work to be done along the way while the ship's crew is resting.

At times, in the case of certain naval vessels passing through, a certain extra chore devolves upon the pilot. The author remembers going through the Panama Canal on a Navy LST during World War II. Throughout the 50-mile journey, as if it were a conducted sightseeing tour, there came over the loudspeaker system a regular running account or lecture concerning the entire operation and the points of interest along the way. Clearly, it had to be the pilot or one of his aides who gave this lecture for the edification of the many first-timers on board.

Forty-Three

Epitome

The word *epitome* is mis-used almost universally to convey the meaning "peak of excellence or perfection," but the dictionary tells us that its true meaning is "a part which represents typically a whole" and that it derives from the Greek words *epi*, meaning "upon," and *temnein*, meaning "cut." The watermelon supplies us with a good exemplification.

It was once a widespread practice, familiar to many of us, for the man offering a watermelon for sale to cut a little cube or "plug" out of it in order to show the prospective purchaser what the entire melon was like inside the rind. That "plug" was the epitome of the melon, so to speak, and probably a similar practice in very ancient times gave birth to the word. It is intended that these added chapters on the pilotage situation in the state of Florida shall be the epitome of the state pilotage system in America, the part which represents typically the whole—with some historical background thrown in for good measure.

In 1821, that part of North America then called Florida was ceded to the United States by Spain, and just about a year later, an act of Congress established it as the Territory of Florida, with a Governor and a Legislative Council at its head.

During those early formative years before it became a state (in 1845), most of the ships putting in to the ports of the new territory, whether from overseas or from the new states to the north, were sailing vessels, and judged by modern standards, they were small. Also, to a great extent, the harbors were shallow, the bars and channels were unstable, and the tempo of shipping activity in general was very slow.

For these reasons undoubtedly, it was many years before the legislative council came up with any specific, comprehensive pilotage laws. Instead, it had delegated authority in piloting affairs to the various local governing bodies of the individual ports. For example, in 1822, the mayors and the city aldermen of St. Augustine and Pensacola were authorized to take care of the appointment and supervision of pilots for these ports. In 1835, a county court was authorized to do likewise for the Port of Key West. In 1836, another enactment provided that "no pilots shall be appointed at St. Johns or at the Port of Nassau who do not reside at or near the mouths of such rivers."

Another statute, enacted in February of 1839, six years before statehood, was the first one that even vaguely conformed to the general tenor of those in the present-day Chapter 310 of the Florida Statutes, dealing with pilots and pilot commissioners. This new law provided, among other things, the following:

> The Governor and the Legislative Council shall be authorized to appoint a board of port wardens at Jacksonville, Tampa Bay, and the mouth of the Suwanee River. Such boards shall constitute the boards of commissioners of pilots, with the power to license pilots.

And so it went from year to year, with new laws constantly being enacted at random to provide for such things as the appointment of pilot commissioners and pilots, the setting of pilotage rates and fees to be charged at the various ports, fixing apprenticeship regulations, et cetera. From 1822 to 1868, there were some 40 of these laws enacted, four of them repealing or amending prior Statutes. The laws vested the supervisory powers—variously—in the Governor, Probate Judges, County Courts, Mayors, Boards of County commissioners, City Commissions, and other government agencies and officials.

Out of this welter of confusion, there finally emerged, in 1868, Chapter 1670 of the Florida Territorial and State Statutes, which was the first general comprehensive law covering pilots and pilot commissioners as a whole. It applied to all maritime counties in the state, and it provided that the Governor, with the consent of the Senate, would appoint a Board of Commissioners of Pilots for each county that had one or more genuine seaports. This chapter was the foundation and framework of the present Chapter 310 of the Florida Statutes.

The full intents and purposes of this Chapter 310 are to provide for the regulation and supervision of the state pilotage system with emphasis on the manifold duties and responsibilities of both the pilots and the pilot commissioners. The pilot commissioners of each county in which there is a port are empowered to examine, license, and appoint a sufficient number of pilots and apprentices, not exceeding a specified quota, to handle the shipping of the port or ports. They also are empowered to discipline pilots, to grant them leaves of absence, to take actions on their grievances, to fix pilotage rates within certain limits, and to make such rules and regulations, not in conflict with existing local, state, and federal regulations, as they may deem necessary.

Chapter 310 also provides, in over two dozen articles or paragraphs, for the paying of a *per diem* allowance for pilots detained in quarantine, for a pilot's entitlement to take out a ship that he has brought in, for the board to receive a percentage of all pilotage fees collected, for the board to examine vessels and their cargoes and records, for the board to keep certain records and accounts, and for other miscellaneous duties and privileges of pilots and commissioners.

Florida, the Sunshine State, with all of its other distinctions, is also a great maritime state, with one of the longest coastlines in the nation and some of the finest seaports in the world. This coastline is 1,146 miles long—472 miles on the Atlantic Ocean and 674 miles on the Gulf of Mexico—and on it are 14 deep-water seaports: Fernandina, Jacksonville, Port Canaveral, Fort Pierce, Port of Palm Beach, Port Everglades, Miami, Key West, Boca Grande, Tampa, Port Saint Joe, St. Petersburg, Panama City, and Pensacola.

The amount of gross tonnage annually passing through each of them varies widely from port to port. Some are less commodious, more remote, and less accessible (from the Atlantic sea lanes) than others—and therefore less patronized by shipping interests. On the whole, however, many millions of tons of valuable cargo as well as many thousands of passengers on liners and cruise ships, some of which have their home bases or hailing ports in Florida, are moved through these ports each year. Before entering or leaving any of them, each and every transoceanic ship takes aboard—is compelled by law to take aboard—an accredited, licensed, *local* pilot to guide it in or out.

All but a very small percentage of Florida pilots are part of Florida's State Pilotage system, which means that they are licensed by state as well as federal authorities and operate under the total authority of relevant State of Florida laws, as elucidated in that Chapter 310 of the Florida Statutes. It means also that they belong to individual, self-governing port pilots' associations patterned on the old-time craft guilds of medieval Europe and England (and just about as exclusive) with rigid apprenticeship programs and strict high standards of conduct and competency.

All of these groups, though autonomous *almost*, are controlled by the state through the various Boards of Pilot Commissioners. Each port group collectively has an intense and abiding interest in the development and prosperity of its own port, and with these objectives in mind, endeavors to serve the shipping interests and the public to the best of its collective ability.

Fundamentally, as previously stated, the federal government is "in charge" with regard to all piloting activity anywhere in the nation, even though it actually is in charge behind the scenes, so to speak; which brings us to that "very small percentage of these pilots" who are not a part of the state pilotage system. These are the ubiquitous, self-styled, so-called "federal pilots," still on the scene in Florida and in other states as well.

Technically, these "federal pilots" are not subject to state control but, according to the jurisdictional set-up, they are authorized to pilot *only* ships under *enrollment* and not those under *registry*, which is to say that they may pilot American *coastwise* vessels but not American and foreign *trans-oceanic* ships. Many of these men are masters, mates, and other deck officers of such ships under enrollment, holding the federal pilot license in addition to their merchant marine "papers."

On such vessels, the master may do his own piloting if he holds that federal license, or he may assign the job to a deck officer who is so qualified, or he may hire and take aboard a free-lance, so-called "federal pilot," or he may hire a properly licensed State Pilots, one who has the required federal (Coast Guard) license as well as the state license and, more importantly, is a member of a long-established local group of similarly documented State Pilots.

It should become apparent that the term *federal pilot* is a misnomer and "phony" in a way, since it connotes some alliance or connection with the federal government. There is no such alliance or connection, except for the insignificant fact that these free lance pilots have a federal or Coast Guard license—which *all* state pilots have, in addition to their state licenses or commissions.

These unattached, free-lance pilots always have been a thorn in the side of the regular state pilotage system, not only because of their recalcitrance in behaving and performing like "real" pilots, but also for their persistent attempts to have the laws changed so that they, the generally itinerant and often unavailable pilots, would be included in the laws' beneficent provisions and be eligible for more of the fringe benefits of the profession.

In Florida, according to clear, authentic, and well-documented evidence presented by the Florida State Pilots' Association, a recent study revealed that, of the total number of American enrolled vessels calling at one of the two largest ports, only a small percentage was handled by the free-lance federal pilots. The rest were handled by members of the state pilots' association of this port. All could have been handled by *any* individual holding that single federal license, with the selection of the individual being entirely up to the shipmasters. This indicated that those federal pilots were not available when needed or were not wanted when they were available.

Yet it is a group of that same class of pilot at that same port who have been the most active and vociferous in seeking the legislative changes mentioned. It seems that they are looking toward obtaining the benefits of the state pilotage statutes but are not doing anything to indicate that they can or will comply with the strict requirements of those statutes. They do not maintain pilot boats on station offshore and remain in attendance there, offering their services to vessels under enrollment, partly because they are not required by law to do so. They may decline or refuse to pilot ships requesting their services and very often do so.

The properly licensed and indoctrinated "state" pilots, however, are not allowed any such leniency or choices. They must comply with the statutes and the regulations of the Board of Pilot Commissioners in every respect, even to the extent of making their services available to all coastwise vessels under enrollment, most of which normally would be piloted by the free-lance federal pilots. For one reason or another, these free-lancers very often are unavailable. On this account, the state pilots' associations in the larger ports, as they arrange their schedules and budgets for men and equipment, must make allowances for the probability that some or many of these neglected enrolled vessels will appear on the scene and request help from the pilot boats on station. This tends to make the thorn prick more deeply.

All of this has the effect of making the state-licensed groups responsible for underwriting the inabilities, for whatever reasons, of the free-lance pilots. All of it tends to validate and justify the compulsory pilotage concept and the tightly-knit state pilotage system, with its influential port pilots' associations, which shape this concept into a functioning apparatus.

All of it tends also to invalidate contentions that the system and the associations exist only to maintain monopolies and little dynasties wielding political influence, obtaining special privileges, and excluding all but a certain favored few from the practice of a lucrative profession.

Forty-Four

The Busy-Body Meddlers

Another thorn-in-the-side and challenge for the state pilotage system stems from an entirely different source, but it is after the same result, legislative changes, without good and sufficient reason, that would unbalance and upset the smooth-running efficiency of the system. The proposed changes would practically destroy the potency and efficiency of the Boards of Pilot Commissioners and the pilots' associations by making them subordinate to "local port governing bodies," which presumably means *Port Authorities*. Instead of being merely a nominal or token take-over, this could be an outright acquisition of all the physical facilities—the pilot boats, the central headquarters offices, the communications set-ups, the licensing procedures, the apprenticeship programs.

This would place the *Port Authorities* (branches of grovernment) squarely in the pilotage business, at quite some expense to the taxpayers, with all pilots automatically becoming government *employees* eligible for many standard employee benefits such as the forty-hour work week, overtime pay, Workmen's Compensation Insurance, pension plans, paid vacations, et cetera, all of which would be of great and lasting expense to these local port governing bodies, and of not much concern to the state pilots now working at their jobs.

Also, additional pilots would have to be trained and hired in order to accommodate to the forty-hour week, and there would be administrative expenses such as salaries for dispatchers, clerks, bookkeepers, boatkeepers, and collectors of pilotage fees. Also, much money would need to be spent—out of the public treasury—for the maintenance of office equipment, pilot boats and gear, and the apprenticeship programs. Under the existing state pilotage system, none of these expenses devolve upon the public treasury and the taxpayers. They are paid by the pilots out of their own pockets, so to speak, as if the pilot groups were independent contractors.

In Florida, the movement to form and so utilize such "local port governing bodies" began under the aegis of the now well-known "Florida Ports and Trade Council." This body was organized in 1959 for the following announced purposes: to further the development of foreign trade throughout the state, to foster a greater awareness of the importance of this trade to the people as a whole, to promote and propagandize Florida's seaports throughout the world, to establish a scholarship fund for selected students showing an aptitude for work in the field of foreign trade, and to develop a kind of uniformity in port practices, terminology, and fees, in order that Florida may be consistently on a competitive basis with other areas of the nation.

This ports and trade council made mention of its legislative objectives, as follows:

> The Council will make itself available in an advisory capacity to the state Executive and Legislative bodies in all matters concerning the best interests of Florida's people relating to foreign trade. The Councial will maintain close contact with the Governor's office, the Cabinet, the Legislature, the Florida Development Commission, and other state agencies. The Council will take the necessary and proper steps to make its opinions felt on national issues affecting the ports and the people of Florida.

Certainly all of these objectives are noble and worthwhile, and no right-thinking, public-spirited Florida citizens could take exception to any of them. However, this council subsequently demonstrated that its members harbored certain misconceptions concerning piloting, pilots, pilots' associations, and pilot commissioners, as all of these relate to foreign trade. This is evidenced by a questionnaire sent out by one of its committees. It revealed that certain council members felt that the Florida pilotage laws were antiquated and obsolete and that the pilot commissioners and the pilots should be placed under the jurisdiction and supervision of the "local port governing bodies."

The initial reaction to this recommendation was a collective and emphatic *No*. It resulted from the sagacious judgements of various groups, among which were steamships agents, insurance underwriters, steavdoring firms, financial institutions, maritime organizations, and pilots' associations of course. Members of these groups evidently knew something of maritime law as it applied to the work of pilots and readily perceived the risks and dangers inherent in a set-up such as this.

At present, by reason of many previous court decisions, there exists a significant body of laws concerning the nature of pilotage. These laws recognize the pilot as *an independent business man* and concede that he best fulfills his duties to industry and the general public if he operates as an *independent contractor under state control* rather than as an individual workman *employed* by the state. As a contractor—and this has been well-established by law—he is liable to the ship owner for any damage caused by his negligence or incompetence, and if the owner and his ship is held liable for damages to others through the pilots fault or neglect, the pilot is legally bound to re-imburse the owner. Nearly all state pilots carry surety bonds of sufficient amount to take care of such deadly eventualities—*to a certain extent, that is.*

If the damage involved happens to be a very great enormity such as the complete loss of the ship and its entire cargo, the remedy or redress against the pilot is financially unreal. There are no millionaire pilots—and one cannot get blood out of a turnip, as the saying goes. Therefore the person or persons injured because of faulty piloting naturally will seek a more substantial and well-heeled debtor or defendant to be cited as the responsible one.

Many legal attempts to reach the pilot *association* beyond the pilot have been made in the past, but none of these were productive. The individual port pilots' associations have a status in the law that is long-standing and well-accepted. In a famous landmark case (Guy versus Donald, 203 U.S. 399—1906), Supreme Court Justice Holmes held that local pilots' associations were "voluntary unincorporated associations" which are not liable for the negligence of any pilot member. The inference here should be quite clear.

If the present state pilotage system were to be abolished, a *Port Authority*, supported by public monies, as an *employer* of a pilot, could be held liable for damages resulting from his negligence or ineptitude. It has long been an established canon of law that when a person is employed to do a job for pay, the employer is responsible for the work done by the employee if the performance of that work is the definite cause of damage to a person or persons.

In G.H. Robinson's admirable book on Admiralty Law, considered to be "the bible" of all maritime interests, on page 700, under the heading "Suits Against Port Authorities as Pilots' Principal," there is this statement:

> Attempts to reach the pilots' association beyond the pilot have not been fruitful. Though it is possible that some association may yet be found to be so organized that it will be liable, the fact set-ups have not been so far favorable for the injured persion. However, if the negligent pilot can be seen as an employee of someone with enough money to seek a recovery from the employer, the Port Authority movement might prove to be a godsend to a shipowner compelled to take for a job risking his ship a person who was merely a wage earner.

The word *compelled* has a special significance in this statement.

In a few case, that very situation or similar set of circumstances *has indeed* proved to be a godsend to shipowners, but at the same time, has been a disaster to certain public treasuries that were depleted by it. Over 50 years ago, the State of Oregon made the Port of Portland "a municipal corporation authorized and empowered to establish and maintain an efficient towage and pilotage service between the corporate limits of the Port of Portland and the open sea."

After an adverse court decision (*Thielbek*, 241 Fed. 209 9th Cir. 1917), by which the Port of Portland was held liable for tremendously costly ship damages (millions of dollars), ostensibly due to a pilot's negligence, the State of Oregon and the port authority officials quickly got out of the piloting business, and the pilots of the port ceased to be anybody's employees.

More recently, in California in 1960, the City of Long Beach was held responsible, as employers of a pilot, in the *Dana Aurora* case. This ship grounded on a breakwater in a patchy fog while entering Long Beach Harbor under the control of a pilot who was on board because of the compulsory pilotage regulation in effect there. The U.S. District Court, Southern District of California (808-57-TC. 187 Fed. Supp. 109 S.D. Cal. 1960) decided that the negligence of the pilot was the sole cause of the grounding, and the City of Long Beach was held liable for full damages—to be paid out of the public treasury.

All of the foregoing should not be taken as an inference that the pilot, as an independent contractor under the present state pilotage system or as an employee under the proposed, disputed system, is automatically responsible and liable for damages on any ship that comes to grief in any manner while in his charge. Many court decisions have produced a prescript which says that a pilot is not liable for damage to a vessel in his charge when he has used his best skill and judgment, even though the end result might show that his best judgment was wrong. An example of this might be a pilot's counter move against a raging storm and its adverse winds that did not quite succeed. There must be proved negligence or obvious gross incompetence.

Besides the expense of securing, operating, and maintaining pilot boats, boat crews, office staffs, and pilots, plus the cost of Workmen's Compensation Insurance, pension plans, apprenticeship programs, et cetera, there is another expensive obligation that would fall on local port governing bodies, and that would be *liability* insurance—if it could be purchased at all! This could be *very* expensive. Accidents involving ships and their cargoes often run into millions of dollars. A local port authority engaged in the pilotage business would have to be so protected or other wise put its city's treasury in jeopardy.

Also, aside from the increased financial burdens, such port

authorities would also be confronted with added administrative problems. For example, as employers, they undoubtedly would become involved in merchant marine and stevedoring strikes. Pilots would be involved in them as a matter of course.

Also, there would be controversial involvement in the assignment of berths (to pilots) and in the arbitration of disputes over priority and seniority in the assignment of duties. At present, under the state pilotage system, such controversy, if it exists at all, is at a bare minimum.

Such port authorities in the pilotage business also would be confronted with another problem, the inability to control any aspect of pilotage on vessels under enrollment, —American vessels engaged in the coastwise trade exclusively—because of the provisions of Federal Law R.S. 4401 (46 U.S.C. 364) enacted in 1871 and still in effect. Simply stated, the substance of this law, as far as state pilotage is concerned, is the removal of all United States coastwise vessels under enrollment from any state control and the permitting of this class of vessel to employ any pilot holding that federal (U.S. Coast Guard) license.

This in itself is not a new situation. It has existed for more than a hundred years along with the operation of the state pilotage system. However, under this proposed port authority take-over, the situation, amplified and exploited, conceivably would hasten the demise of that system, which has functioned satisfactorily throughout those hundred years and has provided an essential public service in every port where it was needed *at no expense to the taxpayers*.

Because of the ever-increasing trend toward federal control over traditional state operations, any significant change in Florida laws relating to pilotage that seeks to liberalize, take over, or modify the relevant statutes can be regarded as an open invitation to complete federal control of this essential public service. In the considered opinion of many eminent shipping personages, such total federal control would not be in the public interest and any attempts to amend those Florida pilotage laws in that direction should be open to serious debate. Similarly, according to these authorities, any such attempts in other coastal states, Atlantic, Pacific, or Gulf, should be met with distrust and counter measures.

Since the first enactment of a federal law on pilotage almost 200 years ago, there have been relatively few additional national laws on the subject. That 1789 law of the First Congress, which left the regulation of piloting to the individual states, was an act of trust and confidence. It called for the highest devotion to duty and honor on the part of the members of that profession.

Later Congresses recognized the special uniqueness of this profession and the fact that the state pilotage system had worked well throughout our coastal areas. Succeeding Congresses in general have approved of the system and have made known their approval officially on many occasions. Continuing to merit this approval is one of the chief aims of the state pilots and their associations. Constant adherence to the principle of rendering the most efficient service at all times has become the keystone of the entire state pilotage system.

Forty-Five

Business as Usual

The stock-in-trade of an accredited port pilot is now and always has been a complete knowledge of local waterway conditions—the shoals, bars, channels, deeps, obstructions, reefs, and other set peculiarities of the sea floor beneath the approaches to the port and its safe harbor. This is the service he sells.

The peculiarities are not constant and unchanging. They definitely do change, sometimes gradually, as in the case of shifting sands and silting, and sometimes suddenly, as in the case of ship sinkings and accidental shifting of channel markers. The pilot always knows about these changes. It is his business to keep himself well-informed concerning all such developments.

Ships change too. They have changed, in shape and size and method of propulsion and handling, over and over again down through the centuries, and they still are changing from year to year, sometimes drastically by conventional standards. The intrinsic value of the pilotage function remains the same, however, regardless of totally new and different ship designs, and these innovations do not detract from the pilot's ability to perform the services required of him. Undeterred by monstrous deviations from what was once considered the normal in ship building, pilots will continue earnestly to pursue their calling, servicing any and all ships of whatever type or size or design or nationality and bringing them into port or out of it expeditiously.

Ordinarily, new hull designs, new propulsion machinery, atomic power, automation aboard ship, and other phases of modern ship construction and operation are matters with which, primarily, only ship owners and operators are concerned. However, the maneuverability of ships, their reversing capabilities, and their response to engine room signals and directional controls on the bridge are matters that, along with their size and draft, are very important to the pilots, especially in maximum confined and hazardous areas.

Ocean liners and oil tankers are the largest movable objects made by man and, in general, their big propellers are designed primarily to move the ships ahead, are moderately inefficient when put in reverse, and thus do not effectively "put on the brakes," as the propellers of yacht-type motorboats do. Consequently, the average big ship of this kind might need a full mile of ocean or river to come to a full stop, after the engines have been reversed, because of mass inertia due to its tremendous size. This means danger—to the ship and its cargo and anything in their path.

Even in the field of small boats and yachts, the embarrassment of an inefficient reverse crops up again and again, and often, when a difficult docking or undocking problem related to adverse winds or currents is being coped with, one hears the question "Has she got a good reverse?" followed by the disconsolate answer "No, she hasn't."

How much greater the embarrassment on a 400-foot Goliath of the sea that cannot be slowed down readily in a bad crossing or passing situation. Undoubtedly, therefore, one of the first questions asked by a pilot when he goes aboard a ship that he has never guided before must be a question about how the ship behaves when her engines are put in reverse.

When the average pilot boards a ship with which he is not familiar, he immediately discusses the operational and underway characteristics of the ship with the master or mate, in order to be able to give a maximum of efficient service. Very often the ship is a foreign flag vessel on which a foreign language only is spoken by the officers and crew. The pilot must surmont this language barrier with his own poor foreign words and sign language or with the help of an interpreter.

Generally speaking, the entire pilotage system is readily adaptable to the unconventionalities of any and all types of ships; and this would include those big freighters and tankers that have their wheel houses or bridges located aft. Pilots do have their design preferences of course, and few have any liking for this type, with the "conn" and the operational controls located back near the stern. This makes maneuvering more difficult in restricted areas and tends to invite accidents, especially in areas where there is an abundance of small boat traffic, recreational and otherwise. For the pilot and others on the bridge, there is an expansive area dead ahead and under both bows that definitely is a blind spot in which various small craft might at any time be underway in the hands of reckless or incompetent operators, unaware or scornful of the danger.

Pilots realize that more accidents are likely to occur with this type of ship, but they realize that its design is based on a sound principle, getting increased cargo capacity and more efficiency in handling it. However, they know also that added turn-around time and more time spent in port because of their awkwardness in being maneuvered in close quarters tends to offset some of that economy.

Certainly pilots will continue indiscriminately to handle these and all other unorthodox design ships, including roll-on roll-off and lift-on lift-off types, the combination ore/oil carriers that come in sizes up to 50,000 tons deadweight capacity, and giant tankers of as much as 100,000 tons "burden." They will do so in accordance with the profession's traditional pattern of service, as they traditionally have followed it, trusting that the ship owners and shipmasters will be ever mindful of the problems involved. There is a very good likelihood of this. The feeling of mutuality of interests between the pilots and the shippers is deep and strong now, as compared with the feebleness of that relationship back in the old days.

The shipping company executives realize more fully the essential need for trained and experienced pilots, with their large passenger ships costing well over a hundred million dollars and their industrial bulk carriers and general cargo ships bearing equivalently high price tags. Safe and expeditious passages through narrow straits and crowded harbors means a great deal to them and to the marine insurance companies that underwrite their commercial ventures.

The pilots as well have become fully cognizant of the fact that only as the shipping industry prospers does the profession of piloting remain sound and stable. The more that industry prospers, the more ships enter and leave our seaports. The more ships that enter and leave our seaports, foreign flag as well as American, the more pilotage services are required. This is not to say the our American pilots have no special interest in American shipping, as opposed to ships of foreign registry. The exact opposite is true.

While all ships, American and foreign, are guided in and out with equal diligence and dispatch by American port pilots, these men are rather intensely interested in the welfare and development of the American merchant marine. Before they are anything else, they are Americans who love their country and consider its general well-being to be of the greatest importance, in peacetime as well as in national emergencies.

They consider the national policy stated in the Merchant Marine Act of 1936 (Section 101), for both peacetime and wartime commercial purposes to be the most worthwhile of any maritime policy ever promulgated by the government of the United States. This act, as amended, declares it to be the national policy that the United States shall have a merchant marine (a) sufficient to carry a substantial portion of our waterborne trade; (b) capable of serving as a military and naval auxiliary for national defense; (c) owned and operated under the United States flag as far as is practicable; and (d) composed of modern, well-

Index